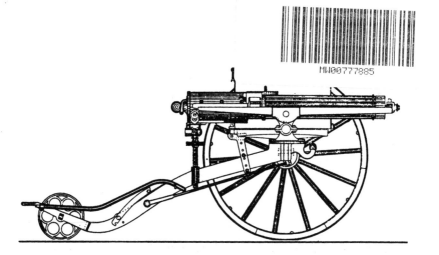

AUTOMATIC ARMS

THEIR HISTORY, DEVELOPMENT AND USE

by

MELVIN M. JOHNSON JR.

Captain, United States Marine Corps Reserve

and

CHARLES T. HAVEN

Co-author of *A History of the Colt Revolver*

SKYHORSE PUBLISHING

Skyhorse Publishing books may be purchased in bulk at
special discounts for sales promotion, corporate gifts, fund-raising,
or educational purposes. Special editions can also be created to specifications.
For details, contact the Special Sales Department, Skyhorse Publishing,
307 West 36th Street, 11th Floor, New York, NY 10018
or info@skyhorsepublishing.com.

Skyhorse® and Skyhorse Publishing® are registered trademarks of
Skyhorse Publishing, Inc.®, a Delaware corporation.

Visit our website at www.skyhorsepublishing.com.

10 9 8 7 6 5 4 3 2 1

Library of Congress Cataloging-in-Publication Data is available on file.

Print ISBN: 978-1-62914-518-1
Ebook ISBN: 978-1-62914-861-8

Printed in the United States of America

EDITOR'S NOTE

MELVIN M. JOHNSON JR. AND
CHARLES T. HAVEN'S

AUTOMATIC ARMS

by Dr. Jim Casada

The coauthors of this work were both well-established experts on firearms and ammunition, and they almost certainly first met while serving their country. In addition to the present book, they also collaborated on two other efforts: *For Permanent Victory* (1942; reissued in 1943 as *Weapons for the Future*) and *Ammunition: Its History, Development and Use, 1600 to 1943 — .22 BB Cap to 40 mm. Shell* (1943). At the time, Haven was a member of the Army Ordnance Corps and Johnson was in the Marine Corps Reserve.

Melvin M. Johnson Jr. was born in Boston in 1909. His father was dean of Boston University School of Law and Grand Master of Massachusetts Freemasons. The younger Johnson studied at Noble and Greenough School before enrolling at Harvard. He became a member of the Marine Corps Reserve in 1933 (commissioned as a second lieutenant) while studying at Harvard Law School. He completed his legal studies in 1934 and practiced law in the city of his birth until 1939, as well as doing some teaching at Boston University School of Law. He married a noted tennis star, Virginia Bingham Rice, and the couple had three sons and a daughter.

By the time Johnson entered law school, he was already deeply involved in the research, study, and design of firearms, and in 1935, while stationed as an observer at the Springfield Armory, he designed the M1941 Johnson rifle. This was a recoil-operated arm that led to the Johnson light machine gun. Both the rifle and the machine gun saw limited use in World War II, their distribution being focused on specialized army and marine units. The processes underlying the two guns' development might be of some interest to students of armaments.

While posted at the Springfield Armory, Johnson was able to watch the Garand and Pedersen trials being conducted at the site. He found the performances unimpressive and determined to design a retarded blowback–operated rifle. This resulted in the acquisition of four patents connected with specific rifle features, and (with financial and other assistance from his father) the creation of the Johnson Automatics Trust in Brookline, Massachusetts. The trust, which later changed its name to Johnson Automatics, Inc., had its production facilities in Rhode Island. The Model 1941 rifles were made under the manufacturer name of Cranston Arms Company. Johnson Automatics also held government contracts to provide barrels for refitting Model 1917 Enfield rifles from the World War I era.

During World War II, Johnson, thanks to his expertise in firearms design, never saw active duty. Instead, the Marine Corps kept him on the home front to utilize his knowledge and insight. With the conflict's conclusion, Johnson diversified his armaments production. This included converting surplus Model 1941s and making air rifles, as well as turning military surplus bolt-action rifles into fine hunting guns through conversion to .270 and other calibers. Early in the 1950s he was hired by Winchester's John Olin as a gun designer and general adviser, and part of this employment arrangement was Winchester's purchase of Johnson Automatics and all its stock.

Meanwhile, Johnson had been promoted to the rank of colonel after his transfer from the Marine Corps Reserve to the Army Ordnance Corps Reserve (in 1949), and two years later he became a weapons consultant to the secretary of defense. He continued active in gun-related matters until his death, which came from a heart attack in 1965. Throughout his career Johnson wrote regularly, and an obituary in the *Boston Globe* credits him as the author of "eight books and more than 80 magazine articles on guns, ammunition and related subjects." Unless the separate editions of his books are counted individually, however, the number of books is inaccurate. In addition to the present work, which was his first, and the two other works coauthored with Haven (mentioned above), his books include *Rifles and Machine Guns: A Modern Handbook of Infantry and Aircraft Arms* (1944) and *Practical Marksmanship: The Technique of Field Firing* (1945).

Charles T. Haven, Johnson's coauthor, was an even more prolific writer. His first book was *Instruction Manual of the Johnson Light Machine Gun, Type H,* and besides the three books written with Johnson during the heart of World War II, his literary contributions include the landmark *A History of the Colt Revolver* (1940; coauthored with Frank A. Belden), *A Comprehensive Small Arms Manual* (1943), and *Shooting Muzzle Loading Handguns* (1947). He was also a regular contributor to gun magazines and annuals such as *Gun Digest.*

Automatic Arms drew considerable attention from the outset. The 1941 first edition from William Morrow and Co. of New York (reprinted here) was succeeded by a second edition in 1942, with both versions having multiple printings. There was also a 1943 British edition from Robert Hale Publishing. Then in 1945 Morrow brought out a massively expanded (from 366 pages to 644 pages) version of the work under a new title, *Automatic Weapons of the World.* All these editions comprised four basic parts, beginning with history and development and including how automatics operate, along with coverage of matters such as accuracy, design, and mechanical workings.

Somewhat surprisingly, given its multiple editions and numerous printings, the book is not easily located in today's out-of-print market, especially copies with the dust jacket present and in fine condition. That consideration, together with the book's lasting importance as a solid source of information on automatic arms from their evolution until the point when the United States entered World War II, makes it a most welcome and deserving addition to the Firearms Classics Library.

Jim Casada

ROCK HILL, SOUTH CAROLINA

J. M. BROWNING

1855-1926

The world's greatest inventor of automatic weapons
with his famous Colt Browning Machine Gun,
Model of 1895-1914, the first Machine Gun made
in this country.

AUTOMATIC
ARMS

TO the two great national associations of the United States of America which have respectively developed, fostered, promoted, and maintained through periods of public lassitude and moments of great national emergency the principle and practice of training our people in the use of their weapons, and of preparing our nation's industry to produce those weapons

To the National Rifle Association of America, founded in 1871

And

To the Army Ordnance Association, founded in 1919

this book is respectfully dedicated.

Author's Foreword

SINCE Roger Bacon, Berthold Schwartz, or some unsung Chinese philosopher first blew the Thursday night stew out through the roof by getting a few stray chemicals too near the cook-stove, gun bugs have been arguing about how to make guns and how to use them.

Probably very few of the disputants have been one-hundred-per-cent right. Certainly, in the rare cases when someone was, no one else admitted it. But out of all the tumult, shouting and shooting has come the progress in firearms from the days when it was necessary to build a fire under a gun to make it go off to the "you press the button and they do the work" automatic arms of the present day.

This development we have tried to outline and illustrate, especially as it applies to automatic arms, as we feel that automatic weapons are of primary importance in modern warfare. Today they constitute the main armament of infantry, cavalry, mechanized forces, the air force, anti-tank and anti-aircraft units, and special service troops, as well as the parachutists and the like.

The percentage of machine guns and light automatics increased tremendously in all armies during the first World War. In the present war, automatic weapons overwhelmingly predominate.

For several years past there has been growing a more widespread interest in automatic weapons on the part of the general public, a section of which now marches in its army's ranks. There has been a great deal of general discussion about various automatic weapons pro and con, and naturally there have been misunderstandings and misinterpretations. While this text attempts to clarify or explain many points, it must be clearly understood that this book is definitely not of a controversial nature.

Both of us are associated with Johnson Automatics, Incorporated, which is engaged, among other things, in the manufacture of Johnson Semi-Automatic Rifles and Johnson Light Machine Guns, the inventions of Captain Johnson. Inasmuch as these are recoil-operated weapons, our natural interest in weapons operated by this method may seem to appear in the text from time to time.

However, this is still a free country, and every man is entitled to his own opinion. We hope that those who differ from us will be interested in our reasons for thinking as we do. Where we have expressed our opinions or indicated our preferences, we have attempted to give in each instance the underlying facts and reasons. The reader is urged to draw his own conclusions. The book is not a collection of operation manuals, describing in detail each well-known weapon, or a sales catalog for any particular manufacturer or arsenal, or a series of essays on what is wrong with any gun, any place, or any organization. The views and opinions expressed herein are entirely those of the authors and do not necessarily reflect or coincide with those of Johnson Automatics, Incorporated, or of any organizations with which the authors are associated.

This book has been written during the second World War. Combat and general military considerations have predominated our discussions, but we are not unmindful of the long-awaited day when world order shall be restored, and when those who enjoy the pleasures and benefits of shooting in its many forms will return in peace to their sport, encouraged and assured by this tragic, yet so oft-repeated proof, that theirs is a pastime of vital, underlying benefit to the national defense of their country. To them, the riflemen and shooters of all peace-loving nations, the year-in and year-out backbone of the national defense, we express the hope that they too will find this book of interest.

We wish to acknowledge gratefully the friendly assistance, in the form of pictures, information and permission to use published material, that we have received from the following friends and organizations: Mr. Kenyon Abbott, Mr. H. P. Abbott, Jr., Mr. Frank A. Belden, Mr. Nathan Danials, Mr. Walter E. Fleming, Mr. J. C. Harvey, Mr. Birnie Pierce, Captain Charles J. Van Ambergh, Mr. Lincoln Wadsworth, Mr. Allen P. Wescott, the National Rifle Association, the Army Ordnance Association, the *Infantry Mailing List,* the Marine Corps Association, Colt's Patent Fire Arms Manufacturing Company and Mr. L. C. Davis and Mr. Albert Foster, Jr., of that company, Harrington & Richardson Arms Company, O. F. Mossberg & Sons, Inc., the Remington Arms Company, the Marlin Arms Co., the Savage Arms Corporation, R. F. Sedgley, Inc., A. E. Stoeger & Company, the Winchester Repeating Arms Company, the Springfield Armory and Mr. William Murphy, curator of the Springfield Armory Museum and the Chief of Ordnance, United States Army.

M. M. JOHNSON, JR.
CHARLES T. HAVEN

Contents

PART THREE

HOW TO KEEP THEM FIRING

Contents

PART FIVE

MISCELLANEOUS CONSIDERATIONS

Illustrations

xiv   Illustrations

Illustrations

XV

PART ONE

History and Development

CHAPTER ONE

Early Multifiring Arms

*Early Machine Gun Types; Automatic Machine Guns
up to and including the First World War*

FROM the day when firearms first came into being, some six
or seven hundred years ago, three problems have confronted
those who have designed and used them. The first is the arrangement of a chamber and barrel through which a projectile can be
driven by a charge of explosive. The second is that of providing
an ignition system to fire the charge, and eventually a container
to hold it as a separate unit. The third, the problem with which
this book will principally concern itself, is that of providing ways
and means to repeat the discharge and fire successive shots as
rapidly as possible.

This third problem has turned out to be for the most part dependent upon the second. For many years the principles behind
most of the modern repeating systems were understood and applied so far as they could be to the arms at hand. But their practical application awaited an ignition system that could be adapted
to making the charge of a firearm a self-contained and self-igniting
unit.

All through the hand cannon, matchlock, wheel lock, snap-
hance, Miguelet lock, and flintlock eras, covering the years from
the middle of the fourteenth century to 1807, there was a common
stumbling block to the progress of multifiring systems. This was
the necessity for applying some regular fire-making apparatus,
such as a lighted match or a flint and steel, to the outside of the
barrel of a gun and then leading the fire so made through an open
hole to the main charge inside that barrel.

Because of this essential requirement, arms to fire more than
one shot—with the exception of double-barreled guns and pistols—

were not common prior to the early nineteenth century, but they did exist. Merely adding barrels to an arm, regardless of its charge and ignition system, was the simplest way to increase fire power, at least temporarily. Multibarreled guns appeared almost as soon as single-barreled ones. Among the mount types, the Ribaudkin or *Orgue des Bombardes* was an arrangement of a number of gun barrels or small cannon mounted together on wheels or on a light cart. It was used in some cases as a mobile arm, and in others,

The French Orgue des Bombardes

especially where pikes were mounted alternately with the gun barrels, as a stationary defense against cavalry.

The Venetian General Colleoni used *Orgues des Bombardes* as mobile auxiliaries in connection with his heavy cavalry at the Battle of Piccardini (Picardy) in 1457. On another occasion, Pedro Navarro, a Spanish commander, protected his infantry at the Battle of Ravenna in 1512 by placing in front of them "thirty carts mounted with arquebuses."

However, the mere addition of barrels to increase the number of shots was never satisfactory in hand arms on account of bulk and weight. Even in mounted pieces it did not allow sustained fire, although the concentrated blast from such arms at the beginning of an engagement could be delivered with telling effect.

Other repeating systems, which have been successfully applied to handguns since the advent of metallic self-igniting cartridges, were tried many times during this early period of firearms development.

Crude revolving arms, some with several barrels and some with a single one fed by a number of chambers at the breech, are met with occasionally from about the middle of the fifteenth century. Magazine repeaters of various types also enjoyed a limited use. Some of them held their reserves of loose powder and ball in the butt, and others in magazines beneath the barrel. They were operated by moving the trigger guard, turning levers lying along the stock, and twisting the barrels on an axis parallel to the bore. All through the flint and steel ignition period these were the acme of the gunsmiths' ingenuity, but they rarely included safety or practicability among their diverse features.

In some of the early repeaters the charges were loaded one on top of the other in the same barrel, like the contents of a Roman candle, and fired by a movable lock which was pushed back to the rear charges after the front ones had been fired. This was a method that was continued until the middle of the nineteenth century. The last arms of the type brought out were the Walch 10-shot, double-chambered, percussion-cap revolver and the Lindsay 2-shot, double-chambered, percussion-cap pistols and muskets, all used in small quantities in the Civil War. The "Roman candle" system was, however, always dangerous with loose ammunition because of possible premature explosion of the lower charges, and of course it was unnecessary after the advent of metallic cartridges.

Champlain, the French explorer, helped the Algonquin and Huron Indians to win a tribal war with the Iroquois in 1608, his party having among their firearms 3- and 5-shot repeaters. Lord Nelson advocated a 7-barreled flintlock carbine for his marines and personally carried a magazine repeating pocket pistol, which, incidentally, is now in the Metropolitan Museum of Art in New York City.

Perhaps one of the weirdest of the early multifiring arms was the invention of one James Puckle, who in 1718 took out an English patent for "A portable gun or machine called a Defence, that discharges so often and so many bullets, and be so quickly loaden, as renders it next to impossible to carry any ship by boarding."

From the patent drawing, Puckle's machine appears to have employed a single barrel with a many-chambered breech rotated by hand and fired by a match. Either the chambers or the whole

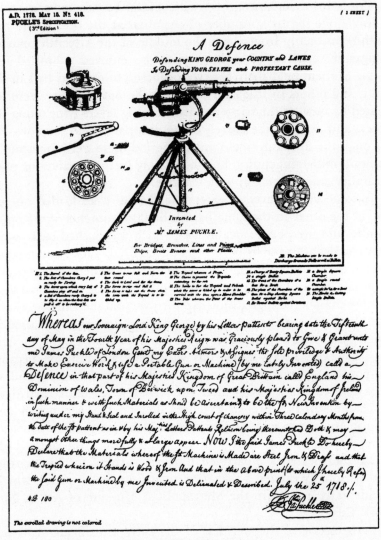

Mr. James Puckle's Defence

breech mechanism were replaceable after the charges were fired. The gun was mounted on a tripod and fitted with a crude elevating and traversing system.

Mr. Puckle also provided what he seems to have considered an added advantage, in designing the arm to shoot round bullets against Christians and square ones against Turks, whom he must have especially disliked. It is probable that none of these arms were ever used in battle, but the patent drawing looks surprisingly modern in some of its features.

However, the gate that was to lead the way to firearms progress in all directions was eventually opened not by a gunsmith nor by a military man but by a clergyman-chemist. The year 1807 marks the end of one era and the beginning of another in firearms design and evolution. Up to this time the ignition systems in use had not progressed in principle since the introduction of the wheel lock, the first flint and steel lock, in 1517. The perfected flintlock of the early nineteenth century was somewhat surer of fire and much more convenient to use than the types which preceded it, but it still employed the sparks struck from flint and steel to ignite powder in an outside flashpan and communicated that flash to the main charge through a hole in the barrel.

In 1807 a Scotch clergyman, the Reverend Alexander Forsyth, patented the application of fulminate of mercury to the discharge of a firearm. He did not "invent the percussion cap" as has been frequently stated. Forsyth's gunlocks used loose detonating powder, but they paved the way for the various types of percussion primers that culminated in the percussion cap about 1816.

Of course, the percussion cap did not immediately become the only type of ignition system for firearms to be used from then on, even though it was the best. Neither the English nor the American government adopted it for army use until after 1840, and best grade flintlock sporting guns were made until the middle fifties. It was, however, available for inventors to work with, and the immediate results of the percussion cap were the various single-shot combustible cartridge breechloaders, all more rapid of fire than the muzzle loaders, and the revolver.

The first multifiring arm that was made and used in any quantity, or that had any real practical value as a military weapon, was in the form of a single-barreled pistol or rifle with a rotating chambered breech holding from 5 to 8 charges. These charges were loaded separately into the muzzles of the chambers and fired by percussion caps on nipples at their rear. The rotating chambered breech, or cylinder, was unlocked, rotated, and locked again with a fresh chamber in line with the barrel, all by the single act of cocking the hammer.

This was the famous Colt revolver, patented in 1836 by Samuel Colt of Hartford, Connecticut. It was first made at Paterson, New Jersey, by the Patent Arms Manufacturing Company, but this company failed in 1841, and no more arms of the type were made until 1847, when 1000 were fabricated at Eli Whitney's plant in

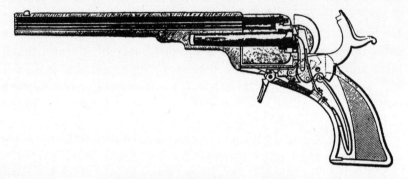

Samuel Colt's First Revolver, 1836

Whitneyville, Connecticut, to fill an order for the United States Army which was at that time engaged in the Mexican War. On the strength of further orders Colt established his own plant at Hartford, Connecticut, by 1848, and the company has been producing rapid-fire arms of many types ever since.

Unheard-of fire power was delivered by the new arms. Accounts of the exploits of the Texas Rangers, the Second Dragoons, and the Mounted Rifles, outfits armed with Colt revolvers, before and during the Mexican War, show the results that were achieved in battle when one force engaged had a marked superiority over the other in this respect.

Instances from the Senate Reports on the use of these weapons include the following: Fifteen Rangers armed with revolvers defeated eighty Comanche Indians and killed forty-two of them. One hundred of the Mounted Rifles, of whom only forty were armed with revolvers, defeated six hundred well-armed Mexican cavalry. Colonel Hays, with sixty Rangers, drove five hundred Mexican cavalry from the field, killing eighty, without losing one man of the Rangers.

Superior speed of fire for the first shots of an engagement, regardless of the time taken to reload or the problem of ammunition supply for the rest of the day, began to show its importance.

The next development to be credited to percussion ignition was the metallic self-igniting cartridge. From the pin-fire paper shells of Le Faucheux in 1836, through the patents of Houillier for all metal cases, rim-fire ignition, and rudimentary center-fire in 1849, the Boxer primer with its own anvil in the middle sixties, and the Berdan drawn brass solid head case of 1870, the cartridge has progressed to the form with which we are now familiar.

Even before this development was complete, the rim-fire copper-cased cartridges of the late fifties and early sixties brought into existence the magazine repeating rifle and the mechanically operated quick-firing gun of a size intermediate between shoulder arms and light artillery, the arm first described as a "machine gun."

Repeating rifles were heard from first. A mechanism originally designed by Jennings and Hunt in 1849—which was eventually to become the basis of the Winchester—was adapted to a .44 caliber rim-fire cartridge under patents of B. Tyler Henry, granted October 16, 1860. This arm was a 15-shot lever-action repeater carrying its cartridges in a tubular magazine under the barrel and feeding them to the action by a rising-link operated carrier block worked by the trigger guard lever.

Another lever-action repeater, also operated by a movable trigger guard, but using a butt magazine of tubular form with a capacity of 8 shots and a rolling block, was patented by C. Spencer, March 6, 1860. The Spencer used a .56 caliber rim-fire cartridge loaded with 45 grains of powder and a 360-grain bullet.

These two were the only metallic cartridge repeating rifles used in the Civil War in any quantity, and such was the respect in which they were held that military authorities estimated a man armed with one of them and operating from cover as equal to eight men in the open armed with regulation muskets. These were the beginning of the long line of military repeating shoulder arms that has stretched toward us through the box magazine, bolt action, clip loading, and finally the automatic types of the present

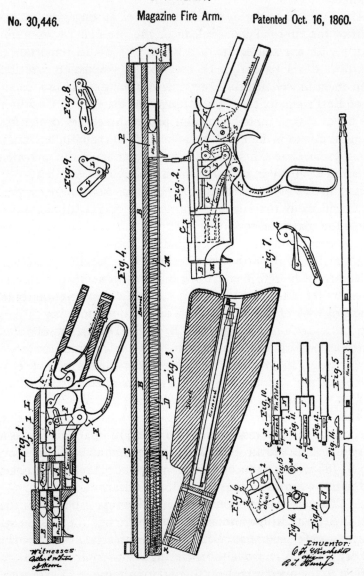

Action of the Henry Repeating Rifle

day. What the future holds we do not know; maybe Buck Rogers' rocket guns are not so wild as they sound.

One of the first of the quick-firing mount guns to appear was the Billinghurst Requa Battery Gun. This arm had a single row of barrels, 24 in number, mounted between wide-set wheels. It was fed by clips of cartridges that had a hole in the base, which were inserted at the breech, fired as a volley by igniting powder in a priming train that went the length of the breechblock and was touched off by a percussion-cap nipple and hammer, and withdrawn as a unit to make room for a fresh clip. This gun was demonstrated in front of the New York Stock Exchange at the beginning of the Civil War in the hope of interesting capital in its manufacture. A few were made, and one was used at Charleston, South Carolina; but the model exerted no influence on the development of quick-firing guns, either from an evolutionary or a practical point of view.

Another gun employing some of the principles of the Billinghurst Requa—although it was much better designed and included several new features, including the use of self-igniting ammunition—was the Montigny Mitrailleuse, also developed during this experimental period. This gun was developed and manufactured in Brussels, Belgium, by Faschamps and Montigny between 1851 and 1869. It was adopted in the latter year by the French government and manufactured for government use at the Arsenal of Meudon.

The Mitrailleuse consisted of a group of 37 barrels contained in a circular housing and mounted on a wheeled carriage of medium weight, so that it had the general appearance of a twelve-pounder field gun. It was loaded by a breechblock or clip having chambers for cartridges corresponding in number and arrangement to the barrels. This was locked into place by a moving member at the breech of the gun, which also contained the firing pins. The firing pin springs were compressed by closing the breech action, but the pins were held away from the cartridges by a movable pierced plate that was moved by turning a crank on the side of the breech. This released the firing pins in succession and the shots could be fired slowly or rapidly, depending upon how fast the crank was turned.

C. M. SPENCER.
Magazine Gun.

No. 27,393.

Patented Mar. 6, 1860.

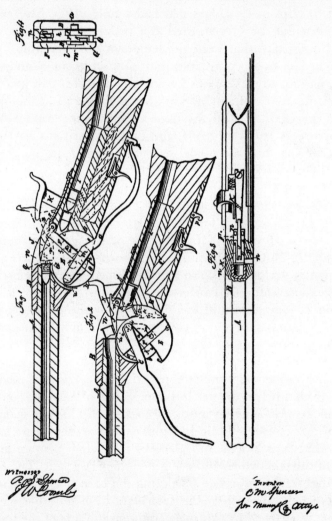

Action of the Spencer Repeating Rifle

Ammunition for the Mitrailleuse was supplied in the 37-shot clips, or plates. With a crew of several men operating it, about 10 clips a minute, or 370 shots, could be fired.

The French army used the Mitrailleuses during the Franco-Prussian War, but unfortunately did not realize the proper

The Montigny Mitrailleuse, 1851-1869

method of employing quick-firing guns. They were used for the most part at artillery ranges, and sometimes even against artillery. Their performance under such conditions was most disappointing to the French, who had advertised the new arm as a "secret weapon" which would make their armies invincible by its terrible destructiveness.

In one battle—by a curious coincidence of names, that of Montigny—the Mitrailleuses did get into action at close range on massed infantry, and performed admirably. The French, however, succeeded in learning nothing at all from this and one or two other similar episodes, and finally lost the war by general mismanagement. Among other excuses for their poor showing, the French blamed the Mitrailleuses because they would not take the place of the field artillery which they looked like, or operate against it. It was, therefore, many years before quick-firing guns overcame the prejudice built up against them in Europe by this episode and were accepted at somewhere near their real value by military authorities.

In this country the first practical quick-firing gun was the invention of Dr. Richard Gatling of Chicago, who patented a "battery or machine gun" in 1862. This was probably the first real "machine gun," in that the charges were fed into the chambers, fired, and extracted by the actual operation of machinery.

One or two arms, such as, for example, the Union Battery Gun, using steel chargers fitted with percussion nipples which were contained in a hopper above a single barrel and fed to it by a crank-operated mechanism, may have been invented at about the same time as the first Gatlings, or they may even have slightly antedated them, but they have left no permanent mark in machine gun evolution, and the few examples of them that remain are museum specimens and little more.

The first model of the Gatling gun also used steel chargers fired by percussion caps, and in this form it was in limited use in the Civil War. The government military authorities did not consider it an especially desirable improvement in small arms, so Gatling hired his own operators to use the guns on the battlefield as a practical demonstration of their capabilities.

By 1866 the Gatling gun was adapted for regular metallic rim- or center-fire cartridges and its manufacture was begun by the Colt company. With various improvements it was made from that date until about 1910.

The mechanism of the Gatling gun consisted of a group of barrels—at first 4 and later from 6 to 10—mounted in a circle within a frame. The barrels were revolved by turning a crank on the right side of the breech housing. Each barrel had its own lock, and the cartridges were fed by gravity from a hopper on top of the breech.

The stationary breech was fitted with camming grooves so that as the barrels turned in a block, the lock of each barrel picked up a cartridge, pushed it into the chamber, fired it, and extracted it so that it fell out through a slot in the housing as the barrel came up past it.

The Gatling was a very satisfactory type of hand-operated machine gun. It was used all over the world in calibers from one

The Gatling Gun

inch down to 6 mm. during the last third of the nineteenth century and the first few years of the present one. The rate of fire was anything up to about 800 shots per minute, depending upon how fast the operating crank was turned. Some of the Gatlings were fitted with an automatic traversing gear as part of the firing mechanism, to insure dispersion at short range. As only one shot in from six to ten was fired from any individual barrel, a fair rate of fire could be maintained for some time without overheating, even though there was no provision for cooling.

The main objection to the Gatling was its weight, as the number of barrels and the heavy wheel mount made it almost a small piece of artillery, although the technique of using quick-firing guns as adjuncts to infantry was fairly well understood before the Gatlings were outmoded.

Another revolving type crank-operated gun of the period was the Lowell Battery Gun. This arm also used a gravity feed from a

The Lowell Battery Gun

hopper on top of the breech. The cartridges were brought to the chamber, fired, and extracted by a revolving mechanism operated by a crank at the back of the breech. The gun was mounted on wheels and had 4 barrels arranged in a circle. It was similar in general appearance to the Gatling, but its barrels did not revolve with the breech mechanism. One barrel was used at a time, and when a barrel became heated, a cool one was revolved and locked into position by hand, to be used until it in turn became hot. This gun was not so good as the Gatling and was nowhere nearly so much used.

Fifteenth Century Multibarrel Revolving Arm

Billinghurst Requa Battery Gun

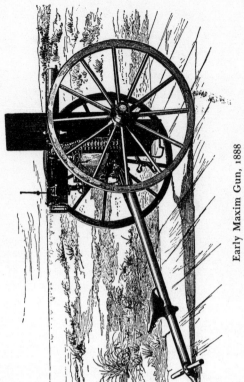

Early Maxim Gun, 1888

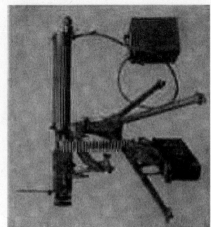

Vickers Machine Gun

Gardner Machine Gun

An even heavier arm of the general Gatling type was the Hotchkiss revolving cannon, used during the eighties and nineties. The Hotchkiss was a 5-barreled gun of great weight, mounted on heavy wheels or fixed mounts, and designed to shoot shells up to 1½ inches in diameter. It differed from the Gatling in that, although the barrels revolved in a block, it had but one lock and firing pin.

Hotchkiss Revolving Cannon

The operating crank on the right side was turned continuously; but, by means of a stop gear in the breech mechanism, after the barrels had revolved to bring a shell in line with the firing pin they remained stationary while it was fired. At the same time, the empty shell was extracted from the barrel on the right of the one being fired and a loaded shell was fed into the barrel on the left. The shells were supplied to the mechanism by gravity feed from a trough inclining to the left at the top of the breech. With a good crew serving it, 60 to 80 shots a minute could be fired from the Hotchkiss gun.

Another quick-firing weapon of large bore, the McLean repeating cannon, was also used in small quantities by the United States forces at this period.

A different multibarreled system was employed in the Palmcrantz-Nordenfeldt machine gun, developed between 1873 and 1878 and used throughout Europe until after the turn of the cen-

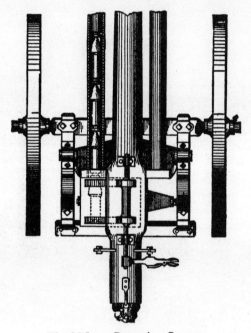

The McLean Repeating Cannon

tury. In the Nordenfeldt gun, from 2 to 6 barrels were placed in horizontal alignment and fired in succession or in volleys by moving a lever on the right side of the breech backward and forward. Hoppers above the barrels supplied the ammunition by gravity. The empty shells fell out of openings in the bottom of the action as they were extracted by the backward movement of the hand lever. Several hundred shots per minute could be delivered from this gun. It was very popular throughout Europe during the eighties and early nineties, especially as a naval fixed-mount gun. Its capacity for volley firing was considered a good defense, particularly with guns of over one-half inch bore, against the light torpedo-carrying boats of small size and considerable speed that were one of the naval developments of the period.

Perhaps the handiest of these mechanically operated machine guns was the Gardner, patented in 1882 by William Gardner, formerly a captain in the United States Army. It was used extensively in the English army up to the adoption of the Maxim automatic gun. The Gardner machine gun was made with from 1 to 5 bar-

The Palmcrantz Nordenfeldt Machine Gun

rels placed side by side and had the usual gravity feed from top-mounted containers. The firing mechanism was a crankshaft and piston arrangement operated by a side crank. When there was more than one barrel, they were fired in succession somewhat similarly to the pistons and cylinders of an automobile. The Gardner gun could be fired at the rate of about 200 shots per minute per barrel.

The Gardner was the first of the really portable machine guns. It was usually fired from a tripod instead of a heavy wheel mount. The single barreled gun, complete with its tripod and 1000 rounds of .45 caliber ammunition, weighed less than 200 pounds. The whole outfit could be carried anywhere on a single horse and handled in a really mobile fashion by a crew of three or four men.

During the period in which these early mechanically operated machine guns were in general use—roughly, from 1875 to 1895—there was no major war by which to gauge their effectiveness. But it was a period of expansion of empire by various European nations. Whatever these guns might have done in battle between well-trained armies, reports of their use against various tribes of "poor benighted heathens" indicate that they were pretty effective civilizers when used against massed charges of our little brethren, brown and black, who were so backward in culture as to carry only spears.

In 1883 Hiram Maxim, an American, was displaying some of his electrical inventions at a science show in Europe, when another American made a very profound remark. "This stuff is all right," he said, "but if you really want to make some money, invent something that will make it easier and quicker for these Europeans to cut each others' throats."

Acting on this suggestion, Maxim set up an experimental laboratory near London, and after two years of work patented a gun which loaded and fired itself by the recoil of its discharge. After further development, the Maxim automatic machine gun was adopted by the English government in 1889 and manufactured by the Vickers company in its original type until after the first World War.

The Maxim gun introduced several new features to quick-firing guns. In the first place, the action was wholly automatic, the operator merely holding his finger on the trigger. The barrel and breechblock were locked together as each cartridge was fired, recoiling for a short distance before a toggle action unlocked the breech and allowed the block to continue its motion. This movement extracted the fired case, replaced it with a new one, fired that in turn and continued this process as long as the trigger was held.

Another feature of the Maxim was a single barrel for all the shots, and this was kept cool by a jacket around it filled with water. A third new departure was the ammunition feed. Instead of the ubiquitous gravity feed with its various troubles and stoppages, the Maxim gun took its ammunition from a canvas belt which ran through the action and was held folded in a box on the

Maxim 37 mm. Automatic Gun, 1898

Colt Browning Gas-Operated Machine Gun, 1914

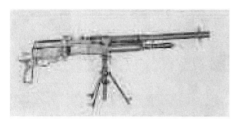

Hotchkiss Machine Gun

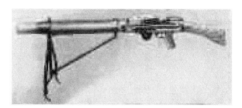

Lewis Machine Gun

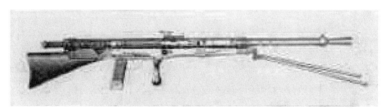

French Chauchard or Chauchat Machine Rifle

Schwarzlose Machine Gun

Early Type Spandau Maxim, German

Revelli Machine Gun, Italian

Early Type Bergmann, German

Fiat Automatic Cannon

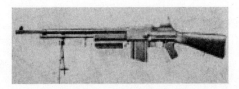

Browning Automatic Rifle Model 1918

Madsen Light Machine Gun

Benet Mercie Machine Rifle M1909

Colt Browning Machine Gun Model 1917

Villa Perosa Submachine Gun

side of the gun. The belt held 250 rounds of ammunition, and box and belt could be replaced in a few seconds.

Water cooling and belt feeding, while they gave no greater cyclic rate of fire, afforded the machine gun a much faster rate of sustained fire and one that could be kept up much longer. The boxed belts of ammunition were also far more easily handled under all conditions than the earlier types. The Maxim gun was the forerunner of many of the automatic guns that are still in use, and a number of its features are retained in most modern guns of the type.

A very large-sized gun of the Maxim type was used in the Boer War and also to some extent in the first World War. This was a 37 mm. full-automatic gun with the Maxim action, belt feed, and water cooling jacket. It was as big as a field piece, and was fed by 25-shot belts containing the 37 mm. shells. From the rapid explosion of the shells as they struck, it was colloquially named the "pom-pom." While it never was considered an especially effective weapon, it is fair to place it as the ancestor of the modern automatic cannon of the same caliber that are being developed and used for aircraft work today.

Another method of utilizing the expansion of gases resultant from the discharge of a gun to operate it was hit upon a few years later by an American inventor, John M. Browning. In the early nineties Browning came to the Colt company with a machine gun operated by gas taken from a port in the barrel near the muzzle. This gas struck the head of a swinging lever under the barrel, causing it to swing backward and down, thus operating a mechanism which drew a cartridge from the canvas belt, inserted it in the chamber, fired it, extracted it, and continued the process as long as the trigger was held back. Guns of this type have since been called gas-operated machine guns.

The Colt company brought out Browning's gun in 1895 as the Colt Browning Automatic Gun. It was adopted by both the Navy and the Army before the outbreak of the Spanish-American War, and saw service during that conflict, as did also the Gatling guns which were still a part of our small-arms equipment. The Colt Browning was an air-cooled gun mounted on a tripod and having a cyclic rate of fire of 400 shots per minute.

A few of the early Maxims were chambered for black powder cartridges, but the fouling was so great with black powder that no automatic arm could operate satisfactorily using cartridges loaded with it. The first Colt Brownings were chambered for the .30-40 Krag-Jörgensen smokeless powder cartridges, and all automatic and semi-automatic arms since the early nineties have used smokeless powder in their cartridges and usually jacketed bullets as well.

Another type of gas-operated machine gun introduced about the same time as the Colt Browning was the European "Odkolek." This weapon tapped its gas from about the same place in the barrel as the Colt, but used it to push on a piston sliding in a cylinder attached below and parallel to the barrel and thus to operate the repeating mechanism. It was the forerunner of the French Hotchkiss machine gun.

These arms were the first of the automatic or "machine" guns as we know them today. They represent the two systems into which most of the present arms of this type fall—recoil operation and gas operation. In their original models they were used up to and including the first World War, but the early types have, for the most part, since been replaced by new or modernized models, and these will be considered in later chapters of this book.

In the Russo-Japanese War of 1904-5, the Russians used the Maxim machine gun and the Japanese used the newly developed Hotchkiss gas-operated gun. Even as late as this war, the real tactical place of the machine gun was little understood, and it played a relatively small part in the conflict compared to what it might have been made to do.

In the years from 1900 to the end of the first World War automatic arms developments came thick and fast. Two types of machine gun were generally adopted by most countries. One type was a heavy mount gun, fired from a fixed tripod, usually belt fed and frequently water cooled, with a total weight of between 50 and 150 pounds. The other was a light machine rifle, fired from a bipod portable rest, if any, usually clip or drum fed, air cooled, and weighing between 15 and 35 pounds.

Great Britain entered the war armed with the Vickers Maxim recoil-operated, belt-fed, water-cooled gun weighing about 85 pounds with its tripod, as the heavy model, and soon adopted the light Hotchkiss gas-operated gun weighing 28 pounds and fed from metal strips or a short belt. In 1916 the Lewis gun was also adopted as a light weapon. This was a gas-operated gun that fed from a drum of 47 cartridges mounted on top of the action. It had a tubular air-cooling arrangement and a light bipod mount. Its total weight was 26 pounds. The Lewis was the invention of an American, but it had been turned down by the United States authorities before it was offered to England. The English used it both in the field with infantry and mounted on airplanes.

France used the Hotchkiss gas-operated machine gun in light and heavy models, both air cooled and strip fed. They also used the Chauchard (or "Chauchat") machine rifle, a long recoil-operated gun fed from a curved box magazine and weighing just under 20 pounds.

Austria had the only simple blowback action machine gun without a breech-locking device that was used by any of the major powers in full rifle caliber. This was the Schwarzlose gun, a belt-fed, recoil-operated, water-cooled arm weighing 90 pounds. The combination of an unusually heavy breechblock and a toggle-joint action somewhat like the Luger pistol was made to take the place of any positive lock in this model.

Germany used as its heavy gun the Spandau Maxim model of 1908. This was a water-cooled, recoil-operated, belt-fed gun weighing from 100 to 125 pounds on different mountings and very similar to the Vickers Maxim in action. A later model made at Erfurt weighed 85 pounds, but was otherwise very similar to the 1908 model.

Germany also used a number of light machine guns, including: the Bergmann, 26 pounds, recoil operated, belt fed; the Parabellum, 22 pounds, recoil operated; the Madsen, 20 pounds, recoil operated, box magazine fed.

Italy used as its heavy gun the Revelli, a 90-pound gun that was water cooled and fed from a peculiar type of clip magazine. It was operated by a combination of recoil and blowback.

The United States, in addition to the Colt Browning of 1895, had adopted the Benet Mercie in 1909. This was a gas-operated, air-cooled gun fed by metal strips of cartridges, and of medium weight. It was very similar to the Hotchkiss. The Colt Browning was improved in 1914 and listed as "Model 1914." It was also manufactured during the war by the Marlin Arms Company, with the variation that the operating lever was replaced by a piston and cylinder.

On our entry into the first World War, Browning designed two new guns for service use. One was a heavy belt-fed, water-cooled model weighing about 90 pounds and operated by a short recoil, locked-breech action. The other was a light gas-operated machine rifle, weighing about 15 pounds and capable of being fired either full- or semi-automatic. It fed from a 20-shot box magazine under the action. Both these arms are still in use and are known as the Heavy Browning Machine Gun and the Browning Automatic Rifle, or "B.A.R." They are made by the Colt Company.

Owing to a shortage of these guns at the time our troops reached France, we borrowed light and heavy machine guns from the other Allied powers—Vickers, Hotchkiss, and Chauchats, as well as other equipment.

In addition to the rifle caliber machine guns, a type of automatic arm was in limited use at the time of the first World War that has undergone further development since, and at the present time bids fair to assume an important place among portable automatic weapons. This is the submachine gun. A submachine gun is generally considered to be a light weapon about the size of a short carbine and weighing from 5 to 10 pounds. It usually employs pistol ammunition and its magazine capacity is limited to about 50 rounds, frequently less. From the light weight, both of the gun and its ammunition, a considerable number of shots can be carried for it by one or two men. While it has no great range, its fire power is something to be reckoned with.

In the first World War the Germans used an arm of this type called the Bergmann Muskete. This was a recoil-operated, air-cooled arm of the appearance of a small carbine. It was chambered for the 9 mm. Luger pistol cartridge and fed from a 32-shot drum placed below the action. The barrel was enclosed in a pierced metal handguard and the arm was designed to fire either full- or semi-automatic.

Two submachine guns were used at this same time by the Italians. They were made by Revelli and by Villa Perosa, and were similar in type though somewhat different from other submachine guns. They were small replicas of larger guns, mounted double, with two actions and with barrels set side by side. They were short and compact, being about 30 inches over-all, with a weight of about 12 pounds. They were recoil operated and air cooled, feeding from box magazines set on top of the action, and holding 40 shots. The two barrels could be fired separately or together. They were mounted on airplanes or provided for infantry use with a light bipod.

These were the general types of full-automatic arms in use up to and including the first World War, of the size that we usually call "machine guns." Some of them are still in use and some new ones have been developed to augment them. Faster movement on the ground and more powerful airplanes have carried the development of these arms toward better mobility, faster rates of fire, and greater power.

CHAPTER TWO

Automatic Pistols

*Early Repeating Types; Early Automatic Pistols; The
Colt Automatic Pistols; Other United States Military
Auto Pistols; United States Pocket Auto Pistols; The
Webley Scott English Auto Pistols; Continental Pocket
Automatics*

EARLY REPEATING TYPES

ASIDE from improvement in ease and speed with which revolvers could be used, metallic cartridges brought to the
small handgun another possibility in mechanism types. This was
the repeating pistol. A curious exception in repeating types of
the percussion-cap period was the Lindsay 2-shot pistol, made in
America during the 1850's. This pistol was loaded with two
charges, one on top of the other, and fired by two percussion
caps on nipples that were struck by two separate hammers which
were released in the proper order by a single trigger. Muskets,
military pistols, pocket pistols, and double-chambered revolvers
were made on this system and were used in limited numbers in
the Civil War.

Some of the earliest repeating pistols, such as the Remington,
Sharps, Marston, and others, gained additional shots by adding
barrels up to the number of 5 or 6, and by providing various
firing mechanisms for discharging these in succession. The Sharps
used an outside hammer with a revolving firing pin which was
automatically turned to strike its 4 barrels in succession as it was
cocked and fired. The Remington had an internal hammer operated by a double-action ring trigger that worked similarly for
either 4- or 5-barreled pistols of .22 and .32 caliber. The Marston
placed 3 barrels one above the other, firing them with a sliding

firing pin moving from top to bottom as the hammer was cocked for each shot.

Other multibarrel types included: the Harmonica pistol, having a row of barrels that moved laterally to bring them under the hammer in succession as the double-action trigger was pulled; pistols with revolving blocks of barrels like the early "pepperboxes"; and heavy English and European Mitrailleuse pistols with 4 stationary barrels and inside revolving strikers, such as the Lancaster and the Breandlin. These arms were usually of .410 bore or larger, with ten-inch barrels.

True repeating pistols that were neither multibarrel arms nor revolvers also began to appear about the middle of the nineteenth century. One of the first of these was a manually operated weapon made by the firm which was also making a rifle-sized mechanism that later became the Winchester rifle. Its action was the same as that of the larger arm.

Smith and Wesson, about 1855, and their successors to the design, the Volcanic and the New Haven Arms companies, between 1855 and 1860, made repeating pistols with a link and carrier block mechanism operated by a trigger guard finger lever which fed to the chamber, from a tubular magazine under the barrel, a succession of hollow-based bullets filled with a priming compound that had enough force to drive them out quite powerfully. There were no cartridge cases, and consequently no extraction problems. This mechanism was not, however, well adapted to pistols. Though it has survived to the present time in many makes of repeating rifles, no handguns of the type were made after 1860.

While the European needle gun cartridges, with their soft paper cases and deep seated primers, were not well adapted for a repeating mechanism, one type of repeating pistol was made to use them. In this arm the magazine lay on top of the barrel and the cartridges were fed to the breechblock by gravity, as the arm had to be held muzzle up when it was cocked. Cocking the arm raised the breechblock so that a cartridge could fall into the chamber in the block, and it was then brought back into line with the barrel. The hammer had a long nose, or "needle," that struck through the powder to the primer at the base of the bullet.

The cartridge was self-consuming, so there was no extractor. This was by no means an ideal weapon, for obvious reasons, but it must have been made in considerable numbers as specimens are met with fairly frequently in antique arms collections.

Another repeating pistol was put out by the Remington Arms Company in the early seventies under Rider's patents. This pistol used a rim-fire cartridge of .32 extra short caliber, which was fed from a tubular magazine under the barrel. The breechlock was pierced so that the hammer struck through it. It was provided with a tang which stood up above the tang of the hammer. The breechblock and hammer were pulled back together to cock the arm. The backward movement ejected the fired cartridge and brought a loaded one up from the magazine into position in front of the chamber. Removing the thumb left the hammer cocked, but the breechblock was carried forward by a spring to drive the cartridge into the chamber and support it for firing. The arm used a very weak cartridge and was never able to compete with the many excellent and powerful revolvers which were available at the time. Relatively few were made and its manufacture was soon discontinued.

Another curious arm was made in the eighties and nineties by the Chicago Arms Company and marketed in this country as the "Protector." The same arm was sold in France. This pistol carried from six to ten small rim-fire cartridges placed like the spokes of a wheel in a magazine inside a casing that was about the size and shape of an old-fashioned watch. A short barrel protruded from one edge of it and a curved lever was pivoted opposite. In use, the pistol was grasped by the whole hand, with the barrel protruding between the first and second fingers. It was fired by contracting the hand to squeeze the operating lever which turned the magazine inside the pistol and fired the cartridges with a central striker as they came opposite the barrel. It was not noted for either power or accuracy.

Several somewhat similar European pistols were in use during the same period. One of these was the Gaulois, and another was made by the Française Armes et Cajdes de St. Etienne. These arms were usually nearly square in the body, with the barrel as a prolongation of the top. They were squeeze operated, the Gau-

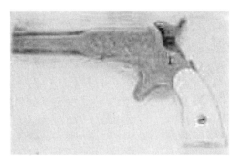

Lindsay Two-Shot Repeating Pistol

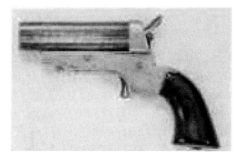

Sharp's Four-Barrel Repeating Pistol

Remington Five-Barrel .22 Repeating Pistol

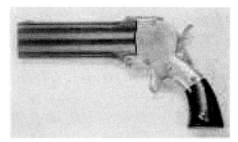

Marston Three-Barrel Repeating Pistol

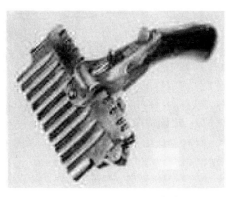

Continental Organ Pistol Made by Jarre

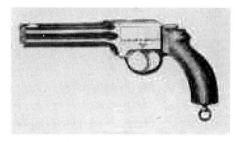

Braendlin Four-Barrel Repeating Pistol

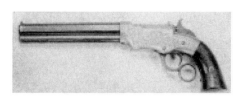

Volcanic Repeating Pistol

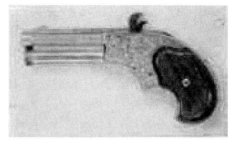

Remington .32 Extra Short Repeating Pistol

French Four-Barrel Repeating Pistol

Repeating Needle Gun Pistol

Protector Palm Pistol

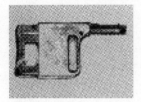

Gaulois Repeating Pistol

St. Etienne Repeating Pistol

French Squeezer Repeating Pistol

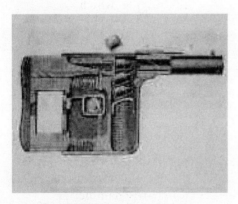

Gaulois Repeating Pistol Section

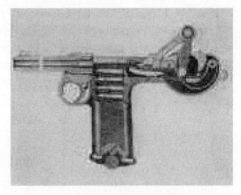

Borchardt Pistol Section

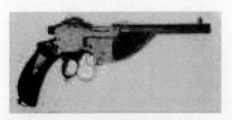

Bittner Repeating Pistol

Borchardt Automatic Pistol

lois closing from the back and the St. Etienne having a moving barrel that came back around the cartridge just before firing. Another type was operated by pressure of the little finger on a ring at the lower part of the front of the frame. These pistols were of small caliber and carried their cartridges in a vertical magazine loaded from the top. Paul Mauser, later the inventor of the Mauser automatic pistol, took out patents for a repeating pistol in 1887.

The nearest approach to the early automatics, both in appearance and mechanism, was, however, in such arms as the Bittner repeating pistol, of which a number of types were made in the eighties, mostly in Europe. The Bittner pistol was made in Germany. It looks very much like some of the early Bergmann automatic pistols. Like them, it carries its cartridges in a box-type magazine under the barrel in front of the trigger guard and it also feeds them to the chamber by the action of a sliding breech-block. But the Bittner was only semi-autoloading. The recoil blew open the action and ejected the fired case, but the action was closed and fired by a double-action ring trigger which was pushed forward and pulled back to seat the fresh cartridge and fire it. In common with all the rest of the trigger-operated repeaters, the Bittner was unsatisfactory because even with a trigger pull that was too heavy to be practical, the action springs had to be too weak for proper operation.

EARLY AUTOMATIC PISTOLS

The first true automatic, or self-loading, pistol was the Borchardt. This pistol, named for its inventor, was invented by a Connecticut man, who also invented the Borchardt hammerless action used in the Sharps Borchardt single-shot rifle, manufactured some years earlier. It was manufactured in Germany by the Loewe Arms Making Company of Berlin. It was first offered to the public in 1893. While it was not entirely satisfactory in its original form, it embodied several features that have been a part of most automatic pistols ever since.

The Borchardt pistol carried its cartridges in a detachable magazine in the butt, in the modern way. It utilized a recoil-operated mechanism with the breechblock locked to the barrel at the moment of discharge. The breechblock was unlocked by a toggle-joint action which was free to move after the breechblock and barrel had recoiled together for a short distance. The cartridge was a powerful bottleneck type, with a rimless case and metal-jacketed bullet of slightly over .30 caliber. Smokeless powder was used for the charge. The pistol could be fitted with a shoulder stock attachment, and it was claimed that accurate shooting could be done with it at 500 meters and over.

The Borchardt was, however, very badly balanced. Its grip was at right angles to the line of sight and the mainspring housing extended far to the rear of it. It was heavy and clumsy in the extreme, and did not give very general satisfaction. It was redesigned by 1900, and appeared as the Luger, or Parabellum, pistol. The Luger retained most of the principles of the Borchardt, but its toggle-breech mechanism and retractor-spring housing were much more compact, and the butt was set in a better position and angle in relation to the barrel. It was manufactured by the Deutscher Waffen und Munitions Fabriken of Germany, whose initials DWM appear on the best Lugers to be found.

The Luger pistols in several models and in 7.65 and 9 mm. calibers have been made and used all over Europe ever since. The Luger is the official sidearm of the German army and also of several other European powers. It was at one time considered by the United States Army but was turned down on account of its small caliber. Some of the models are fitted with a shoulder stock and sighted to 1000 meters. A longer barreled carbine model with a detachable stock and the same action has also been made. In addition to the regular 8-shot butt magazine, a circular drum holding 32 shots can also be used with all types.

During and after the first World War, the Luger pistol was made by many firms besides the original DWM. Some of the other makers turned out good arms, but especially after the war, when the pistols were being made for the export trade, some very poor arms of the Luger type were put together. The best Lugers are those carrying the original DWM mark. Before the war some of these arms made for export to America were stamped with an eagle and stars on the top of the breech. These are always high quality weapons.

The Luger at its best is a powerful, accurate arm which operates very satisfactorily. It is one of the most popular of the European automatic pistols.

Following the Borchardt in point of date was the Bergmann, a German automatic brought out in 1894. The Bergmann was a recoil-operated pistol with the magazine forward of the trigger guard, and it was loaded with a clip dropped in from the side after a hinged cover had been opened out and down. It could also be loaded with loose cartridges. The magazine cover was hinged at the bottom. Opening it compressed the follower spring, and the clip or the loose cartridges were put in place. Shutting the magazine cover brought the magazine follower up and pushed the cartridges into position for firing. The bolt had a rather long travel. In the military model it was locked to the barrel, which recoiled with it until it was released by a lateral swing of the block in grooves in the frame.

The Bergmann was made in calibers 5, 6.35, 7.65, 7.8 mm. and also in larger sizes. The military model of 1897 had a 10-shot vertical magazine in front of the trigger guard, looking in this respect somewhat like the Mauser. The Bergmann was succeeded by the Bayard, which was made in military and pocket sizes and is still manufactured in several types by Pieper in Belgium.

The 5 mm. Bergmann cartridge was peculiar in that it was one of the smallest center-fire cartridges ever made, being .196 inch in diameter, smaller than the .22 rim-fire. The cartridge is further unusual in that it has a tapering case but neither rim nor extraction groove, being blown back out of the chamber by the force of its explosion.

The 1910 military Bayard is very similar in appearance to the Bergmann, but the later pocket model Bayards look more like the pocket Colts in general type and have regular blowback actions, usually with the retractor spring above the barrel instead of below it as is more common in the American arms.

A number of other early types of the period of the nineties, most of which have since disappeared, may be mentioned. Among them is the Claire, a French gas-operated automatic pistol which

fed cartridges from a tubular magazine by a mechanism somewhat similar to the Winchester rifle, operated by a gas-driven
piston. The Dormus, a blowback type loaded by a clip, was
brought out in 1895. Its only useful feature was that of fitting
the retractor spring around the barrel, between it and an outer
casing, a system that has since been successfully adopted for a
number of modern arms. The early Roth, 1900, had a barrel
which recoiled locked to the breech for its full travel. This pistol
has been improved as the Roth-Sauer, and is still in use in its
modern version.

Another of the early automatic pistols was the Schwarzlose,
which was brought out in 1895. At first it had a recoiling barrel,
but later the barrel moved forward instead of recoiling to the
rear. It was held in contact with the breechblock by a rotary
locking device kept in place by the inertia of the bullet in the
rifling. An adaptation of this principle has since been used in
the American Savage Auto Pistol.

The Carola Anitua, Konrad Kromars, Hellfrich, Hauff, Paulson, Simplex, Raschem, and D'Arche are little more than names
now, although they represent various moving barrel and blowback systems that were either experimental or marketed in very
limited quantities between 1895 and 1905 in a number of European countries.

An early system that has survived in improved form is the
Mannlicher, an Austrian arm, first brought out in the middle
nineties. It was not very satisfactory at first, for the barrel moved
forward to operate the ejecting and reloading mechanism, and
it had to be cocked by hand. It was improved in 1898 and 1901,
and several military models have been made in 9 mm. caliber
since that time. The Mannlicher pistols are manufactured by
the firm of Steyr, and they have been the official sidearms of the
Austrian army since before the first World War. They are usually
clip loaded from above into a non-detachable magazine in the
butt. The barrel and breech are locked together by a rotary lock
which is unlocked as they both recoil together.

An interesting English arm was developed during the experimental period of automatic pistols. This was the Mars Automatic Pistol, invented by Mr. Hugh W. Gabbett-Fairfax, and

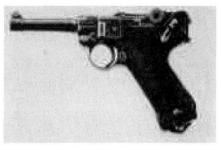

Luger or Parabellum Automatic Pistol

Luger Pistol Section

Early Bergmann Automatic Pistol

Bergmann Automatic Military Model

Luger 9 mm. Pistol Carbine

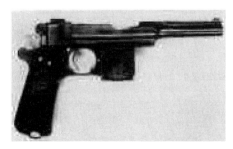

Bayard Automatic Military Model 1910

First Model Steyr Mannlicher Automatic

Steyr Mannlicher Early Military Model

Steyr Mannlicher Military Model 1916

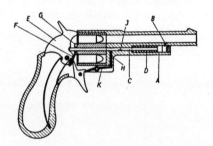

Paulson Gas-Operated Automatic Revolver

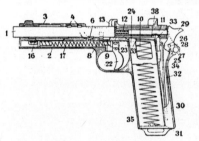

Steyr Mannlicher 1916 Section

Mars Automatic Pistol

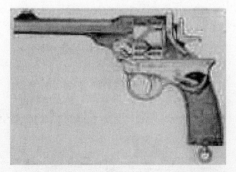

Webley Fosbery Automatic Revolver

manufactured in limited quantity by the Mars Automatic Fire-arms Syndicate between 1900 and 1902. The mechanism of the Mars presents several notable features. The barrel lies above the recoil spring, and an outside hammer is placed at the back of the frame. The magazine is a detachable one in the butt, after the modern fasion. When the arm is fired, the barrel and breech-block recoil together for about two inches. Then the breechblock is unlocked by rotary motion of an interrupted screw, and the barrel is returned to its forward position by the retractor spring. The breechblock remains in its rearward position and the empty shell is thrown out by pressure of the cartridges in the magazine from below. When the trigger is released, the breechblock flies forward, pushing the uppermost cartridge from the magazine into the chamber, and then relocks.

A most unusual feature of this arm is the power of its ammu-nition. It was made in three calibers: 8.5 mm., with a 140-grain bullet at 1750 foot-seconds muzzle velocity and a striking force of 950 foot-pounds; .360, with a 160-grain bullet at 1640 foot-sec-onds and 960 foot-pounds; and .450, with a 220-grain bullet at 1250 foot-seconds and 750 foot-pounds. In relation to any other handgun ammuntion—and especially that of the period in Eng-land when the service cartridge had a muzzle velocity of 600 feet per second and a striking force of 220 foot-pounds—it was a load of almost fantastic power. Writers on the Mars make no mention of any trouble with it that came specifically from the strength of the load, but no handgun since has used factory-loaded ammuni-tion that developed such power, and we know a great deal more about smokeless powder now than was known in the year 1900.

The Mars pistol was a somewhat clumsy-appearing arm, weigh-ing between 2½ and 3 pounds, with barrel lengths of from 8 to 10 inches. It introduced no features that have affected automatic pistol design from an evolutionary point of view, and was appar-ently not good enough to survive competition with the other types of the period that have lasted.

Another unusual English arm developed during this period— 1900-1903—enjoyed a longer vogue than some of the other queer ones, but it has not been made for some years now. This was the

Webley Fosberry Automatic Revolver, made under Fosberry's patents by the English arms firm of Webley and Scott.

The Webley Fosberry Automatic Revolver was chambered for the .455 English service cartridge. The cylinder, barrel, and action were mounted on a slide above the frame and grips. The surface of the cylinder was grooved in such a way that when the recoil of the shot caused the top half of the arm to slide back, a pin in the lower part working in the grooves turned the cylinder and relocked it. The hammer was also cocked by the recoiling action.

The arm set high in the hand with the line of sight a long way above the grip, and it had to be held rather stiffly to make the action work properly. It combined nearly all the disadvantages of both the revolver and the automatic pistol. Consequently, while it was an ingenious weapon, it was never a very popular one.

The earliest automatic pistol that has survived to the present time without considerable change in model is the Mauser military model. The Mauser pistol has been made in Germany under the patents of Paul Mauser since 1898. The same firm also makes pocket automatics and sporting and military bolt-action rifles.

The military model Mauser pistol is a 7.63 mm. caliber ten-shot arm with its clip-loaded magazine in front of the trigger guard. It has a short recoiling barrel, locked-breech action with an outside hammer. The butt is relatively straight up and down and poorly shaped for one-hand shooting. But the arm is fitted with a combination wooden holster and shoulder stock which attaches to the butt. It is sighted up to 1000 meters, and with the stock makes a powerful and compact arm.

The 7.63 mm. cartridge is a bottlenecked case loaded to a muzzle velocity of 1400 feet per second, with an 85-grain metal-cased bullet. This model is also chambered for a 9 mm. Mauser cartridge, and during the first World War, when the Mauser, as well as the Luger, was used as a sidearm by Germany, it was chambered for the 9 mm. Luger cartridge also.

The original model of the Mauser is still made in Germany without much change, but in 1932 a new model was brought out. In this model the cartridge holder, which was originally loaded only from above with a 10-shot clip, was changed to a detachable box magazine. The box magazine is made in both 10- and 20-shot capacity, and can be loaded when removed from the pistol or loaded with clips in the old way while it is in place. The mechanism was also changed so that it can be fired full-automatic as well as semi-automatic, making, with the shoulder stock and a supply of 20-shot magazines, a light submachine gun.

It was with two of these that King Alexander of Yugoslavia was assassinated at Marseille. Several people in the near-by crowd were also killed as the assassin rolled on the ground under the blows of the guard, firing indiscriminately with a full-automatic pistol in each hand.

THE COLT AUTOMATIC PISTOLS

The first automatic pistol experimented with by the Colt company was a gas-operated pistol designed and patented by Mr. Ebbetts, a Colt employee. This pistol was worked on considerably about 1890, but it was never put on the market.

In the middle nineties the name of John M. Browning was for the first time associated with automatic arms. His first product of this type was the Colt machine gun, in 1895, but a small .32 caliber pistol that was the forerunner of many similar models was put out by the Fabrique Nationale in Belgium in 1898, under Browning's patents. At the same time Browning was working with the Colt company in this country, and the "Colt Automatic Pistol, caliber .38, rimless and smokeless" was put on the market in the spring of 1900. This was the first automatic pistol made in this country.

This first Colt automatic pistol was typical of the general principles followed since then in most of the Colt models. The barrel was housed in a moving slide, and locked to the breech and slide by projections on the top of it which fitted into recesses in the slide. The barrel was pinned to the frame by links at the breech and muzzle that acted on the parallel ruler principle, to bring the barrel down from its locked position by the first action of recoil, during which the barrel and slide traveled back together. The slide then recoiled alone to eject the empty shell and recock the outside hammer. A powerful retractor spring under the barrel drew the slide forward to pick up a cartridge from the detachable butt magazine, place it in the chamber, and relock. The cartridge was a .38 caliber rimless case with a metal-jacketed bullet of 130 grains driven at 1260 feet per second by a powerful charge of smokeless powder.

This model was made until 1902. Then a number of improvements were made in the design and two new models were brought out. These were the sporting model, of the same size and type as the model of 1900, and the military model, which had an 8-shot magazine, a square butt and catch that locked the action open after the last shot had been fired. Both these were .38 caliber. In 1903 a pocket model of the same type and caliber, having a 4½-inch barrel, was brought out. None of these models is made at present. The sporting model was discontinued in 1908 and the military and pocket models in 1928.

A lighter pocket model in .32 caliber was also brought out in 1903. This was of the hammerless type, with a simple blowback action as the cartridge was of low power so that a locked breech was not necessary. The model was also chambered for the .380 cartridge in 1908. A few slight changes in design, especially in the forward barrel mounting, were made in 1911. Otherwise the model is still made in both calibers and in its original form. This arm also used a butt magazine and a moving slide with the retractor spring below the barrel.

A military model .45 caliber Colt automatic pistol was brought out in 1905. It had at first a mechanism very similar to the early .38's, but under the spur of government encouragement it was worked over extensively during the next five years and appeared in 1911 as the Government Model .45 Automatic Pistol, Model of 1911. In this form and at that time it was adopted as the official sidearm of the United States services. Its improvements included better shape of grip, grip and manual safeties, and changes in the forward barrel lock.

With little change except the addition of a better checked mainspring housing and a longer grip safety spur for greater comfort in use, this model is made to the present day. To the frame have been added: the Super .38, chambered for a stepped-up .38

Mauser Automatic Section   Mauser Military Model Automatic Pistol

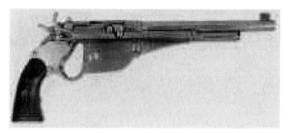

Ehbetts' Experimental Gas-Operated Colt Automatic

Colt Automatic Military Model 1902 .38   Colt Automatic Model 1900 .38

Colt Automatic Military Model 1905 .45   Colt Automatic Pocket Model .32 and .380

Colt Automatic Military Model 1911 .45

Colt Automatic Pocket Model 1903 .38

Colt Automatic Experimental Model .22

Colt Automatic Pocket Model .25

Colt Automatic, Early Woodsman

Colt Automatic, Match Target Woodsman

Colt Automatic Model 1902 Section

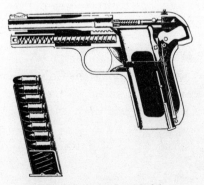

Colt Automatic Pocket Model .32 Section

auto cartridge, in 1928; the Ace .22, in 1930; the National Match Target .45, in 1932; the Super Match .38 in 1933; and the Service Ace .22, in 1938.

The Colt Service Ace and the Service Ace Conversion Unit represent a very interesting application of the recoil principle. The .22 long rifle develops good pressure in firing, but the area in square inches of the case head which receives the backward thrust of the recoil is so small that for many years it was deemed impossible to operate with it an action at all comparable with the service .45, either in kick or spring power, although the advantages of such a combination for training purposes are obvious.

This result has been accomplished within the last two or three years by means of a "floating chamber," the invention of Mr. David Williams, at the breech of the barrel of a .22 caliber unit adaptable to the frame of a standard .45. The "floating chamber" is a separate piece, a little shorter than the .22 long rifle cartridge, fitting into the breech of a barrel of the same outside diameter as the .45 barrel, but bored for the .22. The floating chamber is arranged to allow movement of about $\frac{1}{16}$ of an inch backward. Its front end, which fits into the barrel, is designed to allow gas pressure to operate on an area about the size of a .45 caliber cartridge head. This backward pressure drives the floating chamber back with enough force to operate the pistol similarly to the .45 ammunition in feeling and "kick."

The .22 and .45 units, including barrel, slide, spring, magazine, etc., are interchangeable on the same frame, and provide simulated .45 practice with the low cost and slight report of the .22.

The model brought out by the Colt company next in sequence after the .45 military was the .25 pocket automatic pistol, put on the market in 1908. This was a small compact arm chambered for a .25 caliber rimless cartridge of the same type as the larger sizes. It used a simple recoil-operated blowback system and differed from the other Colt models only in that it employed a straight-drive spiral spring-driven firing pin instead of a regular hammer. It has been made without appreciable change to the present time.

A new style of automatic pistol was brought out by the Colt

company in 1915, listed at that time as the Colt .22 Caliber Target Automatic Pistol. It has since become well known as the Colt Woodsman .22. The Woodsman differs from all other Colt automatics in that it has a fixed barrel with a light, moving breech-block entirely behind the cartridge. It has a well-shaped butt containing a 10-shot magazine, and it looks somewhat like the Luger pistol in outline. It has been made in the original model with very little change ever since it was first brought out. A sport model, differing only in that it has a 4½-inch barrel instead of the 6½-inch of the original, was brought out in 1933, and a Match Target Model, with a much heavier frame and improved trigger pull, was produced in 1938.

This is the story of the Colt automatic pistols, the most extensive line of such arms made in this country. John Browning designed them and Colt continues to make them, which leaves very little more to be said.

OTHER UNITED STATES MILITARY AUTOMATIC PISTOLS

While the Colt company has always been the largest manufacturer of automatic pistols in this country, a number of other types have been made from time to time.

Tests were instituted by the United States government between 1903 and 1911 to determine the best caliber, make, and type of sidearm for the Army and Navy. Although these tests culminated in the development and adoption of the Colt Government Model .45 Caliber Automatic Pistol, a number of other types were offered to the various boards.

At the original test to determine the best caliber, the only automatics tried out were the Luger in .30 caliber and the Colt .38 Military Model of 1902. These tests were carried out by members of both the ordnance and medical staffs on dead human bodies and live cattle. From the relative results obtained with .30, .38, and .45 caliber arms, some of them revolvers, it was determined that no weapon of smaller than .45 caliber, whether it be automatic pistol or revolver, should be adopted. And the arms makers were asked to submit automatic pistols of that caliber for further testing.

In addition to the .45 caliber Colt Military Model of 1905, the following arms were offered: The Knoble, made especially for the test in very small quantity and never sold commercially. This was a .45 caliber recoil-operated, locked-breech arm made in single and double action models. The double action model cocked the outside hammer for the first shot by pulling the trigger.

The White Merrill was a recoil-operated, locked-breech arm of very awkward appearance. It was of .45 caliber and its most unusual feature was a finger lever below the trigger guard, by which the action could be operated if it failed to function by recoil. The White Merrill was never made commercially.

The Shouboe was a Danish weapon of .45 caliber and of most peculiar type. It is the only military automatic chambered for a powerful cartridge ever to use a simple blowback action without a locked breech at the time of discharge. The ammunition, in appearance similar to the regular .45 auto cartridge, was loaded with a bullet made of wood and having an aluminum jacket. The muzzle velocity was close to 1600 feet per second, but the very light bullet gave almost no recoil although the report of the cartridge was very loud and accompanied by a brilliant flash. The idea was an ingenious one, and the bullet showed good striking force, its light weight being counteracted by its high speed. However, it turned out to be extremely inaccurate even at very short range, so it was considered unsuited to military use.

The Phillips was a gas-operated, .45 caliber automatic of very clumsy and bulky appearance. It was one of the very few gas-operated automatic pistols attempted. It was not satisfactory, and probably none but the test models were made.

A number of the foreign military automatics were experimented with to some extent, mostly from a point of view of checking relative stopping power. These included the Italian Glisenti, the Roth, the Bergmann, the Luger, the Mauser, and the Mannlicher. Very early in these tests a few of the Lugers were bought for field trial, but they were adjudged unsatisfactory on the score of caliber as well as performance. They can now be recognized, when they are encountered, by the United States seal on the top of the breechblock. They are much sought after by those in this country who like the Luger action, as they are of excellent quality. None of the other foreign automatics was ever considered seriously by the ordnance board.

The arm that most closely approached the Colt in the tests conducted from 1906 to 1911 was the Savage .45 caliber automatic pistol. This was put out by the Savage Arms Company. It was a recoil-operated arm with the breech locked to the barrel until the barrel rotated to release it with the first rearward movement. It had an outside hammer and an 8-shot magazine in the butt. A considerable number of Savage automatics were made, both for board examination and for field trial, in the course of the government tests. The model, however, did not stand up as well as the Colt under continued firing, and the shape and angle of the grip made it much more unpleasant to shoot. The Colt was adopted and none of the Savage .45's were sold commercially.

In 1917 another .45 caliber military automatic pistol was offered to the government for test. This was the Grant-Hammond, an arm somewhat similar in outline to the Luger, but having a straight recoiling breechblock and an outside hammer. On preliminary tests it showed some defects and no points of superiority over the Colt that were marked enough to warrant extensive experiment under war conditions. Only the few for testing were ever made.

UNITED STATES POCKET AND TARGET AUTOMATICS

The Savage pocket automatic was introduced in 1903 in the .32 caliber, and later was chambered for the .380. It was similar in appearance to the military model but it introduced a number of original features to pocket automatics in this country. The magazine held the cartridges in a staggered column and had a capacity of 10 shots. The breech was locked at the moment of discharge, similarly to the .45, and was the only locked-breech pocket automatic made in this country. After a few years the shape of the grip was improved so that the pistols pointed better than the military model. An outside hammer linked to the firing pin was another unusual feature for a pocket automatic. The arm was well made and easily dismounted. During the period when pocket

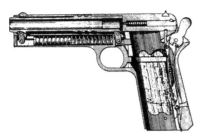

Colt Automatic Military Model 1905
Section

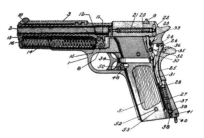

Colt Automatic Military Model 1911
Section

Colt .22-.45 Conversion Unit Section

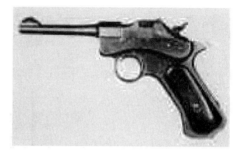

Knoble Experimental Automatic .45

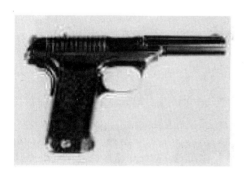

Savage Automatic .45

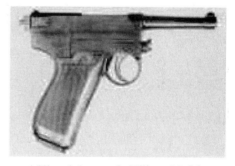

Glisenti Automatic Military Model

Shouboe Automatic .45

Grant-Hammond Automatic .45

Phillips Gas-Operated Automatic .45

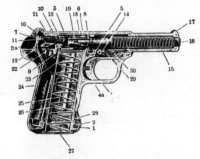

Savage Pocket Model **Section**

Savage Automatic Pocket Model .32

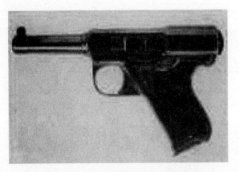

Union Arms Co. Automatic Pistol

Union Arms Co. Automatic Revolver

Smith & Wesson Automatic .35

Davis Warner Automatic Pocket Model .32

Harrington & Richardson Automatic .25

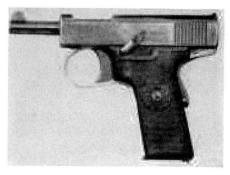

Harrington & Richardson Automatic .32

Remington Automatic Pocket Model .380

Phoenix Automatic .25

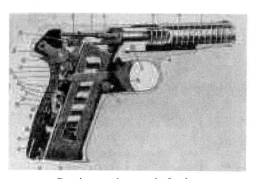

Remington Automatic Section

Fiala Repeating Pistol .22

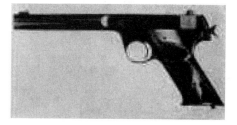

Hi-Standard Automatic .22

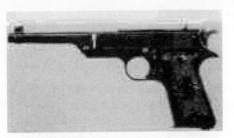

Reising Automatic .22

Reising Automatic Section

Webley & Scott Automatic .455

Webley & Scott .455 Automatic Section

Webley & Scott Automatic .32

Webley & Scott Automatic .25

Early Walther Automatic Pocket Model

Walther Double Action Automatic Pocket Model

automatics were extensively sold, the Savage was a popular model. However, it has not been made for some time.

A very curious arm was introduced about 1904 by the Union Arms Company of Toledo, Ohio. This was a small .32 caliber automatic revolver. The recoil developed by the explosion of the cartridge moved the barrel, cylinder, hammer, and upper part of the frame back in relation to the grips, trigger, and lower and rear part of the frame. A pin in the lower frame turned the cylinder by means of grooves on its surface, and the hammer was cocked as it went back. It was somewhat similar in operation—though much smaller and very different in appearance—to the Webley Fosberry English automatic revolver. It was the only arm of the type ever made in this country. The same concern also made an automatic pistol of .32 caliber having somewhat the appearance of the Luger, and seemingly unnecessarily bulky for a pocket automatic. Neither of these arms seems to have had much to recommend it and but few of them were made. They are very rare collectors' items among American automatic pistols today.

About 1905 the Smith & Wesson Revolver Company brought out an automatic pistol which they listed as .35 caliber. It was a very well-made arm and had a number of unusual features. The grip safety was at the front of the grip below the trigger guard. It opened for cleaning by pulling out and down on the trigger guard, which swung on a pivot at its forward pin and unlocked the whole top of the pistol, which was hinged at the rear and swung up and back to expose the barrel and action for cleaning. It had a release on the retractor spring so that the breechblock could be operated by hand without compressing the spring, thus putting the first cartridge in the barrel with less effort than in the average pistol.

The cartridge was actually close to .32 caliber, but was of special design, for the front part of the bullet was jacketed to operate through the automatic action, and a larger rear section of plain lead was supposed to give better accuracy and less barrel wear than a full metal-jacketed bullet. Like all specialties, the cartridge was hard to obtain, and the arm was later chambered for the regular .32 auto cartridge. Although excellently made, this pistol was never a very popular arm, and it has not been manufactured for some years.

The firm of Harrington and Richardson, well known as the manufacturers of low-priced revolvers and shotguns, put out during the early 1900's a pocket automatic pistol in .25 and .32 calibers. This pistol was almost exactly like the English Webley and Scott models of similar size, in both appearance and action. These arms were, however, made only in very small quantity.

Another concern of limited output was the Warner Arms Company, later the Davis Warner Arms Company, which manufactured first the Warner Schwarzlose and then, shortly before and after the first World War, the Davis Warner .32 caliber pocket automatic pistol. These pistols were sold under the trade name of "The Infallible," but they presented no unusual features and were heavy and bulky for their caliber. They were never especially popular and few of them were sold.

Another very rare pistol of the early post-war period—about 1920—is the Phoenix, a pocket pistol in .25 and .32 calibers, made in Lowell, Massachusetts. Very few of these were made, especially in the .32 caliber, and they are almost impossible to find. They used the simple blowback action and offered no unusual feature, although the retractor spring was placed on top of the barrel, a practice more common in Europe than in this country.

A very fine pocket automatic pistol in .32 and .380 calibers was manufactured for a few years, beginning in 1918, by the Remington Arms Company. It was the design of Mr. Pedersen, a famous designer of automatic arms, and especially in the shape of the grip and natural pointing qualities it was an excellent weapon. But though it was a fine example of its type, it showed no unusual features, as it was a blowback, recoil-operated arm, loading from the usual butt magazine.

The passage of stricter firearms laws by many states during the middle twenties curtailed the sale of the pocket automatic to the general public. Firms whose main business was some form of firearms other than handguns gave up their manufacture, and those whose only product had been such weapons went out of business. Today the Colt pocket automatics, made by the largest firm of handgun makers in the country, are the only ones made here, and they represent a very small part of the company's business.

Two makes of .22 target pistols other than Colts have been produced in the United States in automatic form, and one in a repeating pistol type. Shortly after the first World War a combination was marketed by the Fiala Outfitters, Inc., in the form of a repeating gun and pistol. The set consisted of a repeating pistol action, very similar in outline to the Colt Woodsman, 3 barrels, and an extension stock. It was of .22 caliber and fed from a butt magazine. Instead of being automatic, it was operated by hand, the breechblock being pulled back and forth to eject the shell, to cock it, and to reload it. The barrels were of pocket, target, and rifle length, the attachable butt stock being used with the rifle barrel. It was marketed for only a few years.

Another .22 target pistol of the early twenties—this time an automatic of good design—was the Reising, made for a few years in a hammer model with a 6½-inch barrel and a 12-shot butt magazine. The Reising was a well-designed and well-made pistol, but it never seemed to gain a popularity in line with its quality, and it soon disappeared from the field.

The only other pistol in this class is the Hi-Standard, which started out to be a popular-priced version of the Woodsman, resembling it very much in appearance and action. In recent years it has been improved both in design and workmanship, and now appears in several models, with and without an outside hammer, of light, medium, and heavy weight, and in 4½- and 6½-inch barrel lengths. Its price in the better grades is close to that of the Woodsman, and many shooters consider it an excellent weapon.

ENGLISH AUTOMATIC PISTOLS

The only line of automatic pistols ever extensively manufactured in England is the group made by the firm of Webley and Scott. These pistols have been made ever since the firm first brought out a .32 caliber arm about 1905. They include a .25

caliber pocket model in two types, with and without a hammer, a .32 and .380 pocket model with a hammer, sometimes used as a police arm, a heavier .38 caliber arm designed for the long .38 cartridges, such as the 9 mm. Luger and the .38 Colt automatic, and a .455 caliber service model that is carried by the English navy.

The Webley and Scott automatic pistols are characterized by a very square and somewhat clumsy appearance. The grips are at nearly right angles with the barrel, and the round barrel sticks out of the square frame which meets it with a very abrupt shoulder. The .455 caliber service model has the peculiarity of using a flat V-type retractor spring which lies under the grip on the left side. It is the only automatic pistol made at present which employs a flat spring of this type.

While they are odd and clumsy looking, the Webley and Scott automatics are well made, reliable in functioning, and easy to take apart and put together. They are, however, very rarely seen in this country.

FOREIGN POCKET AUTOMATIC PISTOLS

Shortly after the year 1900, the small pocket automatic pistols, in calibers .25, .32, and .380, designated in Europe as the 6.35 mm., 7.65 mm., and 9 mm. short, began to appear in great numbers, especially from Germany, Belgium, and Spain. Their general characteristics were a compact hammerless design, coil operating springs, simple blowback actions with no breech-locking devices, and varying grades of workmanship, material, and reliability.

In Germany the list of them includes:

Bergmann	Mann	Schwarzlose
Frommer Dreyse	Mauser	Simson
Haenel	Menz	Stendawerke
Kolibri	Ortgies	Stock
Kommer	Rheinmetall	Waldmann
Langenhan	Roth-Sauer	Walther
Liliput	J. P. Sauer & Sohn	Zehna
	Schmeisser	

Ortgies Automatic Pocket Model .32

Walther Automatic Military Model

Roth-Sauer Automatic Pocket Model

Mauser Automatic Pocket Model .32

J. P. Sauer Automatic Pocket Model .32

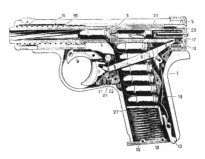

J. P. Sauer Automatic Pocket Model Section

Dreyse Automatic Pocket Model .32

Mann Automatic .25

Liliput Automatic 4.25 mm.

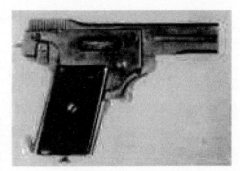

Kolibri Automatic 2 mm.

Steyr Automatic Pocket Model .25

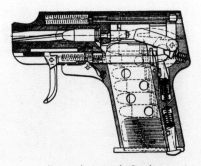

Praga Automatic Section

A few among these show interesting features of one sort or another. Some of the Walther models, including a .22 caliber pocket size which is not made by other firms, and also in the .25 and .32 calibers, are provided with a double action trigger and an outside hammer. These models can be carried with the hammer down. Pulling the trigger fires the first shot double action, and after the first shot they operate in the usual semi-automatic manner, cocking the hammer and reloading each time the cartridge is fired. Walther also makes a .22 caliber target model of the general type of the Colt Woodsman that is one of the best of the European arms of this type.

The Sauer automatics are unusual in that they are among the few pocket models with locked-breech action. The barrel recoils locked to the breech and is only unlocked when the breech reaches the rearward point of its travel, a typical long recoil action more common to larger type arms.

The Ortgies has a grip safety that can be locked out of action when it is not wanted. The Ortgies also has an original method of disassembling. The safety release is pressed in, the slide is drawn part way back, and then it is lifted straight up at the rear. This is a very easy operation, but many people not familiar with it have spent a lot of time trying to get an Ortgies pistol apart.

The Liliput and Kolibri are the smallest automatic pistols that have ever been made, their .17 and .8 caliber cartridges, respectively, weight of less than 7 ounces, and over-all dimensions of less than 3½ inches, make them curious toys but hardly bring them into the class of defense or combat weapons. They present no unusual mechanical features in their operation.

Belgian automatic pistols are usually of good quality. Liége is the arms center of Belgium. Among the pocket arms made in that country are:

Bayard (made by H. Pieper, Anciens Establissements Pieper)
Clement
Delu
Fabrique Nationale d'Armes de Guerre (Browning's patents)
Jeffico

Le Rapide
Melior
Pieper (J. Pieper)
Warnant

The Fabrique Nationale arms are the most interesting to Americans, as they are manufactured under the patents of John M. Browning and closely resemble in several models the Colt automatic pistols made under the same patents. The first model put out was the .32 pocket, made just before the year 1900. It was this model that gained fame as the pistol used in the assassination of the Archduke Franz Ferdinand of Austria at Sarajevo which precipitated the first World War. Other models include: a pocket .25 very similar to the .25 Colt; the Model 1914, .32 and .380, having the retractor spring around the barrel, the only Browning pistol so made; a 9 mm. short similar to the Colt .32 but slightly larger, and with a longer barrel; and heavier military models.

Of the other Belgian pocket automatics the Bayard is notable in that in the .32 and .380 calibers the model is the smallest one made taking these cartridges. It is scarcely larger than the Colt .25. The retractor spring is above the barrel, but otherwise the form and action are regular in all respects.

France has made few automatic pistols, and for that matter few handguns of any type that have warranted much notice. The obsolete Claire gas-operated pistol, Le Française, Metiore, Fiel, and Monobloe are about all the small pistols that were made there. At St. Etienne, however, an arm of medium size is made that displays a most unusual feature. It is recoil operated and of .25 or .32 caliber, although shaped somewhat like the more powerful Luger type arms. Its distinctive feature is that the operation of the action does not leave the firing pin cocked. The straight-drive spiral spring actuating it is pushed back by a long arm reaching up from the trigger when the trigger is pulled. When the spring is compressed to the proper point, the sear arm is cammed out of the firing pin notch and the pin flies forward to fire the cartridge. The St. Etienne automatic pistol is perhaps less liable to accidental discharge than those which are cocked by their recoil, but it is a much harder gun to shoot accurately as the trigger pull is necessarily long and hard.

Italy also has made very few automatics. The Glisenti, Revelli, and Beretta are about the only ones. These are simple blowback action arms in the pocket sizes and show nothing of unusual design.

Spain produced, until its civil war, a great number and variety of small automatic pistols, most of which were of extremely poor quality. They were made for the most part of soft metal by small establishments, some of which assembled, buying parts from other makers, and some of which supplied one or more parts to various assemblers. Consequently, it is almost impossible to assign any especial characteristic—such as even the type of rifling —to a particular maker's name which may appear on any Spanish pistol. One lot of barrels, for example, of a given make might come from one shop, and the next lot from a shop making them with entirely different rifling. On the other hand, one barrel maker might supply barrels with the same rifling characteristics to a dozen different assemblers, which end up in guns marked with as many different names.

All that can be said with any certainty is that Spanish automatics as a group are liable to be pretty bad, both as to quality and functioning, and any of them that use a powerful cartridge may be dangerous to the user. Automatic arms are essentially the products of precision manufacture and good materials. Poor work, bad assembling, and soft metal do not contribute to pistol efficiency.

The city of Eibar has been the center of the Spanish gun trade and manufacture, and while most of the early arms made there were of very poor quality—and plenty of such are still made there —in the last few years before the civil war some efforts were made to turn out better arms. The best and largest of the Spanish arms manufacturers was at that time Bonifacio Echeverria, maker of the Star pistols. His weapons, in various sizes from .25 pocket models to .45 military arms, are almost exact copies of the Colt automatics, and they are of fairly good quality. He made a .22 target automatic that was a pretty good arm. It has won several European matches. The only other Spanish arms that have much to recommend them are the Astra and the Llama, the latter another copy of the Colt Super .38.

The following names are among those found on Spanish pistols. It is perfectly obvious that most of them are merely names to sell cheap and poorly made arms.

Alkar	Kappora	Sharp Shooter
Allies	Liberty	Sprinter
Apache	Llama	Star
Astra	Looking Glass	Stosel
Bristol	Martian	Titanic
Bufalo	Military	Triomphe
Bulwark	Paramount	U.A.E.
Destroyer	Pathfinder	Unique
Eles	Pinkerton	Vencendor
Express	Princeps	Venus
Frontier	Protector	Victoria
Gallus	Royal	Victory
Ideal	Royal Extra	Vincitor
Imperial	Ruby	Walman
	S.E.A.M.	

Austria's large arms-making firm is that of Steyr, making many arms under Mannlicher's patents, but mostly in rifle or military pistol sizes. A small pocket pistol marked Steyr, and two others marked O.W.A. and Little Tom, are about the only pocket automatics we have seen from this country.

Skoda, in Czechoslovakia, turns out the Praga pocket automatic, and some of the other small European countries may make a few arms, but they very rarely reach the United States, and it is doubtful if any of them display unusual features or designs.

Automatic pistols have developed in the last fifty years or so from unreliable curiosities to the standard sidearms of the military of most countries. Their functioning depends to a considerable extent on good ammunition and proper care, but under reasonable conditions they have many advantages as handguns, either for military or private use.

Peiper Automatic .25

Bayard Automatic Pocket Model .380

F. N. Automatic Pocket Model .32

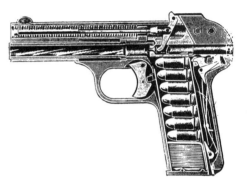

F. N. Automatic Section

F. N. Automatic 9 mm. Short

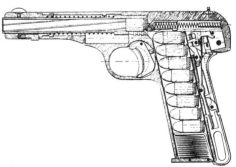

F. N. Automatic Model 1914 Section

Sharpshooter Spanish Automatic .25

Star Automatic .32

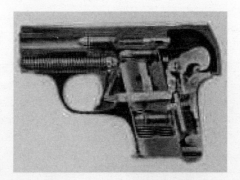

Spanish Automatic Section

CHAPTER THREE

Automatic Rifles up to and including the First World War

*Automatic Pistol U.S. Model 1918; Sporting Automatic
Rifles and Shotguns to the Present*

CONSTRUCTIVE work on the development of the automatic rifle waited upon the arrival of the same conditions
necessary to the automatic pistol and the machine gun. Before
much could be accomplished it was necessary to have available
reliable smokeless powder loaded cartridges of suitable form and
the facilities for precision machine tool work.

But in the case of automatic rifles of military power there are
problems present which do not apply to any other automatic
arm. For this reason, the development of the military automatic
rifle has been much slower than that of either the pistol or the
machine gun.

The automatic pistol employs cartridges of relatively low
power and pressure, so the problems of controlling its various
functions are comparatively simple. The automatic machine gun
is a weapon of from two to ten times the weight of an infantry
rifle, but machine guns were originally designed to use the same
cartridges as the standard military rifles of the countries that
used them. Consequently, here again the problems of controlling
the forces employed are much simpler than in the case of the
rifle.

Military practice based on the capabilities of the average soldier
and the weight of his other equipment has limited the weight of
the infantry rifle to not over 10 pounds. In fact, it is usually somewhat below this figure. The 1903 Springfield, for example,
weighs 8.69 pounds.

Military ammunition has also, in the last forty-five years or so, become standardized within certain limits. Its general characteristics include a bottlenecked rimless shell, a metal-cased pointed bullet of about .25 to .30 caliber and between 150 and 200 grains in weight, and a charge of smokeless powder giving a muzzle velocity between 2200 and 2800 feet per second with a breech pressure of about 35,000 to 50,000 pounds per square inch.

Automatic shoulder arms have occupied the thoughts of inventors since the last quarter of the nineteenth century. Automatic sporting rifles of medium and low power, and automatic shotguns, both of satisfactory performance and not too complicated mechanism, have been commercially available since the first decade of the twentieth century. However, the problem of adapting a semi-automatic action to the weight limits and the power and pressure requirements of the standard military rifle has proved to be a very difficult one.

The two types of magazine used in most bolt action and automatic arms—the box and rotary types—were developed well before 1900. James Lee patented the box magazine in 1879. This design consists of a box, sometimes integral with the gun and sometimes detachable, placed in front of the trigger guard. The cartridges are held either in a single column or staggered for greater capacity and fed up to the action by pressure of a spring from below.

The rotary type magazine—which appeared during the nineties in a number of arms, including the Blake and Mannlicher bolt action rifles and the Savage lever action—lies in the same position as the box but holds its cartridges in some form of wheel-like mechanism and feeds them to the action by spring or mechanical turning of the holder.

These types of magazine have been used in both bolt and lever action rifles and in most automatic rifles of low and medium power. They also led to clip loading, first used in this country in the Lee straight pull bolt action Navy rifle, 1895, and to the rimless cartridge which fed better than the rimmed type. Both these items are very desirable if not absolutely necessary elements of any automatic rifle of much power or military value.

While either one of these magazines is far better than the tubular type ammunition feed for an automatic rifle, the early inventors did not always realize it. Hiram Maxim's first patents for an automatic arm were for a rifle with a repeating mechanism and magazine similar to the Winchester, operated by the recoil on a butt plate hinged away from the stock and connected with the action by a series of levers and springs to work it when the gun was fired. These patents were taken out in 1883, and in the next ten years or so some wonderful and terrible ideas were worked on and patented.

Paulson and Needham in England devised complicated gadgets for making an automatic rifle out of the Martini Henry, an action that no one yet has successfully adapted even to a simple, hand-operated repeating mechanism. Schlund and Arthur, in 1885, also took out English patents that embodied the long recoil locked-breech action, but included various undesirable features as well.

Among the earlier automatic rifles of the beginning of the modern type—although none of them were successful to the point of any general use—was the Griffiths and Woodgate, English, 1894, which employed a box magazine and a short recoil locked-breech action, and used a pivoted hammer-type striker, surprisingly like the modern semi-automatic rifles, instead of a straight-drive, coil-spring driven firing pin of the contemporary bolt action military arms.

English inventors were also responsible for the Clausin (1895) and the Ross (1896), both experimental military type automatic arms that did not get much beyond that stage.

A Mannlicher automatic rifle of the same period was also recoil operated and employed a short recoiling barrel action feeding from a clip-charged box magazine. And the 1905 Mauser used a long recoil system.

Before the first World War the United States had tested several semi-automatic rifle actions, including the Murphy Manning, White Greenman, Farquhar Hill, and arms designed at the Springfield and Rock Island armories. None of them, however, showed promise enough to reach the field issue test stage.

By the early part of the first World War a number of types of semi-automatic rifles were undergoing tests or were in limited use by the warring powers. The one most extensively used was the Mondragon. This was the invention of a Mexican army officer. It was taken to Europe, where it was first manufactured in Switzerland. The German government purchased a limited quantity of Mondragons and issued a few of them to their forces for special purposes. The Mondragon was a gas-operated 10-shot gun, feeding from a box magazine, with a locked-breech system and stationary barrel tapped for its gas port about three-quarters of the way to the muzzle.

Other attempts to construct an automatic infantry arm of the period of the first World War, some of them gas operated and some using short or long recoil actions, include the Rychiger, Liu, Stergian, Bommarito, St. Etienne, Elder, and others. They were tried out by most of the warring nations, but the results were so unsatisfactory that although over twenty years have passed since the war ended none of these systems has been perfected to a point where it has been accepted as an adequate military weapon. Nor, until recently, had any European nation adopted an automatic rifle as its standard infantry weapon.

Another wartime military automatic device—and a most unusual one—was developed by the United States in 1918. This was the "U.S. Pistol, Caliber .30, Model 1918," also called the "Pedersen Device," from the name of the inventor.

This device was a unit for altering the standard Springfield rifle, caliber .30, Model of 1903, to a sub-caliber semi-automatic arm capable of delivering an immense volume of short-range fire. An assembly that took the place of the standard bolt was pushed into position and held by the bolt lock. The front end of it entered the chamber of the barrel and took the place of the cartridge case, extending up to the beginning of the rifling.

It had a simple recoil-operated blowback action controlled by the trigger of the rifle. The ammunition was .30 caliber with a short metal-cased bullet and a straight rimless cartridge case about half again as long as a .32 automatic pistol cartridge. A 40-shot detachable box magazine locked into the unit and protruded at an angle up and to the right of the line of sight. An ejection slot was cut in the left side of the rifles with which the device was to be used. The cartridges develop a muzzle velocity of 1300 feet per second with an 80-grain bullet.

Lee Box Magazine

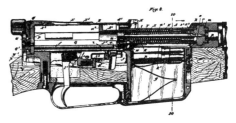

Mauser Automatic Rifle, 1905

Savage Rotary Magazine

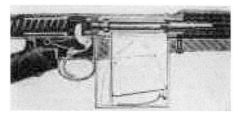

The Griffiths and Woodgate Automatic Rifle

The U. S. Pistol Model 1918 (The Pedersen Device)

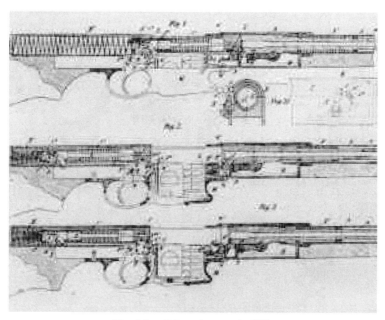

The Mannlicher Automatic Rifle

Pre-War Automatic Rifles of Experimental Type
1. Murphy-Manning Rifle; 2. White-Greenman Rifle; 3. Farquhar-Hill Rifle; 4. Semi-Automatic
Rifle Designed by Springfield Armory; 5. Semi-Automatic Rifle, Rock Island Type

Winchester Automatic Rifle Model 74-22

It was intended that the regular infantry soldier would carry this unit and several magazines in a belt pouch. In close fighting it would be the work of but a few seconds to slip out the regular rifle bolt and replace it with the semi-automatic unit, giving every man a 40-shot sub-caliber weapon, and tremendously increasing the fire power of a given number of troops.

The Pedersen Device was in production, and about 85,000 of them were ready for shipment to Europe, in November of 1918 when the war ended. They remained for some years a closely guarded military secret, and then they were all scrapped except a few examples saved for museums and as collectors' items. It appears that while they had seemed satisfactory under the limited tests that war conditions allowed, further experiment during the leisure of peacetime must have proved that they were not suitable for the purpose for which they had been intended.

In the sporting field, however, quite a number of developments had taken place. John M. Browning, of automatic pistol and machine gun fame, took out patents shortly after the year 1900 for a .22 caliber automatic rifle of simple blowback action that was made in this country by Winchester, and in Belgium by Fabrique Nationale.

Shortly afterward he also took out patents for a locked-breech recoiling barrel automatic rifle designed for cartridges of medium power. This was the basis for the line of automatic rifles brought out by the Remington Arms Company and for a similar line made by Fabrique Nationale in Belgium.

Until after the first World War, the only firms in this country that made automatic sporting shoulder arms in any quantity were Winchester and Remington. Most of the arms made by these companies—with the notable exception of the Winchester automatic shotgun—were designed by John Browning.

Winchester brought out in 1903 the first automatic rifle sold in this country. This was a .22 caliber arm with a simple blowback action feeding from a tubular magazine in the butt. It was chambered for a special cartridge known as the .22 Winchester Auto Cartridge, which was slightly larger in the case than the standard .22 caliber cartridges. This was done because at the time the rifle was brought out, regular .22 caliber ammunition was either loaded with black powder or with smokeless powder of somewhat variable strength. Winchester developed a smokeless load that worked properly with the action of the rifle, and then put it in a case that made it impossible to use the rifle with ammunition that might not be satisfactory. As this situation no longer exists, the model was brought up to date in design and chambered for the regular .22 short or .22 long rifle ammunition in 1933. It has since then been listed as Model 63. The original Model 1903 was discontinued in 1936.

The next Winchester automatic rifle was the Model of 1905, made in calibers .32 and .35, Winchester Auto Cartridges. This gun, also the design of John Browning, was a simple blowback action with no locking of the breech. The cartridges were the straight-case rimless type and of medium to low power. They were similar in ballistic qualities to the .32-20 and .38-40. They were fed from a detachable box magazine forward of the trigger guard. This model was discontinued in 1920.

Another arm of very similar type was brought out in 1907. It was somewhat heavier and designed for a slightly longer cartridge, listed as the .351. In 1910 this arm was also chambered for a cartridge of larger diameter but about the same length. The new cartridge was listed as the .401 Winchester Auto Cartridge. The .401 was discontinued in 1936, but the '07 model, chambered for the .351 cartridge, is still made and offered as a medium-power hunting rifle and also as a police weapon for cruise car and riot work. For this purpose it is an excellent arm, as it is not too powerful for safe use in populous areas.

Within the past two years the Winchester company has added to their line a popular-priced .22 auto rifle, listed as Model 74. It exhibits no new features of mechanical design, as it has a simple recoil-operated blowback action chambered for either the .22 short or the .22 long rifle and similar to other arms of the same type.

The Winchester company also made from 1911 to 1925 a recoil-operated automatic shotgun. This gun was designed by Mr. Johnson of their own plant after a dispute with Mr. Browning over the terms of purchase of a shotgun of Browning's design. It was a satisfactory sporting arm but presented no unusual features in automatic arms design. The original model was discontinued in

1925, but within the last year or so a modernized version of it has been brought out as Model 40 Automatic Shotgun.

The first autoloading arm brought out by the Remington company was the Model 8 Autoloading Rifle, introduced in 1906 and modernized as Model 81 in 1936, from which date to the present time it has been made without further change. This rifle is a Browning design and has a locked breech, long recoil action. It is chambered for a series of rimless cartridges in .25, .30, .32, and .35

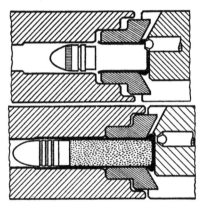

Remington *Floating Chamber* Model 550 for .22 Short and Long Cartridge

Remington auto calibers. These are hunting cartridges of medium power. They are contained in a detachable box magazine in front of the trigger guard. The regular magazine holds 5 cartridges, but a model, listed as the "Special Police," has a 15-shot magazine and is fitted with a military type stock, forearm, and sling.

Remington did not put out a .22 auto rifle until 1914. In this year one was put on the market designated as Model 16. At first this arm was chambered for the .22 short and .22 long rifle cartridges, but regular .22 ammunition was still too irregular in its smokeless loads for satisfactory operation in an automatic arm. After trouble with various makes of ammunition in the regular sizes, the Remington company designed a special Remington .22 automatic cartridge, different from both the regular .22's and from the Winchester .22 auto cartridge, and chambered their rifle for it. The rifle was a simple blowback action with the magazine in the butt. In 1922 it was improved and brought out as Model 24, at which time it was chambered for the regular .22 short and long rifle cartridges, as they had improved to a point where they operate the action satisfactorily. The model was again modernized in 1936 as Model 241, its improvements including greater weight and a better designed stock. As such it is still made.

Within the last few months the Remington company has brought out a .22 caliber Automatic Sporting Rifle which they list as Series #550. This rifle employs a floating chamber similar to that used in the Colt .22′45 conversion unit to adapt it to both short and long .22 caliber cartridges. The chamber is the length of the case of the short cartridge, so that added power is obtained by the recoil action of the chamber when shorts are used. When longs are used, the case goes beyond the chamber into the barrel proper and seals the action so that the regular pressure of the long is employed. This is an interesting mechanism but not one that should affect the design of high-powered automatic arms.

Remington has also made an autoloading shotgun since Browning came to the company with his new design after the dispute with Winchester in 1910. The Remington autoloading shotgun is a recoil-operated arm of good design and is similar in all respects to the Browning autoloading shotgun, made also under Browning's patents both by the Fabrique Nationale in Belgium and, from parts imported from that concern, by the Browning Gun Company in this country. These arms all employ the long recoil action.

Since the expiration of the original patents, similar autoloading shotguns have been put out by Savage, Stevens, and other concerns. The design is very good, and operation is satisfactory whenever the mechanism is made of good quality material, and good workmanship is employed.

An automatic sporting rifle of unusual type was made for a few years by the Standard Arms Company, which was organized in 1909 to make arms under the patent for an automatic rifle taken out in 1906 by M. L. Smith. The Standard automatic rifle was a combination arm. It was nominally a gas-operated semi-automatic rifle of medium power, but it could also be used as a slide, or "trombone," action repeater. It was a hammerless arm

War-Time Experimental Automatic Rifles

1. Mondragon Rifle; 2. Stergian Rifle; 3. Rychiger Rifle; 4. Elder Rifle, Rychiger Type; 5. Bommarito Rifle; 6. Liu Rifle; 7. Liu Rifle; 8. St. Etienne Rifle

Winchester .351 Automatic Rifle Model 07

Winchester Automatic Shotgun Model 40

Remington Automatic Rifle Model 81

Remington Model 81 Police Automatic Rifle

Remington .22 Automatic Rifle Model 241

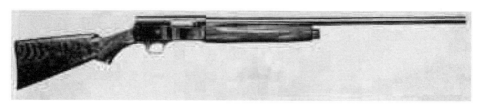

Remington Automatic Shotgun Model 11

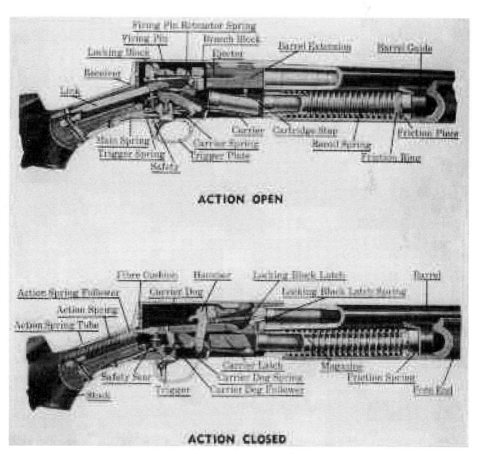

Remington Shotgun Section

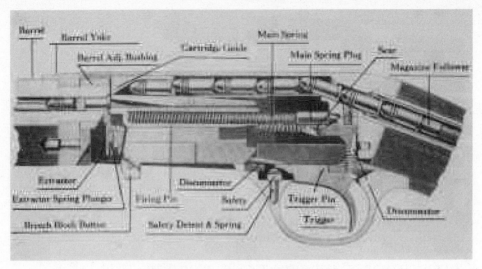

Remington .22 Automatic Rifle Section

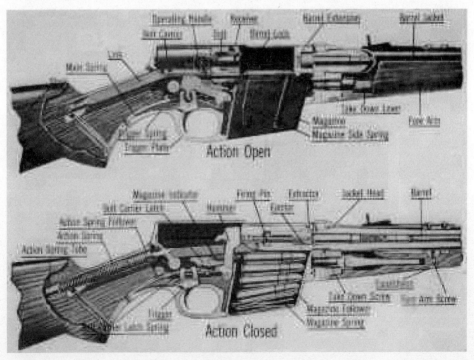

Remington Rifle Model 81 Section

with the action enclosed and the gas port about three-quarters of the way up the barrel. The automatic action was piston driven, with a cylinder beneath the barrel. It had a box magazine holding 4 or 5 cartridges, and was listed as supplied in calibers .25-35, .30-30, and .35. The forearm grip was of cast bronze decorated with a hunting scene, and pressing a button on this grip allowed the arm to be operated as a slide-action repeater.

The Standard automatic rifle was not very successful. It seems to have had the faculty of jamming with exceptional firmness about every third shot, and it was very difficult to release. The manufacture of it was begun in 1910 but continued for only two or three years. So few were sold that they are practically collectors' pieces at the present time.

The popularity of .22 caliber arms has brought to the market in recent years a number of cheap but fairly well-made automatic rifles in this caliber by the makers of popular-priced arms, such as Savage, Stevens, Stevens Springfield, Marlin, Mossburg, and the mail order houses. Some of these rifles are clip loaders and some have tubular magazines under the barrel. The actions are simple blowbacks of sturdy design. The only new feature they present is that some of them are so made that they can be locked between shots and used as bolt action repeaters or single-shot rifles as well as automatics. The very small force of .22 caliber cartridges makes such design possible, so the feature, although it is a new one in automatic arms, presents nothing adaptable to weapons of military power, even if it should be considered desirable in such arms.

For plinking, small game shooting, and not too serious target shooting, these low-priced automatics offer the shooter good fun with a minimum of effort between shots. Automatic shotguns are also put out by some of these concerns, but they also show no new or unusual features of design or performance. Most of them give the satisfaction to be expected from their price class.

Among the foreign makers of automatic arms, perhaps the foremost is the Fabrique Nationale d'Armes of Belgium, which has been making automatic arms under Browning's patents since before 1900. Arms similar to most of the American ones made under these patents are turned out there, including a .22, and a medium-power rifle similar to the Remington models, and a shot-gun like the Remington (which is also imported in parts and sold in this country as the "Browning"), and most of the auto pistol sizes that are made in the United States by Colt.

Other European automatic sporting arms are made by the Walther Arms Making Company of Germany, which puts out a .22 similar to our better models in this caliber, and by Dreyse, who made, as far back as the time of the first World War, a light carbine with a recoil-operated action of the unlocked-breech type for such cartridges as the 9 mm. Luger and the .32 auto pistol.

About the only European sporting arm of the automatic type that offers unusual features is a relatively recent development. This is the Krieghoff Autoloading Rifle, manufactured by the Sempert and Krieghoff Arms Manufacturing Company, of Suhl, Germany.

The Krieghoff is a gas-operated autoloading rifle made in cali-bers corresponding in power and pressure to the regular military cartridges. The action is locked at the time of firing, and is oper-ated by a piston and cylinder, taking its gas from a port in the underside of the barrel at the muzzle. It has a magazine capacity of 4 shots, and an additional one can be put in the chamber, making a total of 5 available cartridges when the arm is fully loaded.

The gun is good looking and apparently well designed, but little data are available on it in this country for the reason that very few have been imported. The sole American agent, Stoeger, of New York, listed them only in the 1939 catalog, and at $500 each. It would appear that the Krieghoff must be an expensive arm to manufacture. War conditions have stopped its import since that year.

Standard Gas-Operated Automatic Rifle

Marlin .22 Automatic Rifle

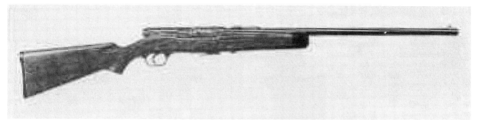

Stevens No. 57 Automatic Rifle

Savage .22 Automatic Rifle Model 7

Savage .22 Automatic Rifle Model 7-S

Stevens .22 Automatic Rifle Model 76

Savage .22 Automatic Rifle Model 6

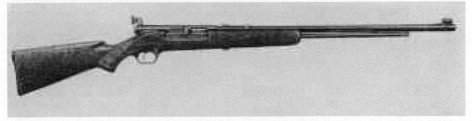

Savage .22 Automatic Rifle Model 6-S

Mossberg .22 Automatic Rifle Model 50

Mossberg .22 Automatic Rifle Model 51

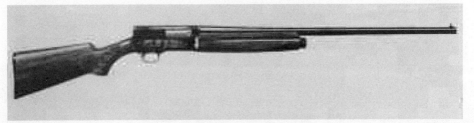

Savage Automatic Shotgun Model 720

Krieghoff Gas-Operated Automatic Rifle

CHAPTER FOUR

Post-War Military Developments

The Submachine Gun; The Semi-Automatic Military Rifle; The Light Machine Gun; The Light Heavy Machine Gun; The Automatic Cannon; Developments in Ammunition

THE SUBMACHINE GUN

WHILE three examples of the submachine gun—the Bergmann Muskete in Germany, and the Revelli and Villa Perosa in Italy—all chambered for the 9 mm. Luger cartridge, were in limited use during the first World War, most of the development of this type arm and the spread of military interest in it have come in the period since that conflict.

The submachine gun shoots pistol ammunition and takes advantage of the lower pressures of this type of cartridge to use a lighter and less securely locked breech mechanism than is necessary with rifle ammunition. Simple or delayed blowback type breechblocks which are usually cocked with the breech open, as are most air-cooled rapid-fire guns, are the general rule. They are light and handy, but the slap of the moving breechblock at the moment of firing limits their accuracy to some extent.

THE THOMPSON SUBMACHINE GUN

In this country the Thompson submachine gun—better known as the "Tommy gun"—was developed shortly after the first World War by the Auto Ordnance Corporation. To the average American it is the best-known weapon of its type, as gangsters and gangster movies of the "roaring twenties" made it a commonplace of civilian life. The Thompson submachine gun is a full-

or semi-automatic weapon chambered for the .45 Colt auto pistol cartridge and operating by recoil with a delayed blowback breech-block. It has a short barrel and removable butt stock. It can be fired from the hip or shoulder, holding it in both hands. It is fitted with a compensator to control muzzle climb. It weighs about 10 pounds and the recoil is not unpleasant even in full-automatic fire. The bolt stays open between shots. The ammunition is supplied from 20-shot clip magazines and 50- and 100-shot drums, which lock into place in front of the trigger guard. The cyclic rate of fire is between 600 and 800 shots per minute, and drums can be changed in about four seconds. It was at first manufactured by the Colt company; but at present it is being manufactured in quantity by the Savage Arms Corporation for orders from the British government.

THE SEDGLEY SUBMACHINE GUN

Another submachine gun being made in this country at the present time is the Sedgley, manufactured by R. F. Sedgley, Inc., of Philadelphia, Pennsylvania.

This is a full- or semi-automatic submachine gun weighing 7 pounds, with an over-all length of 35 inches, and an 11-inch barrel. The action is simple straight blowback, recoil operated. All the springs are contained in the receiver. A detachable 20-shot vertical feed box magazine is located under the receiver and provides a hand grip for the left hand. The bolt remains open between shots. The gun uses 9 mm. Luger pistol cartridges. The cyclic rate of fire is from 450 to 500 shots per minute.

The Sedgley gun is of simple construction throughout, and it is designed for ease of operation and manufacture.

THE HARRINGTON AND RICHARDSON REISING SUBMACHINE GUN

Within the last year or so a submachine gun has been developed by the Harrington and Richardson Arms Company, of Worcester, Massachusetts, under the patents of Mr. Eugene G. Reising. The gun was engineered in the Harrigton and Richard-

The Thompson Submachine Gun

The Sedgley Submachine Gun

Harrington and Richardson Reising Submachine Gun

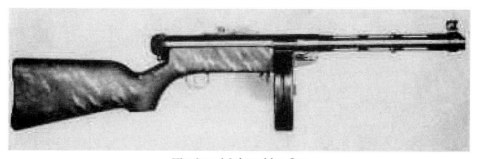

The Suomi Submachine Gun

The Steyr Solothurn-S1-100 Submachine Gun

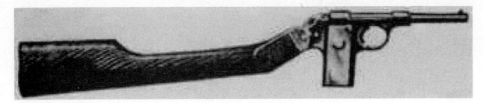

Astra Spanish Machine Pistol

Star Spanish Submachine Gun

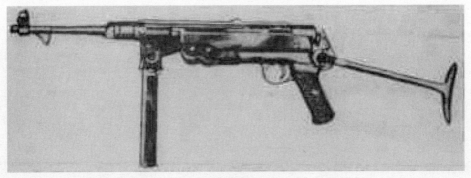

Schmeisser Machine Pistol

son plant to supply a cheaply and easily made full- or semi-automatic gun of light weight, adaptable to present military conditions. The Reising Submachine Gun weighs 6½ pounds, has an over-all length of 35¾ inches, and barrel length of 11 inches. It shoots the standard .45 caliber Colt automatic pistol cartridge from a 20-shot detachable box magazine. The bolt remains closed when firing is stopped and the gun can be fired either full- or semi-automatic at a cyclic rate of 450 to 500 shots per minute. It is fitted with a flash hider and compensator at the muzzle, which makes it a very easy gun to hold during full-automatic fire. The mechanism is a simple recoil-operated design with straight line movement of the parts and a straight-drive spiral spring-driven hammer which strikes the firing pin to discharge the cartridge.

THE SUOMI SUBMACHINE GUN

An interesting foreign submachine gun of recent development is the Suomi, originally made in Finland. This gun is chambered for the 9 mm. pistol cartridge and is notable for its very few parts. It is a simple blowback action without any breech lock, and the firing pin is merely a projection on the face of the bolt, firing the cartridge as the bolt closes. The Suomi is a fairly heavy gun for its caliber, weighing in the neighborhood of 10 pounds, and is very accurate and easy to control. It is fed from a vertical box magazine below the action.

It is said that this gun in the hands of the Finns during the Russian invasion of Finland accounted for nearly 70 per cent of the estimated quarter of a million casualties suffered by the invading Russians.

THE STEYR SOLOTHURN S1-100

Another foreign machine pistol is the Steyr Solothurn S1-100, manufactured at Zurich, Switzerland. This is an 8½-pound submachine gun, 31½ inches long, with an 8-inch barrel. It has a side-mounted detachable box magazine in sizes holding from 16 to 30 rounds. The action is a simple recoil-operated blowback with the bolt stopping open between shots in either full- or semi-automatic fire. The action spring is in the butt and is connected to the bolt by a long link. It is chambered for the 7.63 mm. Mauser, and the 7.65 mm. and 9 mm. Luger pistol cartridges. This weapon appears to be a refinement and improvement of the original Bergmann Muskete.

FOREIGN SUBMACHINE GUNS

In addition to the submachine guns in use at the time of the first World War, a number of German and Spanish machine pistols have been developed. The Star and Astra, Spanish guns, are a relatively simple blowback construction. The Astra looks more or less like an automatic pistol with a long tail, and the Star looks more like the original Bergmann Muskete, having a shoulder stock and left-hand grip under the barrel. A German type, the Schmeisser, has a folding extension stock and a 30-round box magazine below the action. These guns are coming more and more into military use as the present war goes on.

The Russian army is at the present time using a variation of the old Bergmann Muskete in 9 mm. caliber, fed from below with a detachable drum magazine. This is a recoil-operated blowback mechanism.

THE U.S. .30 SRM-1 CARTRIDGE

The United States Government has, within recent months, developed a self-loading cartridge for a light automatic weapon, which is designated as the U.S. .30 SRM-1, or the United States .30 caliber Short Rifle M1 cartridge. This cartridge is a straight-cased .30 caliber, rimless cartridge with a short round-nosed gilding metal-jacket bullet weighing 110 grains. The muzzle velocity is 1780 feet per second, with a breech pressure of about 40,000 pounds per square inch. The United States Government asked inventors to develop for its use a short carbine type semi- and full-automatic arm, with a weight of approximately 5½ pounds, fed from a detachable box magazine. This weapon was to be an intermediate arm between the submachine gun and the standard rifle, as it would have considerably more power than the average submachine gun but would be far more compact and portable than the present rifle.

Among the arms tested were models submitted by the Auto Ordnance Company, Woodhull, Hyde, Savage, Harrington and Richardson, Winchester, and the Springfield Armory. The Winchester was adopted. Its specifications include a 15-shot box magazine with a staggered vertical field; it is gas-operated, taking the gas from near the breech of the barrel, similar to Winchester's experimental .30-06 caliber model and weighs 4.63 pounds. The rifle is 7½ inches shorter than the Garand and is chambered for the .30 SRM-1 cartridge.

From a tactical standpoint, such a weapon fills a very apparent need in the armament of large units. The modern army is full of specialists. There are communications units, engineer units, transportation specialists, and various staff specialists. Above all, there are troops whose primary mission is to carry ammunition to the various weapons echelons. Also there are artillery and tank units whose personnel can profitably employ a 5-pound, 300 yard shoulder automatic.

Last but not least, non-coms and officers of the combat units require a truly effective weapon of this type to augment the fire power of the section, platoon, and company at closer ranges.

For example, crews of heavy machine guns—AT, AA, and artillery units—require a light, portable, medium-range weapon having rifle accuracy up to 150-250 yards. Their primary mission is to operate their big gun, yet they need adequate short-range protection against hostile infantry which may often come within range in the hurly-burly of modern war.

As indicated elsewhere in this book, the increase in automatic weapons results in an increase in the proportion of unit leaders. These, if armed with a 5-pound medium automatic, become far more effective when their unit has reached points within several dozen yards of the enemy.

THE SEMI-AUTOMATIC RIFLE

Despite all the efforts of inventors to perfect a self-loading military rifle, no army in the world is as yet (1941) fully equipped with such an arm. It is fair to say, however, that the United States leads the world in developing this type of weapon.

The semi-automatic rifle has presented great difficulty because of the limitations set on its weight. Inventors have been able to build automatic actions into 15- or 20-pound bipod-mounted guns, but not into 9- or 10-pound shoulder rifles. Sufficient data have already been accumulated to furnish an accurate picture of this future weapon of the doughboy.

The semi-automatic rifle is of about the same weight as the 1903 Springfield or 1917 Enfield. It shoots the standard military rifle cartridge, and has about the same ballistic qualities, suffering no loss of power, velocity, accuracy, or range. It will hold 5 to 10 rounds [1] in a magazine, and every time a round is discharged, the bolt will automatically unlock, extract, and eject the empty case, cock the hammer, and, under pressure of the mainspring, load another round from the magazine into the chamber, and relock. The operator merely pulls or pushes the handle to load the piece initially. After that he squeezes the trigger—once for each shot—until the magazine is empty. Unlike the machine rifle, the semi-automatic is cocked with the bolt locked.

As in any automatic weapon, the force of the explosion is used to operate the mechanism. Therefore some of the kick is taken up and the semi-automatic is more comfortable to shoot than the Springfield. Moreover, because manipulation of the bolt in rapid fire is dispensed with, the semi-automatic. will be less fatiguing in combat firing, and the training time previously required for bolt manipulation will be available for other instruction.

The sights are of the improved peep type, the aperture being close to the eye. It is probable that bayonets will be supplied for weapons of this type, though the trend of opinion indicates the possible obsolescence of the heavy bayonet.

The primary mission of the semi-automatic is to increase the deliverable accurate fire of the rifleman. With the Springfield, a fair marksman can hit 5 man-targets at 200 yards in 25 seconds, or 10 such targets in 1 minute. But the same marksman with a semi-automatic rifle can hit 5 man-targets at 200 yards in 8 to 10 seconds, or 10 such targets in less than 20 seconds.

---

[1] The M1 Garand rifle holds 8 rounds.

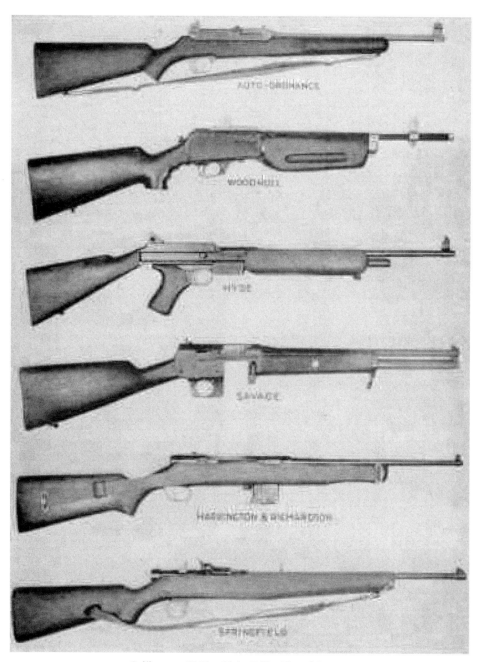

Caliber .30 SRM-1 Light Rifles Tested in 1941

The United States Carbine, caliber .30, M-1. The recently adopted Winchester Carbine using the United States cartridge caliber .30 SRM-1.

Semi-Automatic Military Rifles Tested in 1920

1. Garand Rifle; 2. Thompson Rifle; 3. Berthier Rifle; 4. U. S. Semi-Automatic Rifle, Model 1920, Experimental (Bang type)

It is apparent that a semi-automatic rifleman can deliver from 3 to 6 shots with the same accuracy and within the same time interval that a Springfield rifleman can deliver one.

The semi-automatic rifle is capable of laying down a barrage in much the same manner as a light machine gun. It is, of course, designed and meant to increase the efficiency and effectiveness of the individual rifleman, not to burn up ammunition. With such a weapon the rifleman will fire more rounds per combat minute, but not more rounds per combat day. Squads armed with this weapon will be more carefully disciplined, and it is not unlikely that the number of riflemen under one leader will be decreased to insure fire control. (For example, a squad of four riflemen led by a corporal.)

At the present time two semi-automatic military rifles are in production in the United States and have been adopted by national armies. These are the Garand and the Johnson Semi-Automatic Rifles.

GARAND UNITED STATES RIFLE CALIBER .30 M1

The first semi-automatic rifle to be adopted as standard by any nation is the rifle designated as the United States Rifle Caliber .30 M1, and more commonly known as the Garand Semi-Automatic Rifle, as it is the invention of John C. Garand, employee of Springfield Armory. Mr. Garand started experimenting with his rifle shortly after 1920, when the United States Government indicated a desire to adopt a semi-automatic rifle as a standard military weapon. A number of other inventors also worked on semi-automatic models all during the 1920's. At one time it was decided to reduce the caliber of the standard rifle to .276, and a number of rifles were submitted in this caliber, among them those designed by Thompson, Pedersen, White, and others. However, tests narrowed the field to the models submitted by Mr. Garand. The standard .30 caliber was eventually retained, as it was felt that this cartridge had a very good record for combat use and was best suited for use in machine guns.

After further experimenting, Mr. Garand produced a rifle that showed great promise. Some eighty examples of this model were built at Springfield Armory and given tests. As a result of these tests the Garand rifle was adopted by the United States Government as the official infantry arm in 1936, and tooling for production of the rifle was begun at Springfield Armory. Since then some minor changes have been made in the design, and the rifle is now in quantity production at Springfield Armory, where about 1000 Garands a day are being made at the present time. The government also has a contract with the Winchester company for the manufacture of Garand rifles that are being turned out there.

The Garand rifle is a gas-operated, semi-automatic rifle requiring a separate pull on the trigger for each shot fired. It takes its gas from a port at the muzzle of the barrel to drive an operating rod and operate the action, unlocking the 25° two-lug rotary bolt, by the expansion of the gas in a cylinder beneath the barrel. The rifle is clip fed, with a special clip of 8 cartridges which forms an integral part of the magazine and is pushed into place from the top. When the gun is empty, the clip automatically is ejected after the last cartridge has been fired. It uses the standard model 1905 bayonet. The gas port was at first in a sleeve in front of the muzzle of the barrel, but since 1940 this sleeve has been dispensed with and the gas port is bored in the barrel itself. The rear sight is of the modern peep type, mounted at the rear of the receiver, and it is a much easier sight to use than the open sights of earlier military rifles. The Garand has double the fire power of a Springfield 1903.

THE JOHNSON RIFLE

The Johnson Semi-Automatic Military Rifle, the only recoil-operated, semi-automatic military rifle now being manufactured or that has been adopted by any army, is the invention of one of the authors of this book, Captain Melvin M. Johnson, Jr.

The rifle was invented and the first working model made during the summer of 1936. Patents were taken out the same year. Development went on for some time, during which time 23 model rifles, some of which varied in minor detail while others were of identical construction, were made and subjected to exhaustive tests.

The basic action is a short recoil rotary bolt system locking with

8 lugs and unlocking by the rearward movement of the slidably mounted barrel. The bolt turns 20° to unlock while the barrel is recoiling ⅜ inch. Unlocking is accomplished by cams on the bolt working in a cam chamber and channel in the top of the receiver.

During the development of the rifle, a light machine gun operating on the same basic principle was also designed and patented.

The Johnson Semi-Automatic Military Rifle is 45½ inches long, and weighs approximately 9½ pounds. It is a rotary-feed type with 11-shot capacity, loaded from standard Springfield type 5-shot clips or with loose cartridges. The feed lips are machined in the solid steel receiver and are not part of any light metal magazine or clip. The action can be adapted to any standard military cartridge and is being currently made in 30.06 and 7 mm.

The receiver peep sight is placed well back and is readily adjustable, taking advantage of available improvements in this respect by the receiver design of automatic arms.

A company was formed to market the Johnson arms, and tooling was begun for production on an order for them from a friendly foreign power in the fall of 1940. By arrangement with the Universal Winding Company, of Providence, Rhode Island, part of the work is done by that company and part by the Johnson Automatics Manufacturing Company, occupying space in buildings of the Universal Winding Company.

THE WINCHESTER GAS-OPERATED EXPERIMENTAL RIFLE

This weapon was publicly tested in November, 1940, and is described here because of the interest which its design aroused at that time, as well as for the fact that it is the product of the joint efforts of a cousin of the late John M. Browning, of the well-known Winchester company's renowned engineers headed by Mr. Edwin Pugsley, and of Mr. David Williams, also known as the inventor of the "floating chamber" of Colt "ACE" fame.

The Winchester is a gas-operated, 9.5 pound, detachable box-fed, caliber .30, semi-automatic rifle. In outward appearance it is exceedingly compact and well balanced, resembling in general a conventional military rifle. The magazine is of the "B.A.R."

box type, but the weapon may be loaded by clips in the same manner as the M1903 Springfield.

Gas is taken through a port near the breech. The violent gas pressure diverted hits a small floating piston which is in contact with the operating slide. This piston travels $\frac{1}{10}$ inch, transmitting considerable energy to the slide. Thereafter the piston acts as a valve to prevent loss of bullet power. Rearward travel of the slide unlocks the Winchester model 1895 type rising-wedge breechblock, and the force of momentum plus some residual pressure forces the action rearward.

To insure extraction, several models of this rifle were provided with longitudinally fluted chambers in lieu of oil or grease on the cartridges. This chamber design reduced wall friction and materially reduced resistance to extraction.

A very compact type gas-actuated weapon, this Winchester, like all the products of America's leading rifle factory, showed commendable accuracy in tests closely followed by the authors of this book.

The Winchester plant is now turning out the M1 Garand rifle and the future of the experimental Winchester is not known at this time.

THE LIGHT MACHINE GUN

Inventors have found the problem of designing a light machine gun (or machine rifle or automatic rifle) much easier to solve than the semi-automatic rifle, and a number of such machine guns have been developed since the first World War.

Some of these guns have a few original features, but in general the new ideas amount to little more than the refinement of older designs. In a few, the operating power is obtained from the recoil of the barrel; in a majority, power is gained from the impact of powder gas through a gas port in the barrel against an operating piston.

These guns are fed by box magazines or drums. They are invariably mounted on bipods, the butt stock being held against the shooter's shoulder. In some, the barrel is arranged for quick dismounting, the over-heated barrel being easily replaced by a new one.

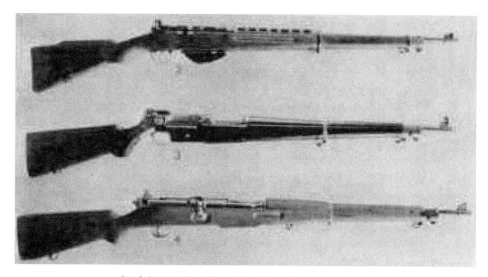

Semi-Automatic Rifles Offered for Test in the 1920's
2. Pedersen Cal. .276, 24-in. barrel, 10 round magazine; 3. Garand Cal. .30, 21½-in. barrel;
4. Thompson Cal. .30, 21½-in. barrel

Semi-Automatic Rifles Tested by the U. S. Ordnance Board in the Late 1920's
Top to bottom, White Cal. .276, with bolt open; Pedersen Cal. .276; Garand Cal. .276; Garand
Cal. .30

John C. Garand with His Rifle

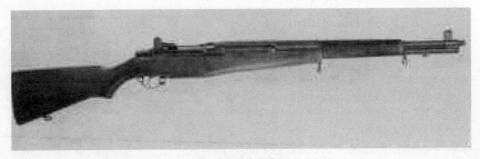

The Garand Rifle

The following list includes most of the more recent guns in this class: [2]

Nation	Gun	Weight	Feed	Operation
U.S.A.	Browning	16 lbs.	20 rd. box	Gas
Britain	Bren [5]	20 lbs.	30 rd. box	Gas
Germany (?)	Madsen	20 lbs.	40 rd. box	Recoil 2 inches
Germany	M-34	26 lbs.	Drum or belt	Recoil
Swiss	Fusil Furrer	18 lbs.	30 rd. box	Recoil 4 inches
Japan	Nambu	20 lbs.	30 rd. hopper	Gas
Denmark	Eriksen	24 lbs.	50 rd. mag.	Gas
Italy	Ansaldo	20 lbs. (?)	(?)	Gas
Italy	Sia	23 lbs.	25 rd. mag.	Gas
Belgium	Chauchard [3]	18 lbs.	20 rd. mag.	Gas
France	Chauchard [4]	19 lbs.	20 rd. box	Recoil 5 inches
France	Light Hotchkiss	19 lbs.	25 rd. box	Gas
Czechoslovakia	Praga	18 lbs.	20 rd. mag.	Probably gas
Czechoslovakia (Brno)	Z.B. [5]	20 lbs.	30 rd. mag.	Gas
Britain	Lewis [4]	27 lbs.	47 rd. drum	Gas

The cyclic rate of fire of the above weapons varies from 400 to 700 rounds per minute. The actual deliverable fire varies from 100 to 250 rounds per minute. Average bursts vary from 3 to 10 shots. Nearly all these weapons can be fired semi-automatically. This type of fire is more desirable on targets not closely grouped, or on any targets ordinarily fired upon by the shoulder rifle.

Recent examples of the Light Machine Gun that show interesting design features include the following:

The Bren Light Machine Gun

Described in other connections elsewhere in this book, the Bren Light Machine Gun is a gas-operated, shoulder-fired, bipod-mounted, magazine-fed, 21-pound automatic arm, the standard of the British army.

Developed in Czechoslovakia by a private manufacturer and known to the late Czech army as the "Z.B.," this design was purchased by the British War Office after tests during 1928-1934 in which the Danish Madsen was a close second. Modified for the .303 ammunition and refined in many respects by British designers, the Bren is an outstanding weapon in its class.

[2] See also Appendix One, pages 312 to 323.
[3] Not to be confused with the wartime French Chauchard or "Chauchat."
[4] These are now obsolete.
[5] Practically identical; based on same invention.

Chief features found in this arm are its quickly removable air-cooled barrel; simple, reliable, rising-block breech lock; straight-line operating slide; straight-line stock with mainspring in the butt; ease of disassembly; simple positive ignition; means of holding open the breechblock on an empty magazine; full- and semi-automatic fire control change lever; self-opening ejection-port breech cover; top-mounted, 30-shot detachable magazine; self-locking, folding bipod with carbon-scraper for cleaning the gas cylinder; shock-absorber butt stock with self-locking shoulder rest; large, easily read, side-mounted peep sight elevation drum; and folding AA mount.

The weapon is made at the Royal Small Arms Arsenal, Enfield Lock, England, and at the John Inglis Co. Limited, Toronto, Canada.

The Solothurn M.34 Light Machine Gun

A very interesting light machine gun was adopted by the German service in 1934 and is now being extensively used by the German armies. It is known officially as the M.34 and also as the "Solothurn." This is a short recoil, air-cooled machine gun chambered for the standard 7.9 mm. German service ammunition. The barrel is enclosed in an air-cooled jacket with a flash hider and a folding bipod mount at the muzzle. The stock is in direct prolongation of the center line of the bore, looking more or less like an old-fashioned crutch with the sights raised above the barrel for comfortable aiming. It is fed from the side with a 20-shot box magazine, or a metallic link belt, or a drum. It can be fired full- or semi-automatically, depending upon whether the upper or lower part of the trigger is pulled. The barrel-locking ring revolves while sliding in the supporting jacket so that the bolt and mainspring recoil in an absolutely straight line, and the action is made up of very simple round parts. The gun weighs slightly over 25 pounds and is a very simple, easily manufactured weapon of good design.

The Dektyarov Light Machine Gun

The Dektyarov Light Machine Gun is the main arm of this type now in use in the Russian army. It is a gas-operated, air-cooled gun, weighing 20 pounds. The barrel is quickly removable as it is held to the receiver by an interrupted screw thread, requiring only a quarter turn to release it. The gun feeds from a flat 47-shot pan on the top, giving it an appearance similar to the Lewis. It can be fired semi- as well as full-automatically. The Russians are using these guns in great quantity, and from the latest newspaper reports with not inconsiderable effect.

The Johnson Light Machine Gun

In the light machine gun field the Johnson short recoil action has been adapted to a light-weight machine gun which is now in process of manufacture by the Johnson Automatics Manufacturing Company. It has been adopted by a friendly foreign power. As we are undoubtedly prejudiced concerning its qualities, we feel that the following article written by Lt. Col. Calvin Goddard and appearing in *Army Ordnance*, May-June, 1941, is perhaps as fair an account of the gun as any we could give:

The years elapsing since the close of the World War have witnessed the introduction of a veritable spate of new machine gun mechanisms, embodied in everything from the tiny "sub" weapons of 6½ pounds and upward firing pistol ammunition, to heavy, water-cooled, tripod-mounted affairs. The intermediate class of "light" machine guns likewise has received attention, and many have appeared—some taking shape as machine rifles of the type exemplified in the United States by the light Browning of 1918, others adapted for use either off-shoulder or with muzzle supports in the form of bipods, etc.

According to Curti ("Automatische Waffen," Frauenfeld, Germany, 1936), the only characteristic possessed by these in common is the absence of a rigid mount. He goes on to say that even without such a support the current German light machine gun can be fired in bursts numbering up to the full capacity of the magazine without the sights riding up off the target, or without any impairment of accuracy up to 1,000 meters. The attainment of such characteristics with a weapon of conventional form is not easy. To achieve them, the makers of the German Solothurn M.34 (the piece to which Curti refers) have undertaken distinct departures from general practice, in the conformation of its "straight-line" stock, and in the mounting of its sights high above the bore.

Both these features are to be found in an American contribution
to the light-machine-gun field—that of Capt. Melvin M. Johnson, Jr.,
Marine Corps Reserve. This arm, the basic elements of which were
invented in 1936, progressed into a fully automatic model in 1937 and,
in 1940, was finally modified into the current form in which it is
capable both of semi- and full-automatic fire. The following is a brief
review of the Johnson's specifications:

Caliber: .30 (M1906), M1 or M2; Action: short-recoil type; Weight
(less magazine): 12.3 pounds; Weight of magazine, empty: 14 ounces;
Barrel length: 20, 22 (standard), and 24 inches; Over-all length: 42
inches; Cooling system: air; Magazine type: single-column box; Magazine capacity: 20 rounds (capacity of gun fully loaded is 25 rounds);
Magazine location: extends horizontally from left side of receiver;
Methods of loading: (1) by inserting loaded detachable magazine; (2)
with magazine in place, by inserting 5-round clips or single rounds
through loading port on right side of receiver; Time required to remove empty magazine and insert loaded replacement: 3-5 seconds;
Line of sight—height above axis of bore: 2 inches; Sight radius: 28
inches; Number of parts to remove for field cleaning: 11; Time required for stripping: 35 seconds; Tools required for disassembly: point
of bullet in cartridge; Cyclic rate of fire with normal buffer tension:
400-450 M2 rounds a minute (rate adjusted by varying tension on
buffer spring); Range of adjustment; from about 300 to 900 rounds a
minute; Time elapsed in firing one full-automatic burst of 20 rounds:
slightly over 2 seconds; Actual number of rounds delivered, full-
automatic, 1-man operation: 180 a minute—with 2-man crew (assistant
replacing magazines): 200-220 rounds a minute; Time required for
barrel removal: 4-5 seconds; Time required for barrel removal and
replacement: 8-10 seconds; Types of fire: semi- and full-automatic;
Safety: positive sear lock.

Reference already has been made to the design of the Johnson stock,
the unusual lines of which will be noted upon inspection of the illustration (p. 80). The atypical outlines there revealed are the result of
a highly successful effort to reduce the usual tendency of an arm of
this class to "climb" during full-automatic fire as well as to eliminate,
in so far as possible, the concomitant vibration. As an additional ges-
ture toward these ends the mechanism is so fashioned that all moving
parts reciprocate along the axis of the bore, the combination of these
novel features constituting one of the outstanding characteristics of the
piece.

Another interesting and apparently highly desirable departure from

Development of the Johnson Semi-Automatic Military Rifle

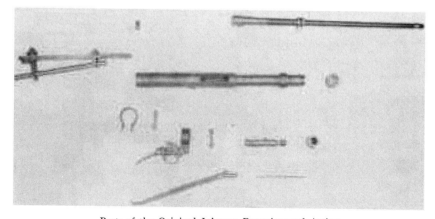

Parts of the Original Johnson Experimental Action

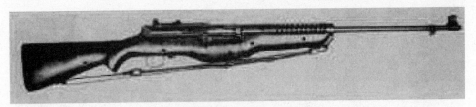

Johnson Semi-Automatic Military Rifle

Winchester Experimental Semi-Automatic Gas-Operated Military Rifle

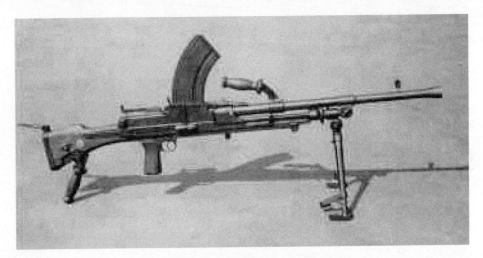

The Bren Light Machine Gun

The Solothurn M-34 Light Machine Gun

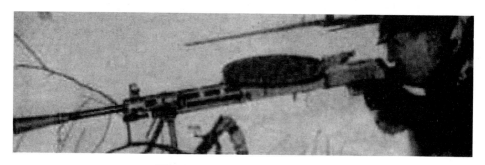

The Degtyarof Light Machine Gun

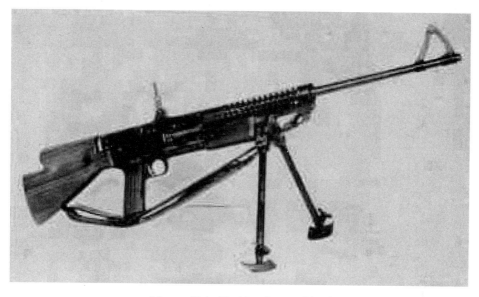

Johnson Light Machine Gun on Bipod

Comparison of Small-Arms Ammunition
(Bullets at left, cartridges at right): Caliber .45 ball; Caliber .30 SR,
M1; Caliber .30 M2; Caliber .50 M2

Captain Johnson and Mr. Haven shooting the Johnson Light Machine Gun

convention appears in the manner in which the bolt functions during semi-automatic, as contrasted with full-automatic, fire. In the Johnson weapon, when set for semi-automatic operation (where the contingency of spontaneous ignition is negligible), the bolt is cocked and locked in the forward (closed) position as in an ordinary bolt-action rifle, a loaded cartridge filling the chamber ahead. Firing takes place in the usual manner—by removing the safety and pressing the trigger, no more vibration being set up than in a non-automatic arm. Should full-automatic fire now be indicated, the change lever is turned to the rear, the bolt thereafter remaining retracted and the chamber empty, until firing is begun. The mechanical design involved provides for engagement of trigger and sear during semi-automatic fire, but when the operation is fully automatic, engagement is between trigger and bolt catch, sear and sear trip. Trigger pressure now releases the bolt which trips the sear in locking, thus releasing the hammer and discharging the piece.

When vertically positioned, the change lever locks both sear and bolt catch, making it impossible to fire with the bolt in either the open or closed position. An additional safeguard is provided in a grip safety located just below the rear end of the trigger guard.

The Johnson possesses yet additional, and seemingly substantial, claims to fame. It manages to eliminate entirely malfunctions due to deformations of magazine lips made integral with a detachable-box magazine, bugbears which long have troubled users of such devices (and it requires but few fingers to count the varieties of box magazines *not* possessing integral lips). The device employed to accomplish this consists of a flat-leaf spring with a rounded hook which fulfills two functions: the first, to engage and retain the top cartridge in the magazine; the second, to act as the magazine retaining catch. Upon insertion of the magazine into its holder on the left side of the action, this hook is cammed upward on a ramp, whereupon it first releases the cartridges from the magazine, then engages upon shoulders in the ramp to prevent the disengagement of the magazine unless and until the proper release lever is actuated.

Once released, the cartridges are forced from the magazine against the cartridge guide or side ramp which constitutes a part of the magazine loading cover. Pressure of the magazine spring against this ramp results in the top cartridge being rolled up into feed lips which are *machined* into the receiver. This mode of construction obviates the danger of lip distortion.

By depressing the magazine loading cover, the ramp formed on the right side of the feed lips is removed, and the contents of the magazine are forced out into the hand of the operator. By means of this same cover it becomes possible to clip-load cartridges directly into the gun from the *right* side of the receiver, a clip seat, identical with that found in the Johnson semi-automatic rifle of rotary-feed type, being provided for the purpose. Furthermore, single cartridges may be introduced in like manner. Since the operator may find an opportunity to refill the magazine after discharging only a portion of its contents, such a feature becomes extremely advantageous. Thus, after firing five or ten shots, he may refill the magazine by the simple expedient of introducing one or two clips of ammunition—the magazine meantime remaining in the weapon. Moreover, should the firing of tracer ammunition suddenly be indicated, a suitable number of rounds of ball ammunition may be removed by depressing the magazine loading cover and replaced directly by as many tracers. Incidentally, the Johnson magazine is of the single-column box type which has much to recommend it by way of simplicity and large tolerances in manufacture.

In the matter of design, Johnson's gun consists of five basic groups of components: (1) barrel group, (2) bolt group, (3) receiver group, (4) magazine group, (5) buttstock and hammer group. For complete field stripping, it is necessary to remove but eleven parts: barrel, butt group, magazine, magazine holder, bolt, extractor, firing-pin stop, firing pin, operating handle, locking cam, and receiver group. Such removal has been accomplished in fifteen seconds and replacement in thirty-five seconds.

The locking action involves a rotary bolt which locks by rotating through an arc of twenty degrees, thereby effecting the engagement of eight locking lugs disposed equidistant one from another about the bolt head. Lug faces are square, without bevel. Lugs mate with a corresponding number of similarly disposed segments or abutments in a barrel-locking bushing, resting against these when in the locked position. A locking cam, positioned at the rear end of the bolt group, effects rotation and locking of the bolt after the latter has reached its fully closed position. Since the cam unit carries the firing pin, unlocking the bolt results in sufficient retraction of both cam and firing pin to prevent discharge until the bolt assembly reassumes its fully locked state.

When the piece is discharged, barrel and bolt recoil together for about one-eighth of an inch, whereupon the angular face of the operating cam contacts a corresponding face in the receiver. This causes the bolt to rotate through the twenty degrees required for unlocking, during which period it travels rearward to the extent of something less than an additional three-eighths of an inch. Total barrel travel in recoil is less than seven-sixteenths of an inch. Unlocking is completed only after residual pressure has fallen to within practicable limits, but there remains at this time sufficient pressure to assist in the retraction of the bolt assembly. Thus recoil alone effects the unlocking; recoil momentum *plus* residual pressure effects the subsequent retraction. Primary extraction derives from the momentum of recoil. Compression of the coil mainspring, which lies on a prolongation of the axis of the bore, results from the rearward movement of the bolt assembly. As the bolt passes the rear of the magazine, the buffer plunger at the rear of the locking cam is compressed as a result of contacting the base of the mainspring tube in the buttstock. The bolt, its motion now reversed, moves forward, engaging the head of a cartridge in the feed lips, inserting this into the chamber, then closing and locking the breech. Ejection is carried out in the same manner as in the Johnson rifle.

Summarizing, we find in the Johnson, a machine weapon so light in weight (12.3 pounds) as almost to place it in the shoulder-rifle class. The only comparable modern piece exhibiting certain parallel characteristics is the German Solothurn, M.34 (which, incidentally, weighs just twice as much). Carefully designed from the standpoints of mechanism, balance, and form to minimize undue vibration during semi-automatic fire and to achieve a degree of accuracy considerably above the ordinary, it exhibits in addition novel features in respect of its feed mechanism, provision for instantaneous barrel replacement, field stripping, etc., and appears a piece worthy of the traditions of American arms makers.

THE FUNCTION OF THE LIGHT MACHINE GUN

The machine rifle, or light machine gun, is designed to be carried by one man and is therefore available for use against targets engaged by riflemen of the squad or section. While the machine rifle is not so suitable as the semi-automatic for shoulder use, it is nevertheless far more effective than the hand-operated, bolt-action repeating rifle.

Until the armies of the world adopt semi-automatic rifles as standard, the machine rifle is likely to serve as an all-purpose weapon. However, as a machine gun it lacks the ability to deliver intense long-range fire for a substantial period of time. As a shoulder rifle, fired semi-automatically, it is frequently much too clumsy, too heavy, and, in most cases, too inaccurate. Its inaccuracy is due chiefly to the fact that it is cocked with the breech open. The shooter, having aimed and pulled the trigger, is handicapped by the movement of the breechblock and the resulting lapse of time prior to ignition. However, this feature is necessary in order to avoid leaving a loaded cartridge in a hot chamber for any length of time. The cooked round may explode accidentally or it may develop dangerously high pressure. The barrels of guns which may be fired in bursts are very liable to reach exceedingly high temperatures.

The light Browning furnishes an excellent illustration of this problem. It is cocked with the breech open. Without the bipod mount it is invariably fired semi-automatically. In fact, the light Browning was originally used as the next best weapon to a semi-automatic rifle. But recently it has been changed by the addition of mounts and is now looked upon as a light machine gun. As such it is generally fired full-automatically in 3- to 10-shot bursts.

The burst from a light machine gun forms a cone similar to the cone of the heavy gun. Especially at short ranges (100 to 1200 yards) the cone is, of course, long and narrow. Thus the fire is most effective from the flank. The light gun is more often fired at targets when they are observed in an area than at predetermined areas occupied or believed to be occupied by targets.

The light gun is fired only by direct laying. It is especially valuable on the offensive because of its comparative mobility and the rapidity with which it can be set up and fired. Though not so easily handled from the shoulder as the pure semi-automatic rifle, it may be used effectively against low-flying planes.

On the defense this weapon can serve as a not unworthy substitute for the heavy machine gun. Against attacks from unanticipated directions by highly mobile forces, this gun is likely to be more efficient than the heavier and less easily moved tripod-mounted weapon. Moreover, the light gun is less vulnerable to counterbattery fire.

The best feature of the light machine gun is its availability to the troops it supports. The heavy guns require liaison. The light guns can actually accompany the rifle squads and sections, mov-

Automatic Cannon of Various Sizes

(From right to left): Cal. .276 (7 mm.) shoulder rifle weighing 9 lbs.; Cal. .30 (7.62 mm.) rifle weighing 16 lbs.; Cal. .30 (7.62 mm.) water-cooled machine gun weighing 30 lbs. without water; Cal. 7.92 mm. (.313 in.) light machine gun weighing 20 lbs.; Cal. .50 (12.7 mm.) aircraft machine gun weighing 55 lbs.; Cal. 20 mm. (.79 in.) air-cooled cannon weighing 143 lbs.

Sizes of Fixed Ammunition
(From left to right): Cal. .276; Cal. .30; Cal. .50; Cal. 20 mm.; Cal. 37 mm.

ing at the same rate of march as the riflemen, and being ever present to cover and protect their movements.

In the hurly-burly of an attack, the heavy machine guns have often failed to deliver effective supporting fires. Such was too often the case in the first World War. In many instances this failure was due to the imperfect execution of the attack, to confused orders, and to other defects of a like nature. However, one must expect errors in combat and plan accordingly.

The light machine gun, on the other hand, is at least under the supervision and control of the platoon leader, who, from this weapon, can obtain instantly the supporting fires he would otherwise be required to request frantically from too far distant company, battalion, or machine gun company commanders.

Thus with the light machine gun, as with the semi-automatic rifle, we can reconcile fire power and mobility.

THE LIGHT-HEAVY MACHINE GUN

We have observed that many of the weapons in the light machine gun or machine rifle class were designed to serve in part as shoulder rifles firing single shots. In this class we find an attempt to combine the characteristics of the pure light-weight machine gun with the endurance and stability of the heavy gun.

For example, suppose a 24-pound machine gun is designed to be mounted on a bipod and fed by a drum or box magazine. This gun could qualify as a machine rifle. But a 40-pound bipod-mount with elevating and traversing gear is provided for the same gun, and a special belt can be used in place of the drum. Thus the light gun becomes the heavy gun, and it can sweep zones, fire with full effect along final protective lines, and fire by indirect laying. The new German army is equipped with such a weapon, known as the M.34.

It is hard to prophesy the future of guns of this class but it is safe to say that every effort will be made to reduce the weight of the heavy machine gun, in which event we may find these all-purpose guns in the height of fashion. The advent of the pure semi-automatic rifle may encourage this fusion of bipod-tripod guns.

Guns of this class will undoubtedly have removable barrels. Instead of fetching water for the cooling jacket, the crews will simply pull out the hot barrel and assemble a fresh one within five or ten seconds. Several spare barrels will accompany each gun.

The demand for mobility has had a material effect upon the development of heavy machine guns. All efforts have been bent toward reducing weight and simplifying parts. Aside from attempting these improvements there has been no change since the first World War in the heavy Browning, Vickers, Hotchkiss, Maxim, Revelli, Schwarzlose, and other such guns.

So many heavy guns were built during the first World War and never used, that some nations had a reserve of these weapons available for the present conflict.

.50 CALIBER MACHINE GUNS

Another development since the first World War is the .50 caliber machine gun cartridge, perfected from the German 13 mm. wartime antitank cartridge in this country in the first years after the first World War. Its characteristics are a muzzle velocity of 2500 feet per second, with a boat-tail bullet weighing 753 grains, to give a striking force of 10,765 pounds at the muzzle. The chamber pressure is 54,000 pounds.

The Colt company developed an enlargement of the regular Browning .30 caliber machine gun to take the .50 caliber cartridge, and mounted it for both aircraft and ground use. The Air Craft Model (MG53A) is an air-cooled gun with a cyclic rate of fire of between 400 and 600 shots per minute. The barrel is surrounded and supported by an air-cooled perforated jacket, and the gun is operated through a synchronizing mechanism the motor of which is attached to the side of the gun and which works from the propeller when necessary. The gun uses a metallic-link belt to feed the cartridges. The gun weighs $58\frac{5}{10}$ pounds unmounted. It is a recoil-operated gun with a locked breech similar to the other Browning machine guns.

The .50 caliber machine gun is also adapted for ground use in the air-cooled model by the addition of a tripod, operating handles, etc. It makes a load packed for transportation of about 250 pounds. It is also fitted to tanks and combat cars, in fixed mounts. While the Colt company manufactures a water-cooled model very similar to the water-cooled .30 caliber gun, the air-cooled model is by far the more commonly used in the United States Army.

AUTOMATIC CANNON

For some years after Hiram Maxim's late Victorian "pom-pom," there was little development in the field of automatic cannon. Machine guns were confined to .30-06, .303, 7.92 mm. or the equivalent.

During the period 1920-1939, various larger calibered automatic weapons were developed in Europe. Calibers included 20 mm., 25 mm., 37 mm., 40 mm., and 47 mm. In addition, so-called semi-automatic, or "self-ejecting," actions were developed for these calibers and up to the 75 mm.

Weapons of these classes include antitank, tank, antiaircraft, and aircraft cannon. Improved armor plate has forced the hurried development of high-velocity, hard-hitting, heavy automatics. The subject of armor penetration and armor-piercing ammunition is beyond the scope of this book. Development is in a state of flux. In general, impact energy is essential to penetrate and shatter armor plate. This means velocity plus mass. Antiaircraft requirements also necessitate long range and higher terminal velocities.

Ammunition in this category raises many problems in the design of suitable automatic mechanisms. Rapid overheating of the barrels and operation with high pressure, plus weight limitations in the interest of mobility, constitute the main stumblng blocks. The actions of such weapons include a few of the gas type. A majority are of recoil and blowback action.

One of the German types uses the short-recoil system. Several other designs employ the long-recoil, especially in the heavier calibers. This system is notably employed in self-ejecting AA cannon, such as the U.S. 75 mm. AA gun.

Another method illustrated in the Swiss Oerlikon 20 mm. gun is the delayed blowback. In this blowback type, a very heavy breech slide operated by a powerful spring closes with force, and the round is fired before the slide is fully forward. The blowback force must overcome the final forward momentum of the slide plus its inertia in opening and ejecting the fired shell. Usually with such types the shells should be greased. Actually there is no breech lock in this system.

The gas and short-recoil systems are similar in principle to those described elsewhere in this book. The long-recoil system used in certain self-ejecting cannon utilizes the familiar French 75 mm. recoil principle. Cams unlock the breech and throw out the shell during the long rearward stroke. The loader shoves home the next round and the breech automatically closes, pushing the loader's hand safely clear. With feed system added, this action becomes fully automatic.

The semi-automatic types can fire from 30 to 40 rounds per minute. The automatics fire up to 100 to 200 per minute. Due to overheating, high rates cannot be maintained over a long period.

Feed systems include loading trays, circular drums, and belts. Projectiles are generally of the solid ball AP type for AT use, and of the impact H.E. type for aircraft and AA fire.

Due to developments in airplane construction, there is a strong trend toward heavier calibers, the .30 and .303 types being used chiefly for strafing ground units. The chief effect of the lighter calibers lies in their high volume. At the outbreak of the current war, R.A.F. pilots were firing 8 Brownings at a rate of 20 shots per second per gun, or 160 shots per plane per 1-second burst. The .50 caliber aircraft Browning is employed in much the same way. The repetition of sudden concentrated hits is extremely effective.

Guns above .55 caliber will when possible be fired semi-automatically to avoid overheating and the wasting of expensive H.E. projectiles.

It is not unlikely that improved automatic mechanisms may make possible the construction of much lighter cannon than are now available. Increases in velocity may substitute for the high explosive shell of the 20 or 25 mm. Much remains to be accomplished in this field.

PART TWO

How They Work

CHAPTER FIVE

Classification of Automatic Weapons

Classification of Automatic Weapons; Functional Outline of Automatic Mechanisms

THE *machine gun*. An example is the heavy Browning M1917, 30 caliber, water-cooled, belt-fed, tripod-mounted; weight without mount, 35 pounds.

The *light machine gun,* or *machine rifle,* or *automatic rifle.* This class requires some explanation to avoid confusion. Primarily, a light machine gun is one which fires the same ammunition as the heavy machine gun, but which usually weighs between 20 and 30 pounds, as compared with 35 and 50, plus the weight of its mount, for the heavy type. The Lewis light machine gun, air-cooled, drum-fed, bipod-mounted, weighs 28 pounds. The Bren light machine gun (new British model), air-cooled, magazine-fed, bipod-mounted, weighs 21 pounds. The Browning machine rifle, .30 caliber, Model of 1918, has been modified for bipod mounting, and weighs 21 pounds. All guns in this class have shoulder stocks, and are fired by one man, usually prone, with the butt held on the shoulder and the barrel supported on the bipod. Some authorities accordingly prefer to use the term "automatic rifle" or "machine rifle." Moreover, nearly all these weapons can be fired full- or semi-automatically. When fired semi-automatically, the arm more closely approximates the rifle. Thus, because the soldier can shoot many of these weapons semi-automatically from the conventional standing, sitting, kneeling, and prone positions, the term "automatic rifle" or "machine rifle" is most appropriate and descriptive.

The *semi-automatic,* or *self-loading,* or *autoloading* rifle, an example of which is the U.S. M1 Garand. Rifles of this type shoot regular rifle ammunition (i.e., .30 caliber, U.S. M1906). Such a rifle weighs from about 9 to 11 pounds, holds from 5 to 10 rounds, and discharges one shot with each squeeze of the trigger.

The *submachine gun*. The .45 ACP Thompson is a leading example of this type of arm. It shoots pistol cartridges full- or semi-automatically, weighs 10 pounds, is air-cooled and drum- or magazine-fed. The 11 mm. Schmeisser is another example. Such weapons are really glorified pistols, having very limited range and accuracy.

The *automatic pistol*. The .45 Colt automatic represents this class. Such a weapon is really semi-automatic or self-loading. The trigger is pulled for each shot.

Automatic cannon. This class includes full-automatic and semi-automatic guns in excess of .46 caliber, but not above 37 mm. Example: .50 caliber Browning, 20 mm. Oerlikon.

FUNCTIONAL OUTLINE OF AUTOMATIC MECHANISMS

Most of us treat firearms like automobiles and radios. We usually know enough to get the correct ammunition, to load, to fire, to put on the safety, and to clean the barrel. We know how to operate a lever, bolt, or trombone repeating action. Some of us use autoloading shotguns or self-loading rifles, keep an automatic pistol under the pillow, fire off boxes of .22 caliber cartridges in an automatic "plinking" rifle, and some of us are familiar with the military automatics of our service. But what, we should like to know, makes a machine gun fire so fast? What causes the "automatic" to eject an empty shell every time we pull the trigger? Why are there so few ultra-high-powered semi-automatic rifles? If a pistol can shoot automatically, how about building a rifle with the same mechanism?

First of all, we should differentiate between the various types or kinds of automatics. Machine guns are self-firing. You hold the trigger back and bullets pour out of the barrel. Theoretically, if you held the trigger for one minute, and there were sufficient cartridges in the belt or drum, the machine gun would fire from 300 up to 1400 shots, depending upon the design of the mechanism involved. Actually, you press the trigger for an instant at a time and the gun fires in bursts of from 3 to 30 shots. Thus, the machine gun is self-firing or "full automatic."

The shoulder rifle, or shotgun, and the pistol are self-loading, or autoloading, or "semi-automatic." Thus they reload themselves every time a shot is fired. The Remington or Browning shotgun and the Colt pistol are examples of this type of automatic weapon.

There are, in addition, certain shoulder arms which may be fired either full- or semi-automatic. Among these are the Browning machine rifle and the Thompson submachine gun.

Now we can dispose of the above differentiations in considering the basic automatic mechanism. We are actually more concerned with the self-loading than with the firing of the "automatic," because all automatics must load themselves in order to be fired.

Instead of operating a bolt handle, a lever, or a slide, in order to throw out the empty shell and shove in a full one, we require a machine to do that for us. Of course we shall be obliged to refill the magazine every 5 or 8 or 10 shots.

Before the gun can be made automatic, we must provide some kind of power or force to operate it. Obviously the operating power must come from the gun itself. Therefore we should examine a typical rifle carefully. Let's take the 1903 Springfield rifle, caliber .30-06, and see what really goes on in an ordinary gun.

The loaded cartridge is pushed into the chamber of the Springfield and locked there by the bolt which slides back and forth in the receiver. The bolt has two locking lugs which, when rotated through ninety degrees, rest against corresponding shoulders in the forward end of the receiver right back of the chamber. In addition, there is a means of hitting the primer of the cartridge when the latter is securely locked in the chamber and the trigger is pulled. The other parts of the Springfield are not essential to this discussion.

What happens when we load the Springfield and pull the trigger? First, the primer ignites the powder and the powder burns, forming a gas which expands with great force in every direction.

The expanding gas develops a pressure of about 50,000 pounds per square inch and drives the bullet down the barrel and out at the muzzle.

Meanwhile, of course, the bolt is locked and cannot move. The neck of the brass cartridge case prevents the gas from escaping to the rear of the chamber. When the gas expands, it presses the walls of the brass case against the walls of the chamber. The walls of the case at the mouth and shoulder of the bottlenecked .30-06 cartridge are thinner than toward the base or rear of the shell.

After the bullet leaves the barrel, the pressure quickly drops in the chamber to zero, at which time we can unlock the bolt and extract the empty shell. Of course if we unlocked the bolt before the bullet had left the barrel, the high pressure would cause the bolt to be blown out and the cartridge case would be ruptured. For a short interval after the bullet actually leaves the muzzle there remains an appreciable amount of pressure in the chamber. This drops rapidly to a point at which it is not dangerous to open the breech, and it quickly reaches zero. In general, therefore, we may say that the bolt must not be unlocked until after the bullet has left the muzzle. Thus we may formulate several general rules or postulates:

1. *The breech bolt of an automatic arm must never be opened until the chamber pressure has dropped to a safe limit.*

2. *There is a powerful force exerted by the powder gas against the face of the breech bolt, which may be used to provide operating power.*

There is another force in the gun which can be used to operate the bolt.

Artillerymen used to set up a cannon, aim it, and fire. The recoil would move it back out of position. Then they would hitch up the gun and haul it back to the firing line. Eventually someone rigged up a cannon so that when it fired, the barrel and breechblock would slide backward on a cradle in the gun carriage. This absorbed the kick, and now the cannoneers sit on the gun carriage while firing.

Hiram S. Maxim once patented a scheme which was arranged like this: He put a movable butt plate on a rod which was connected to the lever of a Model 1873 Winchester type repeating rifle. He set the butt plate back of the stock and put a recoil spring between the butt plate and the stock. When the gun fired, it kicked back against the slidable butt plate. This caused the lever to be pushed open by the connecting rod. The spring returned it. This gives us another rule:

3. *The recoil of a gun furnishes a force which may be used to operate an automatic firearm.*

Suppose, now, that we tried to utilize some of the gas from the barrel to push a piston, as in the case of an automobile engine, for example. In that event we could put a long cylinder directly underneath the barrel. At some point along the barrel and near the muzzle we would bore a hole to let gas enter the cylinder. We would put a piston in the cylinder attached to a rod connecting with the bolt. Thus, gas from the barrel would push the piston which, by means of the connecting rod, would operate the bolt. So we have the next rule:

4. *Powder gas pressure may be made to operate an automatic firearm by putting a gas port in the barrel and arranging a piston upon which the gas can act.*

In one aspect there is only a single primary force, the explosion in the barrel chamber, which actuates the automatic weapon. It may be used in the form of a blow on the breechblock, which is commonly called "blowback" and "retarded blowback" actuation. Or the explosion may be used in its recoiling aspect and be called the "short recoil" or "long recoil." If the propelling gases in the barrel are utilized by means of a gas port and piston, we speak of "gas actuation."

Two operations are performed when we open a Springfield breech. First, when the pressure has dropped we raise the bolt handle, thereby unlocking the bolt. Second, we pull the bolt backward to the rear of the receiver. Thus we extract and then eject the empty shell. In the automatic gun we must cause a force to unlock the breech. That same force, or some other, must be used to push or pull the bolt to the rear of the receiver. The first is called the "unlocking movement." The second is called the "retraction of the breechblock" or the "opening of the breech."

Now let us consider "residual chamber pressure." You will recall that in a Springfield rifle the maximum pressure is about

50,000 pounds per square inch. While the bullet is in the barrel the pressure is extremely high. Just as the bullet leaves the muzzle the pressure is about one-fourth of the maximum, or around 12,500 pounds. Of course this pressure thrusts back with great force upon the bolt. After the bullet has left the barrel the pressure drops rapidly to zero. However, during that brief interval just after the bullet has left the barrel, there is still some pressure in the chamber and that pressure is sufficient to push the bolt back and eject the shell without causing any rupture or breakage. This is sometimes called "residual chamber pressure" or "residual gas pressure." We prefer to call it, however, just plain "residual pressure." In order to utilize it the bolt must be unlocked "on time."

Thus we can formulate a fifth rule:

5. *There is a force called "residual pressure," operative during a brief interval after the bullet has left the muzzle, which may be used to retract the bolt.*

Power being available for unlocking and retracting the bolt, how shall we push the bolt forward, shove in a fresh cartridge, and lock the breech?

We can put a spring behind the bolt. When the bolt is pushed to the rear by the operating force the spring will be compressed. When the bolt has traveled far enough it is stopped by a device such as the "bolt stop" or "buffer block." Then the spring can expand and push the bolt forward again, thus taking care of the reloading and locking. This is called the counter-recoil spring or "mainspring."

Having examined a typical rifle and found power with which to actuate firearms automatically, how shall we harness this power? Let us select a few well-known automatic weapons and describe them. We may as well consider first the blowback, because that is the simplest.

In the blowback there is a strong counter-recoil spring. This spring stores up energy with which to return the breech bolt to its locked position. Next we have a sliding breech bolt without any locking means. Of course we have a barrel and a receiver.

Most of us are familiar with the .22 Colt Woodsman automatic pistol, or the Remington .22 automatic rifle, or the Winchester

.22 automatic, or the Sears Roebuck "Ranger" .22 automatic, or the .351 (or .401) Winchester self-loading rifle. These all are blowbacks.

Suppose we insert a magazine into the .22 Colt pistol and pull back and release the slide, which on this gun is also the breechblock. The pistol is loaded. When we fire it, the bullet—not the breechblock—moves first because the bullet weighs less than the breechblock. More energy is required to start and move a heavy body than a light one. Pressure in a gun starts from zero and builds up to maximum. The bullet starts long before maximum pressure is reached. Now the slide just cannot resist the maximum pressure, so it finally starts backward. Then it is blown to the rear by the pressure in the chamber—more especially by the residual pressure which remains in the chamber just after the bullet has left the muzzle. We should observe that the breechblock does not open materially until the pressure has dropped. Of course, if we put a very heavy block behind the .22, it would not move at all. On the other hand, if we used the blowback system in a .30-06, our breechblock would have to weigh 27 pounds.

The breechblock used in the larger-calibered Winchester .351 or .401 rifle is connected to a heavy steel bar in the fore-end. The special cartridge cases used are comparatively tough, thick, and stubby. They do not tend to stick in the chamber as do the .30-06 or .22 cases. Consequently, because the mere inertia of a blowback type of breechblock does not prevent a slight movement while the chamber pressure is high, the average .22 cartridge case should be lubricated; otherwise it might stick in the chamber. You will note in the instruction manual issued by the factory with each .22 automatic that lubricated cartridges are prescribed.

We are considering as the climax to our study mechanisms for ultra-high-powered ammunition, such as the .30-06. Lubrication is undesirable for such ammunition, and the breechblock would have to be absurdly heavy. Therefore we shall pass on to the "retarded blowback" class.

Retarded blowback mechanisms are quite ingenious. The term "retarded" is somewhat misleading because the pure blowback is retarded by inertia, whereas this so-called "retarded" type is retarded by mechanical means. In either case the bolt or breech-block must not open until the bullet has left the muzzle and the pressure has dropped to the safe limit.

Representative weapons in this class are the "Tommy gun," the Austrian Schwarzlose machine gun, the Pedersen semi-automatic rifle, and the Thompson semi-automatic rifle. The Thompson submachine gun, using the .45 A.C.P. cartridge, has a special sliding wedge which tends during high pressure to retard the rearward movement of the breechblock resulting from the pressure or blow against it. The .45 Colt pistol cases can stand plenty of abuse, having thick brass walls and short bodies which are under relatively low pressure; and this "Tommy" mechanism is regarded as being very close to a pure blowback.

The Schwarzlose and Pedersen employ a particularly ingenious system. To get a better idea of the principle, stand on one foot with your leg bent slightly at the knee. Relax your muscles and let the leg bend. The more the leg is bent, the more effective the weight of your body is against it. You need more muscle to hold up your body with a bent leg than with a straight one. Suppose—in theory—that you sit down, put your feet against a solid bar, and put your back against the sliding "blowback" breech-block of a big gun. Your legs are bent just a little. The breech-block under pressure will push so hard against your back that your legs must bend at the knee, and the more they bend, the easier it will be for the breechblock to push you back. Thus at the beginning your legs would have a mechanical advantage, but at the end it would be the breechblock that would have the advantage.

In the Schwarzlose machine gun there is a breechblock, a connecting rod, and the equivalent of a crank shaft. In the locked position, the connecting rod and crank shaft are just barely off dead-center. The connecting rod and crank shaft are like your slightly bent legs in the situation described. When the gun is fired, the breechblock is forced back by the pressure against it; but during the interval of high pressure, the "blowback" is at a mechanical disadvantage. As the pressure drops, it gains a corresponding advantage, so that it can push the breechblock to the rear and thus operate the gun.

The Pedersen rifle works in very much the same way. The breechblock assembly bends up in the middle like a toggle joint, there being two carefully shaped surfaces which roll upon each other when the breechblock opens. But unfortunately the breechblocks of both these guns move too soon. The cartridge cases must be lubricated to prevent malfunction.

As we have already seen, the forward portion of the cartridge case is pressed tightly against the chamber during the interval of high pressure, and serves as a gas seal. During that interval of high pressure, the base of the case must be supported firmly by the breechblock, otherwise the shell will rupture; for the thin forward portion of the case wants to stay put, while the rear end does not, it being made of thicker brass. To avoid ruptured cartridge cases in the Schwarzlose and Pedersen, the cartridge must be lubricated. Then the forward portion will not stick but will slide back easily, and the empty case can be extracted without sticking or rupturing. This difficulty does not arise with low-pressure cartridges such as the .401, .351, .45 A.C.P., and others.

Residual pressure is partially the source of retracting power; that is, it pushes the breechblock to the rear in these guns.

The Thompson semi-automatic rifle had exactly the same characteristic as the Schwarzlose and Pedersen. Using high-powered cartridges, the Thompson rifle required oiled cases. This rifle used a rotary bolt with inclined lugs. The sloping lugs allow the bolt to act just like a screw. When the pressure pushes upon the bolt face, the lugs give way and the bolt rotates to the unlocked position, whereupon residual pressure pushes the bolt rearward. This is called the "Blish" principle.

The Schwarzlose machine gun was used chiefly in the Austrian army. It is extremely heavy and requires a pump to squirt oil into the chamber. The Pedersen and Thompson rifles were tested by the United States Army and finally rejected. Lubricated ammunition is not good for service use.

Recoiling-barrel actuation is popular, and weapons made on this principle are in common use. Two inventors—Maxim and Browning—are responsible for most of them. After Hiram S. Maxim had patented his peculiar lever-action gun with the special butt plate, he delved further into the idea of harnessing the kick. He mounted a barrel and breechblock in a frame and so arranged the parts that when the gun fired, the barrel and breechblock could kick back or recoil within the frame. After the breechblock and barrel had recoiled a short distance, the bullet left the barrel. Also, Maxim arranged his action so that after the pressure had dropped, the breechblock was unlocked from the barrel by the recoiling force. Due to the momentum gained from the kick-back, the breechblock left the barrel and pulled out the empty case. Thus the breechblock was retracted. The barrel was pushed forward and held in position until eventually the counterrecoil spring sent the breechblock home again, thereby pushing in a new cartridge and locking the breechblock with the barrel in the forward firing position. The Maxim is somewhat complicated in its parts, a fault common to nearly all heavy machine guns.

After unlocking from the barrel, the breechblock is retracted chiefly by the momentum of its own recoil as well as by an acceleration derived mechanically from the barrel momentum after separation. Hiram Maxim's patents were issued in 1885.

During the nineties Paul Mauser, inventor of the famous Mauser bolt-action rifle, patented the Mauser automatic pistol. This weapon was widely used for many years. The barrel recoils in the frame for a short distance while locked to the breechblock. The time taken to move this distance is sufficient to allow the bullet to leave the barrel and for the pressure to drop to within residual limits. Then the breechblock is unlocked from the barrel and the residual pressure thrusts the block back, the empty shell being thereby extracted. The unlocking is effected by a simple cam, and the force of initial recoil furnishes the unlocking power. Momentum derived from the initial recoil contributes in some measure to the retraction of the breechblock, residual pressure being a retracting force as well.

It may be asked why Mauser did not employ some of the momentum of the barrel, as Maxim did, to help push the breechblock. The answer is that Mauser had power enough already. You can easily use residual pressure for retraction in pistols; whereas in high-powered weapons residual pressure is more difficult to use because of the tendency of the cases to stick in the chamber, and also because of the problem of timing. If we wait until the chamber pressure has dropped too low, we must use recoil momentum, as did Hiram Maxim.

George Luger arranged his pistol in the same way. The barrel recoils with the toggle-jointed breechblock. About the time the bullet has left the muzzle, the toggle pin in the breechblock strikes a sloping surface on the frame. This causes the breechblock to bend up in the middle. Thus the breechblock is unlocked by recoil and retracted by residual pressure.

Back in the nineties John M. Browning took out some patents on a pistol which ultimately became the well-known .45 Colt automatic service pistol, model of 1911. Like all the other arms already discussed in this chapter, the Colt automatic has a recoiling barrel. The barrel and the slide—or breechblock—are locked together during the initial recoil of ⅛-inch. The barrel has a pair of lugs above the chamber which engage in slots in the slide. The slide is really the breechblock. There is a device underneath the barrel, called the "link," which is attached at one end to the barrel and at the other end to the frame. The gun is fired and the barrel, locked to the slide, recoils with it. As the barrel moves backward, the link causes it to be pulled slightly downward at its rear end. Thus the lugs at the top of the barrel are disengaged from the slots in the slide, and the barrel stops while the slide continues to the rear, driven by residual pressure as well as by momentum. The counter-recoil spring is compressed by this movement and pushes the slide forward again, shoving another cartridge into the chamber. The action of this pistol is the most reliable of that of any automatic pistol in the world. But pistol ammunition is comparatively easy to handle in an automatic mechanism, as we have seen, and this Colt mechanism would hardly be suitable for high-powered rifle cartridges.

Now let us consider the famous Browning machine gun, caliber .30, model of 1917, known as the "heavy Browning." It was manufactured by Colt, water cooled, belt fed, and issued to our armed forces.

The Browning, like the Maxim, has a slidable barrel which recoils about ½-inch with the breechblock, during which interval the chamber pressure drops. The barrel has an extension, and the breechblock is locked to this extension by the breech lock. A cam on the bottom of the gun causes the breech lock to be disengaged from the barrel extension after about ½-inch of travel. There is a small lever called the accelerator, which, being a swinging lever in contact with both barrel and breechblock, is caused to accelerate the retraction of the breechblock when one end of this lever is acted upon by the recoiling barrel. In effect, the accelerator slows down the barrel to prevent it from striking too hard against the receiver or frame, and at the same time speeds up the breechblock.

Residual pressure is not generally operative in this mechanism. The barrel, being relatively free to recoil, must be slowed down somehow after the breechblock has been unlocked. With pistols this is not necessary as they do not develop so much recoil energy.

Because all the above actions involve the movement or recoil of the barrel in the frame or receiver for a short distance (not exceeding ¾-inch), these mechanisms are said to be of the "short-recoil" type. Practically all automatic pistols of the higher powered calibers are of the short-recoil type.

Recoil-operated automatics derive their power from the familiar kick. We have already seen how the short-recoil types work. After the barrel has recoiled a fraction of an inch, the bullet passes from the muzzle. But the barrel and breechblock can keep on moving for some distance unless something stops them. In fact, they could recoil past the magazine.

Suppose these two parts recoil about 4 inches before unlocking, and that there is arranged a device in the rear of the receiver frame to disengage the breechblock from the barrel. Having provided a barrel-return spring, the barrel alone can then move forward into firing position. A latch-like arrangement holds the breechblock so that the barrel can return without it; thus the empty shell is pulled out. The counter-recoil spring can then push the breechblock forward. This movement permits the loading of a fresh cartridge into the chamber.

Due to the force of barrel recoil it is necessary to use a very heavy barrel-return spring, and a friction-ring or brake, as well. Otherwise the barrel will pound the whole mechanism severely. By the time the barrel has recoiled several inches, all pressure in the chamber has vanished. The chief disadvantage is the length of barrel recoil. For a military rifle this is undesirable. Mounting the barrel is extremely difficult; it may be necessary to put a tube around it, and this retains too much heat. Moreover, the arrangement of the unlocking gadgets, the retaining gadgets, and other parts, together with further complications, leads to the conclusion that the long-recoil mechanism is far from ideal for portable weapons, and better suited for heavier automatic or self-ejecting cannon.

The Browning autoloading shotgun and the Chauchat machine gun operate on the long-recoil system. The Remington autoloading shotgun is based upon a Browning patent. So is the Remington Model 81 rifle, made in several medium-power calibers. Observe the tube surrounding the barrel on the Remington rifle.

Gas actuation is next on the list. John Browning invented the first gas-actuated machine gun in 1889, four years after Hiram Maxim had developed his short-recoil gun. Briefly, Browning bored a small hole in the barrel about a foot from the muzzle. He fitted this hole with a piston on the end of a swinging lever. When the gun was fired, the bullet passed this hole, and the gas, under high pressure, struck the piston and knocked it downward with great force. The piston caused the lever to which it was attached to swing downward and to the rear, operating a connecting rod which unlocked and retracted the breechblock.

Shortly after Browning's invention, the Austrian Baron Von Odkolek produced a machine gun having a tube, or cylinder, and piston parallel to and underneath the barrel. As in Browning's gun, the gas was allowed to act upon the piston through a hole in the barrel. The piston moved straight to the rear and unlocked and retracted the breechblock by means of a connecting rod. Later on this mechanism was developed into the well-known Hotchkiss machine gun.

The Hotchkiss or Odkolek weapon is quite representative of the general scheme used to harness the powder gases in a gun by means of a gas piston. The reader may be familiar with the Browning machine rifle, caliber .30, model of 1918, otherwise known as the "Browning Auto Rifle" or "B.A.R." This weapon operates by means of gas taken from the barrel into a cylinder, where the gas acts upon a piston, which through a connecting rod unlocks and retracts the breechblock.

The Lewis machine gun, used by the British during the first World War, is gas operated, air cooled, and drum fed. This weapon has been used quite extensively on aircraft. Recently the British adopted the Bren light machine gun, also gas operated, which weighs about 21 pounds (7 pounds less than the Lewis).

As a result of many years of thorough study, research, and tests of various semi-automatic military shoulder rifles to replace the Springfield, the United States Ordnance Department developed the gas-actuated Garand. This rifle, the invention of Mr. John C. Garand, is without question the simplest, neatest, and lightest gas-actuated rifle ever developed. Basically this weapon in its action is not unlike the Lewis gun.

The old standard gas-actuated sporting rifle was sold to the public in limited numbers some years before the first World War. The Winchester company is at present developing a gas-operated arm.

Generally speaking, there are two methods of using gas to operate a gun. When the gas is allowed to hit the piston and literally knock it back, we speak of an "impinging-gas arm." Where gas is admitted to a cylinder and allowed to expand against the piston, we speak of it as an "expanding-gas arm."

An unduly complicated mechanism is required to allow powder gas to expand within a cylinder. Some gas must be admitted through a hole in the barrel, and then the hole closed quickly. But expanding gas gives an extremely smooth action. On the other hand, impinging gas is not so complicated to harness up. That is the system used on the B.A.R. and on the Garand. But impinging gas gives a rougher, harsher action. A gas cylinder is needed in either case, but the expanding-gas type in a rifle is likely to be more delicate, and it must not leak.

One difficulty with gas actuation is the likelihood of powder fouling in the cylinder and on the piston. On the Browning machine rifle there is a device with various-sized holes in it so that when the gas port, or hole in the barrel, gets plugged, the hole can be enlarged.

The following authoritative comment is quoted from an article by Brigadier General Julian S. Hatcher, Ordnance Department, United States Army, published in *The American Rifleman,* March, 1933.

A great many years ago the Army recognized the desirability of the semiautomatic rifle, but for many years little success attended the efforts to design such a weapon. Numerous gas-operated guns were tried. These had the disadvantage of having the piston and gas cylinder under the barrel or at the side of it, which added weight and bulk. Then another trouble with these guns was that gas was tapped off the barrel at such tremendous pressure that it was hard to handle it without introducing severe strains on the gun. When the bullet passes the gas port in the barrel, the pressure at that point will be anywhere from 40,000 to 10,000 or 12,000 pounds per square inch, depending upon where the port is located. The closer to the breech it is, naturally, the higher will be the pressure. Assuming that the port is at the point where the pressure is 25,000 pounds to the square inch, a sudden application of this enormous pressure on the head of the piston slams the breechblock open with extreme violence, and the result is not only undesirably quick opening, tearing the heads off the empty cartridge cases, and such troubles as these, but also excessive breakages of parts.

The logical thing to do was to move the gas port as far forward as possible, where the pressure would not be so great, and reduce the area of the port so that the gas was throttled down to a lower pressure before striking the piston. By doing these things a number of very successful gas-operated guns have been made; but there is another disadvantage to the gas-operated system, and that is the hole bored in the barrel to form the gas port. It is difficult to clean this hole, so that it is always a point where rust and corrosion are likely to start.

Gas operation has been more successfully applied to machine guns than to shoulder rifles. In machine guns the moving parts can be made heavy enough so that the very sudden blow of the gas is partly absorbed by the inertia of the piston. Moreover, the pressure of the gas on the piston endures only about one one-thousandth of a second, and if these parts are made heavy they will absorb sufficient energy from this blow to continue their rearward motion against the action of the return spring and complete the opening action even after the gas pressure is gone.

With the shoulder rifle, conditions are very much more difficult. The piston and other moving parts cannot be made heavy or the gun will weigh too much; and light parts do not have enough inertia to carry through the rearward motion after the gas pressure is gone unless the impact of the gas is made extremely violent. The result has been that in most gas-operated shoulder rifles the light piston gets up energy enough to open the breech against the spring action by being slammed to the rear with very high speed, and this violent action is conducive to very high breakages.

Some of the objections raised by Brigadier General Hatcher may also be applied to recoil-operated rifles and to light automatics, for while these eliminate the gas port, piston, and cylinder, they, too, have light-weight parts which must start off at high speed unless some medium besides recoil is added and applied.

For rifles, the chief disadvantage of recoil-action is a lack of suitable mounting for the bayonet. Such a mechanism does not lend itself to the inclusion of wooden handguards around the barrel.

The technical authorities of the leading nations are generally open-minded on the gas versus recoil argument, which is really of little consequence because it all is dependent upon the particular weapon under consideration. For example, the British and the United States use both gas and recoil weapons. The United States has recoil-operated Browning pistols and machine guns, gas-operated Garands, and Browning automatic rifles. The British have gas-operated Brens and Lewises, recoil-operated Vickers, and Browning aircraft guns. The French used gas-operated automatics almost exclusively, while the Germans use chiefly recoil-operated arms, such as the Solothurn light machine gun.

A further and more detailed technical discussion of automatic mechanisms will be found in Chapter Eighteen, "A Design Critique of Automatic Mechanisms."

CHAPTER SIX

Factors Affecting Design

LET us analyze the restrictions and discuss various requirements which must be met and considered in the process of
developing automatic weapons. By way of introduction the following anecdote is appropriate.

Recently we had the pleasure of conferring with a well-known
colonel of the Infantry. We were discussing machine guns and
semi-automatic rifles. He warned of the disadvantages which arise
from too much complication in our weapons, and by way of illustration told about a certain French machine-gun school held for
our officers during 1918, in which a French instructor addressed
the school as follows: "Messieurs, it is wiz ze most great pleasure
I inform you zat we have exceedingly simplify and improve ze
light machine gun by ze mere addition of a numbair of parts!"

Machine guns and semi-automatic rifles have many features in
common. We should keep the fact of their basic similarity in
mind. In truth, their only mechanical differences are these: one
is generally fired from a tripod or mount, "full automatic," having belt or drum feed, and air or water cooling; the other is fired
from the shoulder, "semi-automatic," having magazine feed and
no artificial cooling. Because of their tactical employment, machine guns can weigh from 20 to 50 pounds; because they must
be carried by individuals and fired from the shoulder, rifles must
weigh under 11 pounds. Generally speaking, a semi-automatic
rifle can rarely be designed from a machine gun, whereas a machine gun can invariably be designed from a semi-automatic.

Machine gun units in the service are obliged to put up with
cumbersome weapons because inventors have not been able to
produce lighter mechanisms. There is an increasing demand for
light-weight machine guns. If we have a semi-automatic rifle, we
can undoubtedly use that mechanism as the basis for the design

of a light machine gun. Military experts are constantly seeking
to increase mobility, and weight naturally decreases mobility. At
the same time, these experts seek to increase fire power. Thus
there is presented the problem of reconciling mobility with fire
power, which to date has been difficult due to the weight of machine guns and the lack of automatic shoulder rifles.

For the benefit of readers interested in military problems, it
should be pointed out that the service desires to standardize
weapons so far as possible. Thus, if an army is equipped with a
semi-automatic rifle having the same basic mechanism as that of
the machine gun, the problem of training the enlisted personnel
to operate their automatic weapons would be greatly simplified.

Ammunition must be considered in connection with the design
of automatic weapons. The reader will recall discussion elsewhere relative to the characteristics of high- and low-powered cartridges in the various mechanisms.

For some years following the first World War the Ordnance
Department of the United States Army considered using the .276
cartridge, mainly because it was better adapted to the available
semi-automatic rifle mechanism, and also because it was smaller,
weighed less, and could be carried in greater quantities by the
infantry. The Pedersen and Thompson rifles, for example, were
built in this caliber, as well as the first gas-actuated Garand. However, the necessity for interchangeability of ammunition led to the
retention of the .30-06 cartridge for which machine guns are calibered.

It is clear that any mechanism which will function with .30M1
ammunition ought to function with any less powerful loads, such
as the new M2. As a matter of fact, however, the .30M1 cartridge
is about the hardest type of ammunition for adaptation in automatic arms. For example, the pressure is about 46,000-50,000
pounds per square inch. The head space must be carefully adjusted. Due to the pressure, every precaution must be taken to
prevent blown-out primers, and variations in the annealing of
the brass cases may have some effect upon the action of the
weapon. In general, any difficulties encountered in the Springfield with this ammunition are likely to be accentuated in an automatic, especially during periods of hasty wartime manufacture.

A designer may be tempted to introduce some form of special automatic cartridge, but his efforts, particularly at the present time, should be met with extreme hostility. Great quantities of standard ammunition are on hand; both government and commercial plants are tooled up for existing specifications. In short, the present-day gun must fit the ammunition, not the ammunition the gun.

Manufacturing requirements are of paramount importance in this connection. Many inventors ignore this problem in designing their weapons. Any inventor's scheme which would be difficult to produce in an average arms plant today ought to be discarded without further experimentation.

We must ask ourselves the following questions:

1. How many parts are required?

2. How many of the parts are more complicated to manufacture than those of a normal rifle?

3. Can we use a normal type rifle barrel as generally manufactured, with minor changes, or must we have a radically different design?

4. Do we require any costly metals of which there is a limited supply, or can we use the conventional steel alloys for all our parts?

5. Are there likely to be any manufacturing operations far beyond the present comprehension of the average skilled machinist or gunmaker?

6. How will the manufacturing operations and tools necessary for the automatic compare with those required in the production of conventional bolt-action military or sporting rifles?

7. Must the fittings and tolerances be much closer than those of a conventional rifle?

8. How much will it cost to tool up for this weapon?

9. How much will the complete weapon cost to produce, compared with a Springfield or similar rifle?

These questions are inevitably asked, often ignored, and rarely answered.

Component parts of the semi-automatic rifle must be carefully considered. Some of them we have already referred to, more particularly the breechblock, or bolt.

The barrel, so far as possible, should be conventional. If possible, it should be readily dismountable so that the chamber and tube can be cleaned, and also that the barrel itself, when worn or overheated, may be replaced in the field. The barrel of a semi-automatic rifle or machine gun should be exposed to the air as far as possible so as to facilitate the radiation of heat and consequent cooling of the barrel.

The extractor is one of the most important parts of any rifle, more especially of an automatic. It must be rugged, for it is invariably subjected to harsh treatment in that it is forced to yank at the sticky case when the brass is pressed against the walls of the chamber. On the Springfield we find an extracting cam which aids in loosening the tapered case, but on many automatics it is impossible to make such provision. However, it is for a more fundamental reason that the extractor is subjected to great strain on any automatic. Sufficient power must be provided to carry the breechblock some four to five inches against a heavy spring, at the end of which movement the breechblock must not have been retarded so much that sufficient ejection power is lacking. Thus the breechblock must start off at high speed, and in consequence the extractor is subject to a severe yank. If this sudden movement does not break the extractor, it is likely to rip off the brass rim which is barely $\frac{1}{32}$ of an inch in depth. Moreover, simple means for dismounting and replacing a broken part should be made available. One should never presume to have designed an unbreakable extractor for an automatic weapon. And if possible, the extractor should be removable without dismounting the breechblock.

The ejector, too, should be readily dismountable. It may be installed in the frame or in the receiver. On some rifles it is mounted in the head of the breechblock.

The firing mechanism should be as simple as possible, but the semi-automatic rifle is, in this respect, more complicated than the machine gun, in that the sear must slip with each movement of the trigger, thus necessitating a distinct release and squeeze of the trigger for each discharge. In general, it is preferable to use a hammer mechanism, having a separate firing pin, rather than designs of a type similar to the Springfield "striker." The fact that a hammer is used on the Colt .22, the Colt .45, the Remington autoloading rifle and shotgun, the Browning autoloading shotgun, the Winchester self-loading rifle, the Garand rifle, and many others, is ample evidence that this method is more desirable. The most popular semi-automatic sear is that found in an early patent of John Browning, and incorporated in both Remington autoloaders as well as in the Browning shotgun and the Garand rifle.

Safety features should be considered in designing the firing mechanism. Under no circumstances should it be possible to discharge the automatic until the breech is fully locked. This feature is essential in any rifle. For example, when the bolt of the Springfield is partially locked, the release of the striker causes the energy of the striker spring to be expended in closing the bolt. Moreover, until the bolt is closed, the striker cannot hit the primer. An examination of the cocking cam will disclose the reason. But such a feature is more important in an automatic because the operator does not close the bolt by hand. If, for a number of reasons, the breechblock of the automatic failed to lock, the operator would not be aware of that fact and might discharge the weapon with disastrous consequences. This feature cannot be emphasized too strongly. It should be incorporated as an integral part of the design.

Mainsprings are a source of some difficulty in automatic shoulder weapons. Like all other parts, the spring should be utterly simple. The ordinary coil spring, mounted in a tube and located in the stock, has much to recommend it. Several patents disclose novel devices, and the Lewis machine gun illustrates a unique method of storing up energy in a spring-actuated cogwheel. Such weapons as the Bren machine rifle, the Browning shotgun, and the Remington autoloaders, use a simple coil spring in the stock, which is connected with the breechblock by means of a strut. The location of the mainspring under the barrel has an advantage in that it permits a straight pull, all movements being parallel. However, a connecting rod is generally needed for such springs, which must extend from the breechblock to the further end of the spring. On the other hand, the stock-mounted spring tends to thrust the breechblock against the top of the receiver. The strut must move in an arc, and there is a slight tendency with such an arrangement to cause the parts to bind. Nevertheless, the spring and strut are not exposed, and the average rifle stock provides ample room for the housing. But for the necessity of having a curved stock, it would be highly preferable to mount the spring directly in line behind the breechblock. This is done in the Solothurn light machine gun used by Germany.

Receivers on some rifles are extremely long, and it is felt that long receivers may give poor balance. The use of a rotary bolt in an automatic rifle of .30-06 caliber raises some difficulty in the design of a compact receiver. Breechblocks such as that of the Pedersen rifle are ideal in this respect. But the rotary bolt certainly has its advantages in an automatic. Suppose, for the sake of argument, we used a modified Springfield bolt. The bolt must be long enough to cover the magazine plus the lugs and bolt head. That makes the bolt about four or five inches long. The operator cannot duck his head when he pulls the trigger, so the bolt must be enclosed. Thus the receiver must be nine or ten inches long. We might contrive to locate the lugs somewhere within the limits of the magazine and thus reduce the bolt to the length of the cartridge used in the magazine. This has been done on the Garand, which has excellent balance and an unusually short compact receiver.

In the last analysis there are two reasons for shortening receivers: one, to get all the weight in the breech centered in a short space so as to improve the balance and handling qualities of the weapon; the other, to cut down total weight. However, when we examine the Springfield and measure the distance from the front end of the receiver to the rear end of the bolt in its cocked position, we find that by adding about two more inches we can accommodate an automatic rotary bolt without any appreciable difficulty. The resulting receiver would have an ejection port a sufficient distance from the tang, so that a left-handed shooter would not be discomforted when the shells were ejected.

Rifles should be designed if possible to be readily operated without modification on either the right or the left shoulder. Many men are left-handed, or perhaps their left eye is their master eye. The gun should be fitted to the man, not the man to the gun. With the exception that the receiver should be not so long that the operator must obtain a railroad ticket to get from the tang to the chamber, the agitation over long receivers is of minor importance.

The magazine need not be necessarily different from the conventional types in common use. Some prefer the clip-loaded type, using the standard Mauser or Springfield clip. Others prefer the detachable-box type, similar to that of the Colt pistol, self-loading Winchester, or Browning machine rifle, or the eight-shot, en bloc clip of the M1 Garand. If possible, the magazine should permit the mounting of a telescope close to the receiver.

The second point relates to the number of rounds in the magazine, and, incidentally, to the questions of cooling and of ammunition supply. The semi-automatic rifle is designed to permit the hunter, whether he be in pursuit of animals or men, to discharge a rapid succession of *aimed* shots. The rifleman so armed is not a walking machine gun. The hunter wants to get in a second and third shot because too often his quarry does not drop or is not, at least, vitally wounded with the first. Any honest deer hunter will admit that a second and often a third shot is needed to put the animal down. The automatic is merely a logical improvement over the repeater or double gun. The soldier attacked by two or three men from an enemy squad can be most efficient with a semi-automatic. But from five to eight or ten shots in rapid succession are enough. The semi-automatic is not primarily a bullet squirter. Machine guns are used for barrages and the sweeping of sectors. The rifleman must not burn up his ammunition. The interval necessary to re-fill an empty magazine allows a cooling period for the barrel. In fact, it cools off the rifleman as well. Pumping out bullets is a great temptation when under stress. Consequently, the magazine need not hold more than ten rounds. Unless these points are kept in mind, each semi-automatic rifleman must be given a water-cooled barrel—and a large *safari* to transport his ammunition.

Sights for automatic weapons are generally designed on conventional lines. With the increasing use of aperture or peep sights located near the eye, the average automatic and semi-automatic weapon gains added popularity due to the design of the receiver which permits much better mounting of such sights than was practicable on the average repeating rifle. Telescope sights are also well adapted to those automatics which do not load or eject from the top of the receiver.

The peep sight is regarded as superior for most purposes to the open sight, except in dim light or after dark. The Germans use open sights on the Solothurn light machine guns.

Sights are usually located in conventional positions on many weapons. However, on those light machine guns which have top-side magazines, the sights are offset to the left; while on straight-stock weapons, such as the German Solothurn and the Johnson light machine gun, the sights are set several inches above the bore.[1]

"Fore-sights," as the British call the "front sight," are usually of the post or barleycorn type, often with protection ears similar to the Enfield M1917 rifle sight. Such are found on the Bren, Garand, and the Johnson rifles. A detailed discussion of rear sight features is beyond the scope of this book.

By some designers it is believed undesirable to cover a semi-automatic rifle barrel with wood, due to the increased heating of the chamber which in turn gives rise to greater extremes in pressure. For example, a cold rifle gives pressures of 48,000 pounds per square inch. Suppose we fire thirty shots rapidly. If the barrel is wood-covered, the pressure developed in the thirty-first round will be substantially higher; consequently, the dispersion will be much greater, due to this variation in pressure.

Moreover, fewer rounds are required to heat the wood-covered barrel sufficiently to cause pre-ignition. In this connection it should be observed that "cooked rounds" give rise to extraction difficulties.

One of the reasons for cocking machine guns and machine rifles (i.e., B.A.R. M1918) with the breech open is to avoid leaving a round of ammunition in a hot chamber. To obtain accuracy, a rifle must be cocked with the breech closed. It is, therefore, believed by some designers undesirable to aggravate this condition by preventing the radiation of heat from the barrel.

1 See page 71, description of Johnson Light Machine Gun.

As an example of the benefits to be gained from the exposure of the barrel of an automatic weapon to air, the following comparisons are submitted, based upon tests and demonstrations at Fort Benning, Georgia.

FIRING TEST AT 100 ROUNDS PER MINUTE

WEAPON: Browning Automatic Rifle.

With standard wooden forearm the wood was smoking in 60 rounds (40 seconds); the target was obscured completely in 100 rounds, forearm was in flames in about 400 rounds (4 minutes, 10 seconds); gun was out of action, mainspring had lost its tension and gun would not fire in 700 rounds (7 minutes).

With cut-down forearm the Browning fired 1,750 rounds in 17 minutes 30 seconds before becoming unserviceable. (See *Infantry Journal,* March-April, 1939, page 180.)

FIRING TEST AT 30-40 ROUNDS PER MINUTE

WEAPON: Gas-operated semi-automatic rifle with wooden handguards.

The wooden handguards and forearm began to char after 328 rounds fired in about seven minutes (46 rounds per minute). In another test a similar rifle fired 30 shots per minute for about nine minutes (270 rounds) when the vision was obscured by smoke. In ten minutes the rifle was out of action, having failed to extract the 298th-300th rounds, inclusive, requiring the use of a cleaning rod to clear the chamber.

WEAPON: Recoil-operated semi-automatic rifle, with air-cooled barrel, cal. .30-06.

1. 247 rounds at 30 shots per minute with no stoppages, using F.A. Lot 1889 (excessively soft brass cases, failed to eject 247th round. Rifle continued to fire up to 500 rounds at 30 rounds per minute, with 23 stoppages due to the soft brass-cased ammunition.

2. The barrel was then cleaned and the rifle fired continuously at a rate of 25 up to 50 shots per minute for 2,000 rounds, when the rate of fire was increased to 60 and finally 80 rounds per minute for 400 more rounds. The rifle was not put out of action; there was no charring or smoking of the forearm. Out of the first 895 rounds there was one failure to feed. The mechanism was not lubricated or cleaned for the entire 2,900 rounds. At the end of this firing the barrel showed

wear in the breech, but was not so worn as to impair the functioning of the rifle. From these and other tests it appears that the exposure of the barrel to air doubles its life, and materially increases the capacity of the weapon.

However, other designers believe that the rifle will not fire enough to raise excessive temperatures, and they prefer hand-guards for protection of the hands, for bayonet work, and for drill. The final answer depends upon each user's requirements.

THE BAYONET

The soldier's rifle should have a bayonet, or pike, or some other effective type of pointed instrument attached to the muzzle of the piece.

The most modern and efficient bayonet is the new British type, which consists of an 8-inch triangular, pointed blade locked to lugs on the muzzle of the S.M.L.E. This bayonet is designed to reduce weight and to insure easy withdrawal after the thrust.

It is interesting to note the similarity of this bayonet to our Civil War type. Eight inches of blade can inflict death quite as effectively as sixteen.

Bayonet tests with a short-recoil barrel indicate that the thrust is facilitated by the punch of this barrel against the recoil stop, in the manner of a can opener.

With regard to the necessity for wooden handguards, it is be-lieved that such protection is essential for the short jab.

The British bayonet might be provided with a handle of the handguard type, if necessary. However, with a short 8-inch bayo-net on a 44- to 48-inch rifle, the soldier can readily execute the short jab. The British intimate that a short bayonet facilitates the parry, permitting the soldier to step inside the enemy's guard.

The bayonet controversy wages hot and furious. There are many divergent views backed up by undoubted authorities. The authors understand that the Russians favor bayonet fighting in attacks against the Nazis. Rumor has it that the Germans run from cold steel. This may be because they do not like to be cut up, but as long as they can obtain ammunition the German army seems determined to outweigh bayonets with fire power. So far their score is noteworthy. Burgoyne complained that American farmers would not face the bayonet and shot his men from behind cover. The farmers did not have bayonets so Burgoyne's men fared badly under Morgan's rifles at Saratoga. Modern examples are too plentiful to require reference here. The authors can only remark: Do not launch mass bayonet attacks against the well-directed fire of modern automatic weapons. Bullets travel faster than bayonets. But if the gun jams or ammunition gets too low, a blade is indispensable.

"Armament conditions organization, and a tactical system is implicit in the organization adopted." So states Major General George A. Lynch, Chief of Infantry.[2] Major General Lynch further points out that tactics should be adopted to exploit improved weapons, such as the semi-automatic rifle.

If we conceive of the semi-automatic rifle as a rifle, we instinctively fail to exploit its superior capacity. For example, in the above-mentioned firing of the air-cooled rifle which fired 25-80 shots per minute for over an hour, this weapon was actually performing as a machine rifle, or, to a lesser extent, as a substitute light machine gun. Two of these rifles, firing at 50 shots per minute, would equal the intensity of fire per minute of the Browning machine rifle, and could fire for as long a period or longer.

Not that this would be a normal procedure, yet half a loaf is better than none. Moreover, these weapons are designed for combat, and actual combat procedure is rarely normal.

Thus in the last analysis our objective is to give each soldier the maximum power or force consistent with the mobility of shank's mare. Our tactical concepts should be broadened to exploit the maximum potential power of the weapon in question.

Those who are alarmed about the problem of ammunition supply are urged to ponder over the fact that the Americans ran out of ammunition at Bunker Hill. Soldiers have run out of arrows, powder and ball, food and water since the beginning of mortal combat and will continue to do so until the end of time.

[2] *Infantry Journal,* 1939-40.

Component parts of machine guns are generally similar to those of the semi-automatic rifle, except for the mount, the firing mechanism, and the feed.

The most common type of mount found on heavy guns is the tripod, having traversing and elevating wheels which permit adjustment in "mils" or minutes of angle. The "mil" system has found great favor in artillery circles for computing the deflection. There are 6400 mils in a circle. One mil subtends one yard at one thousand yards. Operated from such a mount the machine gun can provide indirect fire, and with the M1 ammunition our guns could lay down effective barrages at ranges up to 3500-4000 yards.

The other type of common mount, used more frequently on the lighter weapons, is the bipod, which, combined with a special butt, permits the gun to be fixed. No provision is made for deflection, the gun being aimed like a rifle. The tripod mount on the heavy Browning and the bipod on the Lewis are familiar illustrations of these mounts.

Feeding of cartridges is a difficult problem in machine guns.[8] The Maxim and Browning use belts, the Hotchkiss a metal strip, the Lewis a drum, the B.A.R. a box magazine located underneath the gun, the Bren a box magazine located centrally on top of the gun, the Madsen a box magazine located on top of the gun at the left-hand side of the breech. These are the representative types of feed. In a word, the question narrows down to the belt versus the magazine when one considers light machine guns. For a number of reasons the drum and strip are not so desirable.

The belt permits a large number of rounds to be fed without reloading but complicates the operating mechanism considerably. The magazine, holding from 15 to 30 rounds, permits a simple operating mechanism; but of course it must be replaced after two or three short bursts. Magazines increase the weight of the gunner's load.

The use of a water-cooling device on a light machine gun is hardly practicable. To be light, the gun must have an air-cooled barrel. The use of a belt in such a weapon would undoubtedly

---

[8] See also Chapter 7, page 116, on feed systems.

cause over-heating. The short interval required to recharge or change magazines permits the barrel to cool appreciably.

Rate of fire is a matter of extreme importance in connection with our consideration of the objective, and it concerns all classes of automatic weapons for this reason.

For example, the Browning heavy machine gun, model of 1917, fires at a "cyclic rate" of from 300 to 500 rounds per minute. The Thompson submachine gun, commercial model, fires about 800 rounds per minute, Marine Corps model about 600 rounds per minute. Aviation models of the heavy Browning can fire as high as 1200 rounds per minute. The present demand for aviation guns is somewhat extreme, a cyclic rate of 2000 rounds per minute. It is respectfully submitted that no practical gun, using standard type .30 caliber ammunition, can be designed to fire at such a rate, 1500 per minute being practically the absolute maximum. When fired at a rate in excess of 1000-1200 rounds per minute the machine gun has very much the effect of a shotgun. Due to the great speed of modern airplanes, the gunner is on the target such a short time that he requires a very high rate of fire to obtain an adequate concentration of the burst on the enemy plane.

If a gun firing .30 caliber ammunition were operated at a rate of 1200 rounds per minute, the bullets would be roughly fifty yards apart along the trajectory. Without attempting any mathematical calculations, it is obvious that a gun firing at a rate in excess of 1000-1200 rounds per minute must unlock its breechblock during the interval of residual pressure. If the pressure is too high, the shells will not extract, for reasons stated previously in this book.

The amount of heat generated by full-automatic fire will necessitate more frequent cooling intervals on ground guns. This is another reason for preferring the magazine to the belt in adopting a system of feed for the light machine gun.

Due to vibration, heating, and economy of ammunition, the light machine gun generally fires at a cyclic rate not in excess of 450 rounds per minute, or about 7 to 8 rounds per second.

Accuracy is a virtue which the average repeating rifle now possesses.[4] Few riflemen are sufficiently expert to uncover inaccu-

[4] See also Chapter 17, page 265, on accuracy.

racies in a modern Springfield or a similar rifle. Our service ammunition is of the highest quality. Our barrels are superb. What about the automatic weapon? Will the semi-automatic rifle necessarily prove to be less accurate than the Springfield?

Probably not. Of course in a weapon which utilizes gas taken from a port in the barrel, a small amount of pressure may be taken from the propelling force with a consequent loss in velocity. The Garand rifle, however, furnishes good groups and normal velocities.

Fixed-barrel rifles, utilizing residual pressure for retraction, will not show any loss of accuracy or velocity. This is true also of weapons in the recoiling-barrel class. The velocity of .30 caliber ammunition in the heavy Browning is practically the same as that in the Springfield, and this machine gun is not inaccurate.

Rifles which have their sights on a housing within which the barrel slides, may vary as to sight settings. The sights might not be exactly parallel to the axis of the bore. It is believed preferable to have the front sight fixed to the barrel for this reason, and the Luger pistol may be said to be superior to the Colt .45 in this respect.

In the last analysis every rifle barrel is allowed to jump and vibrate. Provided the jump or movement is uniform, the amount, within reasonable limits, should not affect the accuracy.

It has been asked if a recoiling barrel reduces the velocity. Every barrel recoils more or less on the shooter's shoulder. The variation in recoil would be measurable merely by the difference in weight between a complete rifle and the recoiling parts of the automatic. In one test a recoil-operated semi-automatic rifle averaged higher velocities than a fixed-barrel weapon.

For the above reasons and as a result of exhaustive tests, it is concluded that where a standard type of ammunition is used in both weapons, the semi-automatic will prove quite as accurate as the conventional repeater. To compare a .30-06 Springfield with a .401 or .35 cartridge fired from one of the commercial automatics is manifestly unfair. The B.A.R., due to its moving breechblock, is not at all comparable in this connection. Target shooters may cling to a single-shot match rifle for fine shooting, slow fire, but the day is rapidly coming when military rifle ranges will echo to the roar of rapid-fire programs.

Kickless rifles, hairless faces, noiseless nights, and holeless socks have been the goal of mankind for many years. Some of the contrivances submitted to reduce the recoil of shoulder weapons should be exhibited in a zoo.

The question of combining reduced "kick" and a semi-automatic rifle has puzzled many serious inventors. One unfortunate individual demonstrated a weapon which multiplied the normal kick from fourteen to thirty odd foot-pounds. He later used his model to commit suicide, but the coroner could not determine which end of the gun was responsible for his demise.

In the preceding section of this book we discussed three basic methods of actuating an automatic. With respect to the question of reduced recoil it is submitted that the use of residual pressure in a retarded blowback tends to reduce the recoil slightly; that the recoil of gas-actuated weapons, such as the Garand, is much less than that of the corresponding Springfield; that some weapons having short-recoiling barrels tend to produce less recoil or kick than other types, and in one case up to 25 per cent less kick than the Springfield.

If we use some of the force which ordinarily produces the unpleasant kick to actuate the mechanism, we shall necessarily reduce the kick by the amount of force used for the automatic operations. In other words, we can reduce the kick by making it perform work. Thus we may utilize a force ever-present in all firearms which might otherwise be wasted.

We might be led to conclude that the recoiling-barrel system would necessarily reduce the kick. However, .30-06 barrels which are allowed to move too freely a fraction of an inch will develop an excessive pounding on the frame or receiver. Some means must be provided to slow down, or decelerate, the movement.

Malfunctions in automatic weapons are a source of great annoyance.[5] The percentage of jams experienced in machine guns and certain types of pistols gave such firearms an established reputation for unreliability. The ideal automatic mechanism should be incapable of jamming. We venture to predict, however, that no

---

[5] For complete discussion refer to Chapter 8, page 127, on malfunctions.

automatic made in large quantities will function absolutely 100 per cent perfect on the basis of 10,000 rounds. Pistols, such as the .45 Colt automatic, turn in fine performances. As stated in other connections, pistol ammunition is much easier to handle.

Consider the average Springfield. Not infrequently when one is firing a string "rapid," a shell sticks and the operator loses time in trying to unlock the bolt. Primers have been known to be defective. Cases have been known to rupture. Variations in the dimensions of the case, thickness of the head or cannelure, and other deformities in a cartridge are likely to cause difficulty in an automatic chambered for high-pressure loads.

Aviators during the first World War inspected their own ammunition and loaded their own belts. Factory inspection, especially in wartime, cannot be relied upon too much.

The chamber of the automatic must be inspected and cleaned. The most vulnerable part is the extractor. Other parts being well made, the extractor is more often the source of difficulty, for reasons dealt with in another connection.[6] Most malfunctions not directly attributable to defective ammunition may be said to originate at the moment of primary extraction. If the brass case can be loosened just a fraction of an inch, it will probably be ejected without any difficulty.

From a practical standpoint those few malfunctions which necessitate merely a yank on the operating handle to clear the empty cases and reload, are hardly serious. If the weapon is inclined to break down every few hundred rounds, the mechanism is not a very ideal substitute for a hand-operated weapon. Overheating will cause the shells to stick, and jams for this reason are more frequent in machine guns.

The reader is reminded that this subject is rather large, quite capable of filling many volumes. In setting forth the foregoing discussion it has been attempted to answer the sort of questions most generally asked about design features. Countless other questions can be raised, and perhaps the answers are not so easily forthcoming. After the publication of an article in a certain military magazine, the editor informed the writer that an inquiry had been made by a gentleman who enclosed six dollars and wanted

6 See page 301.

"five dollars' worth of patents," one dollar being for the editor and the writer "for their trouble." One writer was requested directly by several "patent lawyers" to tell them how to obtain a patent on certain automatics. Several "inventors" wanted a writer to help them finance and market their weapons.

CHAPTER SEVEN

Methods and Systems of Feed

*Single-Column Vertical Feed; Staggered-Column Verti-
cal Feed; Rotary Feed; Belt Feed; The Hopper System;
The Metallic Strip System; Drum Feed*

HEREIN it is intended to survey the various methods of conveying cartridges into the action of automatic (and repeating) weapons. The feed systems will be considered in relation to
the various types of weapons in which they are used.

TYPES OF MAGAZINES USED IN MILITARY RIFLES, SEMI-
AUTOMATIC AND AUTOMATIC RIFLES, AND PISTOLS

Single-column Vertical Feed

The most common feed system is the single-column vertical
feed. In weapons using this action the magazine is usually detachable and consists of a box containing a follower or cartridge plat-
form urged upwardly by a flat leaf or round wire spring. It is most
commonly used in pistols.

Examples are found in the Colt automatic pistol, in the Russian rifle, and in the Johnson light machine gun with its side-
mounted magazine. This type of magazine is easly removed but
it increases the weight of the ammunition when the magazines
are carried in quantity for instant re-loading.

Staggered-column Vertical Feed

This system is usually referred to as the Mauser, as it was probably originated by the famous inventor of the Mauser rifle with
its well-known 5-shot, clip-loaded magazine. The follower is so
shaped that the cartridges load alternately, one above the other,
on each side of the magazine well.

In such weapons as the Mauser, the Enfield M1917, and the Springfield M1903, rifles, this magazine is not detachable, although the floor plate can be removed quite readily.

In the Browning machine rifle, M1918, the Bren, Z.B., and other similar light machine guns, the magazine is of the detachable box type, mounted underneath the receiver on the Browning and on top of the receiver in the Bren and Z.B., as well as in the French Light Hotchkiss and others.

The Mauser-type feed is quite compact, is well adapted for clip loading, but requires the breech to be open for loading, and is subject to malfunctions resulting from the acute angles at which the cartridges must enter the chamber. Moreover, the cartridges occasionally jam together side by side in the magazine well.

The British S.M.L.E. rifle (Lee-Enfield, short model) has a detachable magazine holding 10 cartridges, which can be loaded like the Mauser with clips of 5 cartridges each. Normally this magazine is not detached.

The Ross magazine is of the staggered-column type but is actuated by a lever arm which is hinged under the forearm.

The Garand magazine, holding 8 cartridges, operates on somewhat the same principle as the Ross. The cartridges are inserted in a steel charger or clip, en bloc. This clip functions in the body of the magazine, actuated by a special follower. When the last cartridge has been fired, the clip is ejected by a spring, the bolt remains open, and a fresh clip is inserted, the bolt closing on the top cartridge. This system is very ingenious but it is more likely to get out of order than the Mauser, due to dependence upon accurately machined clips, a clean magazine well, proper functioning of the clip-ejecting components, and absence of excess friction in the clip.

The Garand magazine, unlike the Mauser, cannot be easily refilled when partially empty without first removing the clip and then inserting another. It is not well adapted for loading single rounds into the magazine.

Under normal conditions the Garand clip magazine is extremely well adapted for rapid recharging, as the operator need only insert the 8-shot clip and pull the trigger. It takes up a minimum of space and is extremely neat and compact, and the clips are easy to carry in belts.

A variation in the Mauser type feed is found in such arms as the Madsen light machine gun and the Reising submachine gun. In these the body, feed lips, and follower are arranged so that the cartridges are staggered below the feed lips but are forced into single column as they are fed from the magazine.

This system eliminates the disadvantages of the Mauser system and is more compact than the single-column magazine. However, such systems are more difficult to design and manufacture correctly and are quite susceptible to malfunction.

An interesting improvement on this system was developed by the Finns for their famous Suomi submachine gun. Their latest design magazine held four columns of 9 mm. cartridges which were forced into a single column at the feed lips. An exceedingly strong spring is necessary in these systems.

Rotary Feed

The most common type of rotary feed is found in the Mannlicher rifle, a slight modification of the Mannlicher type feed being found in the Savage lever-action sporting rifle, model 1899. In feeds of this type the magazine is charged with the bolt open by means of single rounds, or by a clip not unlike the Mauser. The follower consists of a rotating spool or wheel with separations to accommodate each cartridge. The follower is usually actuated by a torsion spring. As the cartridges are pressed down they fall onto their respective ribs or separators which are machined in the follower. As on the Mannlicher, they feed into the magazine counterclockwise, and are fed out through the magazine in firing by a clockwise rotation of the rotating follower. The right-hand feed lip of the Mannlicher magazine can be compressed so as to permit the instant emptying of the magazine without operating the cartridges through the chamber. This type of magazine normally holds 5 cartridges. The 5-shot capacity Mannlicher magazine contains the cartridges in practically the minimum possible space.

The Johnson rotary feed magazine loads through an aperture parallel to and just below the ejection port, which is on the side of the receiver. Cartridges are introduced by clips or by single rounds past the spring-actuated magazine cover. The cartridges are loaded in counterclockwise against a flat, thick, spring leaf follower actuated by a coil spring. The cartridges lie against each other in a single, curved column, and the angle which the cartridges form by reason of their taper is compensated by the follower arm. The Johnson magazine holds two 5-shot clips or a total of ten cartridges, plus an eleventh cartridge in the chamber. This magazine can be loaded with the bolt in the closed position as well as in the open, and so can be refilled when partially empty without opening the breech. The Johnson magazine bulges somewhat below and around the line of the stock. This magazine can be emptied by depressing the magazine cover, which permits the cartridges to be forced out of the magazine by the action of the follower, operated by a torsion spring. This magazine is well adapted to the loading of single rounds into the magazine as well as directly into the chamber.

The Krag-Jörgensen magazine is unique in design as the cartridges are fed by a follower arm which is hinged at one end and acts as a lever. The magazine is loaded by opening a hinged box which permits the insertion of 5 cartridges. During the insertion of these cartridges the follower is retained in the cover of the box. Closing the box causes the follower arm to go into action, pressing the cartridges clockwise into the feed lips. This magazine, like the Johnson, can be loaded with the bolt closed or open. It is not well adapted to clip-loading, however. The cover of the box sticks out on the right-hand side of the rifle.

Tubular

It is not practical to use tubular magazines with center-fire ammunition having spitzer or sharp-pointed bullets in the cartridges. An earlier model of the French Lebel rifle had a tubular magazine. Tubular magazines, located under the barrel or in the butt stock, are most commonly found on American lever-action sporting rifles, such as the Winchester and Marlin, and on a variety of .22 caliber weapons including autoloading, bolt-action, and slide-action .22 caliber arms.

TYPES OF FEED SYSTEMS USED IN LIGHT AND HEAVY
MACHINE GUNS

Belt Feed

This is the most common type of feed used on heavy machine
guns. As a considerable amount of work is required to operate
the belt-feed system, it is best applied to guns of the heavier type
having heavy operating parts which develop considerable momentum during the firing of the piece.

The conventional type of belt is made of a webbing material
or similar fabric having loops through which the cartridges are
inserted. One end of the belt is inserted in the breech of the
machine gun, and the belt is pulled across through the gun either
by the action of a lever in turn operated by the reciprocation of
the breechblock during firing or by a feed wheel or skeletonized
cylinder similarly actuated. The original Maxim gun used the
feed-wheel system as did the original Browning gas-operated machine gun, known as the "potato digger" and made by the Colt
company. The M1917 heavy Browning uses a lever arm to feed
the belt across.

As the belt is fed through the gun, an extracting means is provided to pull the cartridge rearward from the loop in which it is
retained and place it in a position where it can be fed into the
chamber of the gun. This action is performed on the heavy
Browning M1917 gun by a piece described as the "extractor."

On airplane guns it is common to use disintegrating metallic
links which are so arranged that each cartridge holds two links
together. When the cartridge is moved from the loop, one section
of the link drops off. This is desirable where a long fabric belt
would inconvenience the pilot or operator.

The belt-feed system is an excellent one for maintaining a
more or less continuous fire. However, the materials from which
the belts must be made, whether fabric or metal, are such that
considerable difficulty is encountered in extracting the cartridges
from loops. Moreover, a great deal depends upon the condition
of the loops and the tightness of the cartridges in them. The cartridges must be properly positioned or there will be considerable

difficulty in feeding them into the gun. Difficulty is also encountered especially with rimless ammunition in pulling the cartridges from the loops by an extracting means. The belts have to be examined very carefully to insure their correct condition before firing. The mechanism required to operate the belt is necessarily complicated and naturally subject to malfunction which in turn will put the gun out of action either temporarily or permanently.

The Hopper System

The hopper system was one of the earliest and was used originally in the old Gatling gun, which was operated by a crank, and by other early machine guns. The hopper system is not very reliable, and it is of course impracticable where it is necessary to fire the gun at considerable elevation or depression.

In modified form the hopper is found in a Japanese gas-operated machine gun, the Nambu. This gun is a modification of the gas-operated Hotchkiss, and has a hopper which accommodates rifle cartridge clips placed horizontally in the hopper. A means is provided for pulling the cartridges from the clips, ejecting the loose clips, and thrusting the cartridges into the path of the bolt for feeding into the chamber. This hopper holds approximately 30 cartridges.

The Metallic Strip System

This system is commonly associated with the Hotchkiss gas-operated gun used chiefly by the French. A metallic strip with serrations holding 30 cartridges is inserted into one side of the breech and an actuating means is provided to feed this strip across the gun so as to place cartridges successively in position to be removed from the strip and chambered for firing. Strips are subject to considerable criticism as they may stick or be improperly formed, or they may become bent or broken, or the holders in which the cartridges are placed may become deformed or otherwise unfit for use. The strip feed system was used in the United States Benet-Mercie light machine gun which was a standard in the United States Army from 1909 to 1916. This gas-operated arm was discarded at that time.

Drum Feed

The most typical example of this type of feed is found in the Lewis light machine gun which was used extensively by the British during the first World War. In this type the cartridges are placed in vertical groups of approximately 5 cartridges each, distributed radially around a circular drum which is located on the top of the machine-gun receiver, lying horizontally and rotating either clockwise or counterclockwise during the process of presenting the cartridges for feeding into the chamber. Lewis drums hold from approximately 47 to 97 rounds, depending upon the style of the gun. A similar system is found in the Russian Dektyarov gun.

Modification of the drum feed is found in the Thompson submachine gun which is provided either with a 20-shot staggered column vertical feed magazine or with a drum magazine holding the cartridges spirally and actuated by a clock spring. With this type of drum it is customary to locate the body of the magazine in a vertical position lateral to and below the receiver, giving the weapon the appearance of having a shield. Fifty cartridges are carried in the Thompson drum. A somewhat larger capacity drum is used optionally in the Finnish Suomi submachine gun.

Box Magazine

An interesting type of box magazine is found in the Revelli machine gun which has several vertical columns and partitions placed parallel to each other in such a way that when one vertical column is empty, the assembly moves over one space and presents a full column for refeeding. This type of magazine has a capacity of 25 to 50 shots.

GENERAL COMMENTS

It is impossible in the space allotted to this subject of feed systems to give a complete evaluation of all the different kinds of rifle and machine-gun feeds. From the point of view of design the subject of feed systems for automatic weapons in particular is most fascinating and vexing. It would seem almost humanly impossible to develop a really perfect feed having a capacity much in excess of 5 or 10 cartridges. Invariably there must be some objections to whatever feed is presented, for the simple reason that so many factors are involved. By way of illustration, a few of the factors which bear upon feed systems are listed as follows:

1. Adequate capacity for the purpose intended.
2. Reliability of feed.
3. Simplicity of design.
4. Minimum number of parts.
5. Balance. (If the cartridges are all placed on one side or the other or on the top or the bottom of the gun they may affect the balance of the weapon.)
6. The method of feeding should be not too complicated, and it should be possible to clear jams. The design should prevent the entrance of dirt and grit so far as possible.
7. The magazine should be of such a type as not to increase materially the weight of the ammunition load. For example, magazines of the detachable box type are usually criticized because the ammunition must be carried in these magazines and they materially increase the weight of the ammunition loads. This is particularly bad considering the needs of regiments, brigades, and divisions.
8. On machine guns it is generally desirable to have if possible greater capacity without necessitating any reloading or recharging, and without requiring the attention of a member of the gun crew.
9. For certain uses it is desirable not to have a belt unless the belt disintegrates after the cartridge has been removed from it, round by round.
10. The feed must not be exposed to external objects which may interfere with its operation of conveying the ammunition into the gun. For example, belts may get twisted and stuck, thereby preventing the cartridges from entering the gun.
11. The actuating means must be positive, and on guns requiring a large capacity feed it is impossible to use operating springs. This in turn puts the load of feeding on the already somewhat overtaxed operating mechanism of the gun.
12. In general, if the feed has too great a capacity the gun becomes much less mobile, and if the feed capacity is not sufficient to permit a fairly prolonged, sustained fire, criticism will be leveled at it, notwithstanding the full mobility.

13. On light machine guns in particular it is difficult to satisfy the requirements of those who would like to have a feed capacity equal to that of the heavy guns, yet at the same time to have as nearly as possible the mobility of rifle-armed troops.

14. Cartridges having rimmed cases make the feed problem extremely difficult where magazines are used. Rimless cartridges having a tapered case, as they all do except in pistol ammunition, also present a problem where a very large capacity is desired, as they create a very difficult angle to contend with. With rimmed ammunition, the rims are always catching and upsetting the process of feeding, and in magazines such as the Bren gun it will be noted that the body of the magazine has to be curved on account of the angle formed by the rimmed cartridges when placed on top of each other in rows. In order to simplify feed, it would be desirable to have ammunition shaped like a true cylinder without any taper. But there are so many other considerations which prevent this, that it is hardly worthwhile hoping for such a boon to designers of feed systems except in short-range types such as the new U.S. .30 S.R. M1.

15. There is also the point that one cannot put a whole flock of healthy rifle cartridges into a space any smaller than the cubic displacement of those cartridges necessitates. And even if one could, what could be done to feed them out?

16. The users of automatic weapons are therefore exhorted and beseeched to be as lenient as possible in contending with the feed problem as it is not so easy to solve as it may seem. Simplicity and reliability are of primary importance.

PART THREE

How to Keep Them Firing

CHAPTER EIGHT

Malfunctions and Stoppages

Types of Stoppage; Analysis and Field Remedy

THIS chapter is offered in the hope that it will be of some aid to that harassed, mud-encrusted, much-exhorted, little-appreciated, generally exhausted individual who actually pulls the trigger, as well as to his equally harassed and over-worked squad and section leader, platoon, and company commander.

If perchance any hard-hearted bearers of gold braid and rank should cast their logistical-data-scarred eyes upon this humble page, it is hoped that they will reflect upon wisdom of worthy Chinese philosopher, Confucius, who say:

One loud bang worth thousand lousy duds.

Which, in modern language means that all the weapons and ammunition in the world are of no use in combat if you cannot "keep them firing."

Unfortunately there exist great confusion and misunderstanding over the following terms:

Stoppage; Malfunction; Functional Failure; Jam.

Stoppage. This is an accidental cessation of fire for any reason. It may be caused by defective ammunition, by a defect in the magazine or feed mechanism, by a defect in the gun itself, by careless or improper loading of belt or magazine, by dirt in the mechanism, or by the fault of the operator.

Malfunction. This is a failure of a *designated* element to operate or perform in a proper or normal manner.

In other words, there is really no such thing as a plain "malfunction." A "stoppage" may be the result of a malfunction of the ammunition, or a malfunction of the gun mechanism, or of the feed system.

For example, if a cartridge misfires during the process of firing, this constitutes a stoppage. It may be due to a malfunction of the ammunition (primer defective), or to a malfunction of the gun (weak hammer or striker spring, defective or broken firing pin, excess headspace). But this misfire may be due to the fault of the operator in failing to manipulate the gun correctly, or, in the case of a new gun, in failing to clean off the grease or cosmoline from the striker.

A malfunction generally results in a stoppage. However, the slide on an automatic pistol may fail to remain open after the last shot, due to a malfunction of the catch, yet this need not cause a stoppage.

The use of the term "malfunction" conveys nothing unless we know *what* malfunctioned.

The following illustration is submitted to emphasize the point that malfunctions must be described by reference to the defective element, and evaluated.

Gun A100 fired 1000 rounds and had 10 "malfunctions."
Gun B200 fired 1000 rounds and had 200 "malfunctions."
Which of these two guns would you choose?

First, you must analyze the malfunctions of Gun A100:

Total rounds fired....................................	1000
Malfunctions of ammunition..........................	None
Failures to feed.....................................	None
Explosion of breech, resulting in serious injury to operator, due to defective design of breech-locking mechanism, and requiring replacement of receivers (5), bolts (5), extractors (4), barrel (1), stocks (3), magazine assemblies (2)	5
Failures to extract due to broken extractors.............	5
Total	10

Gun B200 malfunctioned for the following reasons:

Total rounds fired....................................	1000
Failures to feed due to defective magazine spring found to have been improperly heat-treated and having insufficient tension to lift more than 50 per cent of the capacity of	

the magazine 200
Other failures of any part of the mechanism to operate... None

NOTE: Spring was replaced after 400 rounds and the last 600 rounds were fired without any stoppages or malfunctions whatever.

Technically, gun B200 should have been examined after the first twenty rounds, the defective spring should have been discovered, replaced, and the test *then* continued. Therefore, the report should have read:

Defective magazine spring, replaced after 20th round.... 1

Functional failure. This is a failure of the operating mechanism to function normally due to a fault of the mechanism.

For example, a feed failure due to the magazine in a weapon having a spring-actuated feed system is not a functional failure. A failure to extract due to a defectively designed extractor would be a functional failure, as would a failure to eject due to lack of sufficient operating power in the mechanism of an automatic weapon.

Jam. This is a colloquial expression meaning a stoppage. On explaining an automatic weapon to a group of British soldiers, the question was asked by an inquiring recipient of His Majesty's shilling:

" 'Ow many bleedin' *jems* do yer 'ave?"

Probably the term *jam* is used because of the comparative frequency of actual jams in the magazine of several types of well-known rifles and light machine guns.

TYPES OF STOPPAGES

It is of course impossible to cover all possible types of stoppages and malfunctions, their causes and remedies, because each weapon has its own peculiar characteristics, and reference must be made to the instructions furnished with the weapon issued. Moreover, because of their particular design, some weapons are more likely to develop certain types of stoppages than others.

For example, failure to extract the empty shell from the chamber due to a broken extractor is quite possible in the M1918 Browning Automatic Rifle but almost impossible in the M1917 Browning Machine Gun, for the latter has a T-slot in the face of the breechblock which engages the extracting groove in the shell, while the B.A.R. has the conventional extractor.

Again, the B.A.R. may have stoppages resulting from excess fouling in the gas cylinder and on the gas piston, whereas the B.M.G. has no gas cylinder nor piston. Instead, the barrel of the B.M.G. may fail to recoil due to a tight muzzle gland.

Consequently, we shall not attempt to explain the possibilities for failure in each specific gun but, rather, we shall describe the parts common to all types of guns—such as barrels, bolts (this means breechblocks), extractors, ejectors, magazine feeds, firing pins, hammers, etc.—which may be the cause of stoppages.

The most common kinds of stoppages in rifles, semi-automatic rifles, automatic (or machine) rifles, light and heavy machine guns, pistols, submachine pistols, and submachine guns are as follows.

TYPE I: Failure to fire or misfire.

TYPE II: Failure to unlock the breech.

TYPE III: Failure to extract the empty case *primary* (this means failure to loosen case from chamber).

TYPE IV: Failure of the breech to open, or failure of secondary extraction, or failure to pull shell out of the chamber. (TYPE IV-B: In belt-fed weapons, failure to extract cartridge from belt.)

TYPE V: Failure to eject the empty case.

TYPE VI: Failure to engage the head of the cartridge in re-loading.

TYPE VII: Failure to load the cartridge into the chamber.

TYPE VIII: Failure of the breech to close fully, or failure to lock.

ANALYSIS AND FIELD REMEDY

It is not intended within these pages to do more than indicate what might be done by the operator or gun crew to make the best of a bad situation.

Unless reference is made specifically to a gun, this analysis and list of remedies covers military repeating and automatic weapons. Tabulations are avoided so far as possible because the table system is too far from being readable.

So here we are, in a mud hole, aching in every joint, dog-tired, and hungry, but battle mad. The enemy is coming on relentlessly. We cannot afford to be out of action for more than a few minutes. We must "keep them firing."

Alas, we press the trigger in vain. Misfire!

Question: *How could we have guarded against this stoppage* before we reached the combat zone, *and what can be do* now that we have it?

Type I

Failure to fire, or misfire.

1. CAUSE: Bad primer in cartridge.

   REMEDY: Wait about ten seconds for a hangfire, but not too long if the chamber is hot from firing. Yank the cartridge out and fire the next one. Or, if you insist, cock and try again. If the next few rounds also misfire, you probably cannot blame the ammunition, so—

2. CAUSE: Weak hammer spring, or weak striker spring, or equivalent.

   REMEDY: You could have checked this before. Watch your empty cases in practice firing, and note whether *your* gun or guns are delivering healthy blows to the primers. But here you are, and the best you can do is to procure another spring, or clean and oil the ignition parts *to reduce the friction as much as possible*. Maybe it is a borderline case, and every little bit will help.

3. CAUSE: Perhaps the trouble is with the firing pin, which may be worn, broken, or jammed due to dirt or fouling; or it may be sluggish in cold climates due to gummy oil.

   REMEDY: Replace the pin, or clean the affected parts. Again, you could have corrected this difficulty in practice firing. Watch your firing pins and the primers in your empty cases. A bad pin discloses itself in the fired primers. DO NOT OIL A GUN IN COLD CLIMATE.

4. CAUSE: Not infrequently misfires result from either too

much headspace or not enough headspace. This is especially likely to be the case in such weapons as the Browning machine gun (M1917—"heavy Browning"), in which the headspace is adjusted when the barrel is assembled.

REASON: The significance of headspace is often misunderstood. For a complete explanation of headspace refer to the section entitled *"Headspace"* at the end of this chapter. In this connection it may be stated that if the headspace is insufficient to permit the bolt to lock the cartridge in the chamber, the gun cannot fire. If the headspace is excessive, the firing pin cannot reach the primer of the cartridge in most guns.

REMEDY: Refer to instructions pertaining to your particular gun and, if possible, adjust the headspace. You could have checked this before moving up. If the headspace can only be adjusted at the factory, content yourself by writing a nice juicy letter of complaint which the stretcher-bearers may find among your personal effects. Nevertheless, you could have discovered the trouble in practice firing and turned over the gun to the armorer. That's what he's there for. You must be expected to know enough to see that something is wrong with the functioning on the range.

5. CAUSE: The trigger may be jammed, bent, or broken. The sear may be jammed, bent, or broken. The sear spring or its equivalent may be broken or defective.

REMEDY: Consult the instructions furnished for your gun, and correct the difficulty by cleaning, replacing, bending back, etc. But suppose you lack time or facilities for this. The following is an example of emergency measures with an M1903 Springfield or its equivalent. Your sear is broken and the rifle will not stay cocked. (a) Hold and aim rifle, using left hand only for support. (b) With thumb and forefinger of right hand pull cocking piece fully to the rear and release it smartly. Probably you will succeed in firing your rifle.

"And how can man die better
　Than facing fearful odds"—*etc., etc.*

Type II

Failure to unlock the breech.

1. CAUSE: Usually dirt or fouling in the mechanism. In gas-operated weapons the gas port may be plugged, or the operating rod may be jammed, bent, etc. In recoil-operated weapons the barrel may be jammed due to foreign matter, etc.

   REMEDY: Know your gun and follow the instructions furnished for it.

2. CAUSE: Defective cartridge. The defect may be due to soft brass in the cartridge case, or, in automatic arms, insufficient pressure; although sometimes there may be too much pressure.

   REMEDY: Remove the cartridge case by force if necessary. Oil or saliva on the case may help if you can introduce any. A cleaning rod will help in some instances. Consult instructions furnished.

3. CAUSE: On bolt-action repeating rifles a dirty mechanism, especially dirt on unlocking cams (primary extraction cams on M1903), or a bad cartridge chamber may create this difficulty.

   REMEDY: Keep the parts clean and use oil if the climate is not too cold. Always keep the chamber as clean as possible. You could have discovered machining defects in the chamber during practice firing by examining the condition of the empty cartridge case bodies.

4. CAUSE: This type of stoppage can be caused by innumerable mechanical defects, or by errors or weaknesses in design, resulting in burrs, breakages, etc.

   REMEDY: Letter of complaint, etc.

Type III

Failure to extract empty case—primary.

Introductory comment: This is undoubtedly the most frequent serious stoppage. It is especially serious in automatic weapons. In most instances, if you can't *fire* the rifle or gun *and* loosen the empty case, then you are "in for it."

1. CAUSE: See Type II. If it will not unlock, it cannot extract.
   REMEDY: See Type II.
2. CAUSE: Broken or defective extractor.
   REMEDY: Replace the extractor. Beware of guns in which the change of extractors is not very readily accomplished, regardless of sales talk. They will break, and not always because of a fault of the extractor. So carry a spare extractor (as well as a spare firing pin if possible) in your butt stock trap or your pants' pocket.
3. CAUSE: Fouled, sanded, or defectively machined chamber which causes the brass case to stick tightly to the walls.
   REMEDY: *Keep chamber clean.* Do not load dirty cartridges into your gun. Keep belts, magazines, and clips out of sand and dirt. Keep magazine clean.
4. CAUSE: Defective ammunition, having soft brass cases, or excessive pressure due to improper loading or due to a *hot chamber.*
   REMEDY: If you have sticky brass-case ammunition, try to *wet* the cases with water, saliva, or a few drops of oil, etc. Do not use oil unless you have to. It is not safe to use oil on cartridges fired from the M1903, M1917, etc. This can be done in the B.A.R., the B.M.G., or in other rifles or guns having extra breech-locking strength.
   Do not leave a cartridge in a hot chamber very long. It may preignite, but apart from this, the pressure will be excessive when you fire it, and the case may stick and fail to extract. This difficulty is avoided in automatic weapons which are cocked with the breech open; as, for example, the B.A.R., the Bren gun, etc. It is avoided in certain rifles by providing for heat radiation from the barrel. The use of ammunition having reduced chamber pressure, such as M2, reduces this hazard.
5. CAUSE: Broken cartridge case rim, in turn due to defects in the brass, or due to jamming the rim of a sticky case which refuses to extract for reasons given above (chamber, soft brass, etc.).
   REMEDY: This is a bad stoppage. If you can exchange barrels, do so at once. If you have a rod, push out the case. If

you can get at the chamber, you may be able to pry out the case. An ounce of prevention is worth a ton of cure in this instance. You should have kept your chamber clean. If the gun showed a tendency to extract badly, you should have resorted to saliva or water or oil on the cartridges. In this situation a rainy day is distinctly advantageous. Even muddy water is an asset. Good clean soft watery mud is useful.

6. CAUSE: Occasionally, due to defective ammunition, the primer of a fired cartridge may blow out, or "pop." A popped primer may cause trouble in an automatic weapon. Sometimes the primer will allow gas to escape which in turn may cause the extractor to be ripped through the rim of the cartridge. This is beyond your control, unless you have excessive headspace which would contribute materially to blown or popped primers, there being insufficient support for the primer during the interval of high pressure. Therefore, check your headspace. Aside from this, you can resort in emergency to saliva, water, or oil on the cartridges. This remedy will cure popped primers in many instances.

Type IV

Failure of the breech to open, or failure of secondary extraction, or failure to pull the shell out of the chamber. (Type IV-B. In belt-fed weapons, failure to extract cartridge from belt.)

1. CAUSE: The empty case may be ruptured in firing, and the forward portion left in the chamber while the head or rear portion is pulled out. This may be due to excessive headspace or defective ammunition.

REMEDY: Correct the headspace. Use broken shell extractor, if any. Put wet sand on a live cartridge, jam it into chamber, and try to extract broken portion of fired round. If you suspect the occurrence of this stoppage, again resort to saliva, water, or oil on the cartridges.

2. CAUSE: Sluggish action resulting from dirt, sand, fouling, rust, etc.

REMEDY: Clean your gun, and try to keep it clean. Most guns

will perform better if they are clean. Lubrication is necessary on some automatic weapons, but must be avoided in cold climates. Under normal conditions and in temperatures above freezing, a little oil does no harm. (On weapons which require special lubrication, such as graphite, grease, etc., follow instructions carefully as far as possible.)

3. CAUSE: Excessive tension in mainspring (automatic weapons).
   REMEDY: Reduce tension if possible. You should have adjusted this in practice firing.

4. CAUSE: Empty case may fall out of bolt head due to lack of proper support on head of case, in turn due to defective extractor in most instances.
   REMEDY: Correct or replace the extractor.

5. CAUSE: Excessive friction on bolt resulting from: (a) too much pressure from hammer (in guns of this type) actuating spring (or equivalent); or (b) too much tension in magazine follower spring when the magazine is fully loaded; or (c) in belt-fed guns, too much resistance in pulling the cartridge from the belt.
   REMEDY: In emergency use lubricants or water, etc., except on belt. Free up cartridge loops if possible or change belt. If springs have too much tension, you should have ascertained this in practice firing, and then you could have consulted your armorer. If you have a belt-fed gun you should study your instruction manual carefully. Web belts are affected by the weather. New belts are inclined to be very stiff. Metal links rust, often jam, and should be carefully inspected. You should pay careful attention to the extractor claw which pulls the rounds from the belt loops.

Type V

Failure to eject the empty case.

1. CAUSE: Broken, bent, or defective ejector.
   REMEDY: Correct ejector if possible. There is very little you can do now except operate the gun as a single loader.

2. CAUSE: Any of the preceding types of stoppages may cause

a failure to eject, except, of course, misfires and failures to unlock. Type IV is the most likely cause.

3. CAUSE: This may be due to defective ammunition, lacking sufficient pressure to operate the mechanism adequately.

REMEDY: You might oil your cartridges to increase the operating power. Otherwise, you can operate the weapon by hand and write a letter of complaint.

Type VI

Failure to engage the head of the cartridge in re-loading.

1. CAUSE: See Type IV and Type V. The bolt failed to travel sufficiently rearward to engage the next round. This may be due to a basic defect in the weapon, or to dirt, or to lack of lubrication, etc., in guns depending upon lubrication for proper functioning. It should be noted that in most weapons ejection takes place before the bolt head has reached a point in rear of the magazine or feed path. *Thus, the empty case may be ejected, yet the weapon will fail to feed due to defects other than those of the magazine feed itself.*

REMEDY: See Types IV and V. In emergency use lubrication if possible (saliva, water, oil, etc.).

2. CAUSE: Defective or broken magazine spring, or jammed follower, or jammed cartridges, or deformed cartridges.

REMEDY: Try to correct defective item. Be careful in loading ammunition. You may be forced to fire by single-loading.

3. CAUSE: In weapons having a staggered feed (M1903, M1917, Mauser, Enfield, etc.), the cartridges may jam side by side.

REMEDY: Remove floor plate, drive out cartridges, replace, reload.

4. CAUSE: In weapons which accept the charger as a functioning part of the magazine, care should be used to insure that the chargers are not rusted, dented, or otherwise defective as these may otherwise cause a serious stoppage.

REMEDY: Inspect chargers before using. Be sure the chargers are not bent, rusted, or dirty.

5. CAUSE: This type of stoppage may occur in belt-fed machine

guns due to causes which prevent the breechblock from moving rearward with sufficient force. For example, a Browning M1917 gun failed to feed because the barrel chamber was unduly rough due to careless finishing. After the chamber was smoothed up, the weapon functioned perfectly.

REMEDY: In emergency use saliva, water, or oil on the cartridges.

6. CAUSE: Sand in the action may cause this stoppage, as the bolt may be prevented from traveling fully rearward.

REMEDY: Clean the mechanism.

Type VII

Failure to load the cartridge into the chamber.

1. CAUSE: Broken shell or piece of shell or foreign matter in the chamber.

REMEDY: Clean out the chamber.

2. CAUSE: Deformed cartridge.

REMEDY: Check on cause of deformation. This may be due to the ammunition or it may be due to a fault in the rifle—usually the magazine, or the point of the cartridge may be deformed in passing from the lips of the magazine toward the chamber. This is more frequent in weapons having a staggered feed as the points of the cartridges must cross as well as rise to enter the chamber. (Example: B.A.R. M1918.)

3. CAUSE: Bent or deformed feed lips in the magazine.

REMEDY: Repair or replace magazine if detachable. If the lips are machined this is less likely though more possible if the cartridges are staggered.

4. CAUSE: In weapons which feed the cartridges at a sharp angle, or in any weapons which have weak ejection due to dirt, excessive mainspring tension, etc., there may occur what is known as "riding the cartridge." The bolt will start the cartridge by barely touching the perpendicular face of the base of the case. As the bolt moves forward, the base of the case drops below the bolt face while the point of the cartridge is rising into the chamber. The bolt then

"rides" on the cartridge, pushing it forward until it jams the bolt.

REMEDY: For immediate action, pull the operating handle rearward slightly and shake the gun. This may permit the cartridge to loosen so that the base of the case can be contacted by the bolt. The round may then be chambered, except in weapons cocked with the bolt open, such as the B.A.R. In such guns the round should be removed from the breech. This may be done by releasing the detachable magazine. If this stoppage is a recurring one, check the action for dirt, check feed lips, check magazine spring, check detachable magazine to insure proper engagement in the magazine aperture.

5. CAUSE: Insufficient clearance for base or head of cartridge to slide under extractor claw into bolt face, or deformity in cartridge.

REMEDY: Examine extractor claw. Check for dirt or brass around claw. Examine extracting groove in cartridge. This difficulty is more likely to be encountered in feeding from a staggered-feed magazine as the angles are more acute in loading.

6. CAUSE: Weak mainspring, dirt in the action, friction of operating parts, excessive tension in magazine spring, or a combination of these.

REMEDY: In emergency push the operating handle forward with hand, or pull out the round. Oil may alleviate this condition momentarily, but check the cause at the first opportunity.

Type VIII

Failure of the breech to close fully, or failure to lock.

1. CAUSE: This may be due to causes listed under Type VII above.

REMEDY: See remedies listed under Type VII above.

2. CAUSE: Insufficient headspace.

REMEDY: If possible, increase the headspace. (Example: M1917 heavy Browning). You should have learned this in practice firing. In emergency you will find that you can recock the gun and lock it. The cartridge will probably be reduced in size after its first chambering so that the bolt will lock on the second trial.

3. CAUSE: Defects, dirt, burrs, etc., on locking components, cams, etc.

REMEDY: Try oil in emergency. Examine and correct this condition at the first opportunity.

NOTE: Failure to lock generally results in a misfire. The cycle of operation is now completed by stating a cause for Type I, misfires, as "Failure of the bolt to lock." If the weapon can fire with the bolt unlocked, your troubles may be over unless you have a very strong, well-designed receiver to protect you. But do not be alarmed. Modern weapons are well designed in this respect.

CHAPTER NINE

Headspace

Special Note on the Browning M1917 Heavy Machine Gun

A DISCUSSION of stoppages and malfunctions necessarily requires considerable reference to "headspace," a greatly misunderstood and somewhat mysterious term describing a very simple matter.

To simplify the explanation of headspace, it is best to ignore the term for the moment, and consider the cartridge, the barrel chamber, and the breechblock or bolt.

Rimless cartridges, as the term implies, have no rim to arrest their entrance beyond the barrel chamber. Instead, the rimless cartridge is positioned by its shoulder, which rests against the corresponding shoulder of the chamber. (Examples of rimless cartridges are the .30 U.S. M1906 [M1, M2], the 6.5, 7, 7.65, 7.9 mm., etc. Among cartridges with rims are the British .303 Mark VII, the 7.62 mm. Russian, and 8 mm. Lebel.)

When the cartridge has been pushed into the chamber, the bolt (or breechblock) must lock, so that the face of the bolt rests snugly against the base or rear end of the cartridge. The bolt must have room enough to lock on the cartridge. For example, on the M1903 Springfield, the rear faces of the bolt lugs must clear the front faces of the receiver abutments or shoulders in order that the bolt may be rotated into the fully locked position.

The .30 U.S. M1906 rimless cartridge stops when its shoulder rests on the chamber shoulder. Therefore, the shoulder in the chamber is a locating point. Assume in all instances that the bolt lugs are resting on their abutments in considering the location of the bolt face, against which the base of the cartridge case must obtain support under the pressure of the gases generated in firing.

Now suppose that the distance measured from the shoulder of the cartridge case to the base of that case is 1.943 inches. Suppose that the distance measured from the shoulder of the chamber to the face of the bolt (locked against its abutments) is 1.933 inches. Can the bolt lock under these conditions? No, because there is no clearance.

Suppose the cartridge measurement were 1.942 inches and the chamber-to-bolt-face measurement were 1.952 inches. Can the bolt close? Yes, with plenty to spare.

Why, then, all this fuss? Why not allow plenty of room for the bolt to lock, as in the last illustration? Why not allow an extra amount of clearance or space for the head or base of the cartridge?

The chamber-to-bolt-face measurement represents the *head-space* and the reasons that this must *not* be excessive are numerous in rimless cartridge weapons. For example:

1. FIRING. The firing pin will literally push the cartridge forward against the chamber shoulder as the pin falls against the primer. This would so cushion the firing pin blow that a misfire might result. If the cartridge were already snugly thrust against the chamber shoulder, the firing pin might not be long enough to reach the primer effectively.

2. CASE RUPTURE. Under pressure, the brass case expands tightly against the chamber walls. The head of the case stretches back sharply because it is thicker than the forward portion of the case and is therefore less elastic under pressure. Unless the bolt face is close to the case head, the case will stretch beyond its limit toward the rear and *rupture*. Oiling the whole case permits it to slide rearward in one piece until the bolt face is contacted, but such oiling materially increases the thrust on the locking lugs and may rupture them unless they are very strong.

3. HAMMERING THE BOLT. Excessive headspace permits the bolt lugs to be out of actual contact with their abutments. In firing, the bolt is violently thrust back in such a way as to hammer the locking lugs against their abutments. This may prove serious, and it invariably creates burrs and fractures on the lugs.

4. ACCURACY. Excessive headspace destroys accuracy, for accuracy is essentially dependent upon uniformity. The cartridge cases and, especially, the bullets must be seated uniformly in the cham-

ber and throat of the barrel. Excessive headspace makes it possible for the cartridges to be seated with sufficient variation to upset the accurate grouping of shots from the weapon.[1]

On bolt-action rifles, such as the M1903 Springfield, the usual headspace for best performance is about 1.942-1.943 inches. Service maximum limits are 1.946 inches for new rifles and 1.950 for used arms. The minimum is 1.940 inches.

Semi-automatic rifles having rotary bolts are usually held around 1.942-1.946 inches.

Because of the dimensional variations inescapably encountered in the production of any weapon, it is not entirely practicable to hold the headspace limits much below plus or minus $3/1000$ of an inch (± 0.003).

The headspace problem is less acute with rim-cased ammunition. The thickness of the rim is a controlling and more easily established dimension. The rim serves as a more positive means of arresting the cartridge in the chamber. For this reason misfires are less likely with rim-cased ammunition. Unfortunately, however, rimmed ammunition is very badly designed for magazine feeding, especially in automatic weapons.

To summarize, the headspace in a rifle or machine gun is the distance measured from the shoulder of the chamber (in rimless calibers) to the face of the locked bolt.

If the headspace is insufficient, the weapon will not lock. If it is excessive, the following difficulties may result: Misfires; Ruptured cases; Damage to locking components (lugs, etc.); Loss of accuracy.

Headspace is normally determined by employing a headspace gauge, which is a steel plug shaped like a cartridge case without the neck. However, it is possible to obtain a rough check on the condition of a weapon by closing the bolt carefully on any undeformed empty cartridge case which has been fired in a weapon known to have correct headspace, or, in emergency, on an unfired case. In fact, with a little experience, it is possible to determine the headspace within reasonable limits by trying the fit of live cartridges. In doing so, one must be sure not to mistake a tight bullet seat in the chamber throat for a tight chamber.

[1] See Chapter 17, page 265, on accuracy.

SPECIAL NOTE ON BROWNING M1917 HEAVY MACHINE GUN

In order to obtain maximum accuracy and the best general performance from the heavy Browning, the following method of adjusting the headspace is recommended.

1. Assemble the barrel to the barrel extension, screwing in the barrel till it stops on the shoulder.

2. Assemble the entire gun.

3. Pull the operating handle to the rear and release it smartly.

4. Pull the trigger.

5. If you cannot pull the trigger, the headspace is too tight. Therefore, open the cover, and, using the wrench provided in the parts' kit, unscrew the barrel *one* notch on the ratchet.

6. Pull handle and release it.

7. Try the trigger.

8. Repeat, if necessary, until the trigger can be released. When this is possible, you will have obtained the minimum headspace for your gun. If desired, you may then unscrew the barrel one extra notch on the ratchet to approach the medium and maximum limits.

CHAPTER TEN

Ammunition

The Functioning of Automatic Weapons; Comparison of Ammunition Caliber .30 M1-M2 and M1906; The New 1941 M2; Certain Tactical Considerations

AMMUNITION has necessarily been given some consideration in other chapters of this book in various connections. Nevertheless, no treatise on automatic weapons can be complete without a chapter devoted exclusively to the fodder which makes the wheels go round.

In the following pages ammunition is discussed from the standpoint of the functioning of automatic weapons, their power, and their effective range.[1]

Inevitably there are several angles from which this subject must be considered. To this end a table of ammunition is submitted in the Appendix, followed by explanatory comments. These tables do not include every cartridge or caliber in existence, but they do include the most important ones used in automatic weapons. Those interested in ammunition are urged to read any of the many excellent and complete treatises available on the subject.[2]

THE FUNCTIONING OF AUTOMATIC WEAPONS

This topic can best be presented by indicating the features which we should like to see incorporated in a cartridge to make it the most ideally suited for functioning in the most simplified type of automatic mechanism; such as, for example, the pure blow-

---

[1] *Accuracy* is more specifically discussed in Chapter 17, page 265. *Ammunition supply* is specifically considered in Chapter 16, page 254. The matter of *headspace* is covered in Chapter 9, page 141.

[2] The authors especially recommend J. R. Mattern's *Handloading Ammunition*, and P. B. Sharpe's *Complete Guide to Handloading*. On ammunition, cal. .30 U. S. M1906 and M1, read E. C. Crossman's *Book of the Springfield*.

back type already described in other connections. In the first place, we are most concerned with the problem of extraction of the cartridge case from the chamber. If we can accomplish this with minimum difficulty, functioning is virtually assured. Therefore, the first requirement for the ideal cartridge would be an extremely tough, thick, and rugged cartridge case.

In the second place, we do not want any more pressure than is absolutely necessary, and we particularly desire that the pressure shall be comparatively low in proportion to the strength and toughness of the cartridge case. This would result in a combination capable of sliding freely in the cartridge chamber under pressure but without the use of lubrication, and without the complication resulting from the excessive expansion of the case against the chamber walls during the interval of high pressure. Cartridge cases which are thrust tightly against the chamber walls under high pressure are very often more difficult to extract after the pressure has dropped than those which are not stretched with great force. Thus, for example, a 70 per cent charge in a caliber .30 M1 cartridge furnishes a much simpler type of ammunition for functioning in any automatic gun chambered for this caliber, subject to the consideration of operating power, which can be taken care of if the pressure is standardized.

In the third place, we desire a cartridge case which is shaped as a true cylinder, having no taper, and, preferably, having no bottleneck or shoulder. The best example of this type of ammunition is found in the .45 automatic Colt pistol cartridge and the S.R.M1, which have very tough and rugged cartridge cases, comparatively low pressure, and are shaped as true cylinders.

Finally, to facilitate feeding we not only desire the cylindrically shaped case but we desire a rimless case. The rimless case materially facilitates the feeding problem.

The lower-powered load causes much less wear and tear on the mechanism, and less care is needed in the design of the weapon for such ammunition. On the other hand, ammunition having very high pressure and a maximum pressure consistent with the strength of the case, is correspondingly much more difficult to contend with in the design of the weapon. In designing arms for high pressure cartridges, more attention must be paid to the extractor, to the breech-locking needs, in the unlocking type to delaying needs, and to the general strength and durability of all the parts.

Where the ammunition develops very high pressures, it is particularly desirable to provide a wide extracting groove and a thick rim, in order to avoid the possibility of broken rims in extraction.

Certain weapons of the blowback and retarded blowback types generally require lubricated cartridge cases. It is perfectly obvious that lubrication of the ammunition facilitates functioning in automatic guns, provided the breech lock is designed to keep the breech substantially closed until the pressure has dropped to a safe limit. Where the breechblock moves back during the interval of critical pressure in any measurable degree, it is essential that the rear end of the cartridge case wall should be extremely rugged so as to withstand the pressure developed in the case without the support of the chamber wall.

The conventional .22 autoloading rifles and automatic pistols generally require a certain amount of lubrication on the cases. In these weapons the breechblock can actually move back somewhat before the bullet is out of the muzzle. However, the case is sufficiently strong to stand a small amount of movement prior to the time when the pressure has dropped to a safe limit. Incidentally, a very large percentage of the malfunctions experienced with .22 caliber automatics could be avoided by the use of a little extra lubrication in the form of oil or grease on the cartridges or applied to the magazine body. The application of a light oil to the magazine tube or its equivalent is especially helpful in cold weather, when the grease on the greased cartridges is usually too hard to be effective.

With reference to the ammunition table to be found in the appendix, it will be noted that such cartridges as the .45 ACP, .32, .351, and .401 Winchester, and the .25, .32, .380, and .38 ACP are, by comparison, the easiest cartridges to incorporate into the average automatic arm. Because of the weight latitudes permissible, such ammunition as the .45 ACP is especially simple to incorporate in a so-called submachine gun. The .22 long rifle cartridge, because of the nature of the cartridge case material, requires lubrication, but with lubrication this cartridge is very easily incorporated in an automatic.

Similarly, in submachine guns, and to a slightly lesser extent in pistols, such cartridges as the 7.63 mm., 7.62, and 9 mm. Mauser and Luger pistol cartridges are relatively easy to adapt in an automatic mechanism, especially in a submachine gun.

Because of their relatively medium or low-medium pressures, such cartridges as the .25, .30, and .35 caliber Remington are far from being the most difficult to adapt into an automatic mechanism, notwithstanding the necessity for a breech-locking means.

A cartridge which was not mentioned in the tables because it has never been standardized is the special .276 caliber which was developed and experimented on by the United States Army up until about 1931 or 1932. This cartridge, which was slightly smaller than the caliber .30 U.S. M1906, was of .27 caliber, had a pressure of approximately 38,000 pounds per square inch, and a bullet weighing approximately 130 grains. Compared with the caliber .30 U.S. M1 or M1906, this cartridge could be much more easily handled in an automatic weapon, especially in a semi-automatic rifle. Earlier models of the Garand rifle, as well as models of the Pedersen and Thompson semi-automatic rifles, were chambered for this cartridge. So also was an early model of the White gas-operated semi-automatic rifle.

Chiefly because of the rimmed case, the .303 British, 8 mm. French, and 7.62 Russian cartridges are far from being ideal for the average automatic mechanism. Less difficulty is encountered with rimmed case ammunition where the cartridges are fed through a belt. In fact, the rim tends to facilitate the extraction of the cartridge case from the belt to some extent. But in magazine feed, the rimmed case ammunition is very undesirable. With reference to pressures, the above-listed rimmed case cartridges are by no means the easist, yet they are far from being the hardest types to adapt in an automatic mechanism.

The famous well-known Mauser series, ranging from the 6.5, 7, 7.65, 7.9 mm. calibers, all having rimless cases, are by no means the most difficult for adaptation, yet they develop fairly high pressures in proportion to their cases, and too many liberties cannot be taken with the mechanism of the weapon chambered for these cartridges.

Due to the attention which has recently been given in the United States to the question of the two types of caliber .30 U.S. ammunition, namely, the M1 and the M2, special reference will be made to the comparative merits of their respective loads in the following section of this chapter.

Generally, with regard to functioning, it is sufficient to point out that the pressure of the 1939 M2 load is 38,000 pounds per square inch approximately, whereas the pressure of the M1 load is 48,000 pounds per square inch approximately. It is obvious, therefore, without further comment in this connection, that the 1939 .30 M2 load is far easier to adapt into an automatic mechanism, more especially into the mechanism of a semi-automatic rifle, than is the M1. As compared with the M1 load, the 1939 M2 is virtually a reduced load. We are, however, considering merely the question of pressure developed in the load, and are not in this connection for the moment considering the exterior ballistics of the two loads, or the need or lack of need for such ballistics as those of the M1 in comparison with those of the M2.

The original well-known .30 M1906 load developed a pressure of approximately 50,000 pounds per square inch, and this load, as well as the M1 load, represents perhaps the most difficult of all for adaptation in an automatic mechanism, more especially in the mechanism of a semi-automatic rifle. This fact is aggravated by the nature of the groove and rim of the .30-06 case, the groove being none too wide and the rim being none too thick.

One incidental consideration relates to the seating of the primers. Functioning in an automatic weapon is improved definitely by seating primers tightly in their pockets. A blown primer is very likely to cause a stoppage.

COMPARISON OF AMMUNITION CALIBER .30 M1, M2, AND M1906

The M1906 ammunition has a 150-grain flat base bullet, a chamber pressure of approximately 48,000-52,000 pounds per square inch, a muzzle velocity of approximately 2700 feet per second, and an extreme range at an angle of 30 degrees of approximately 3300 yards. Ammunition caliber .30 M1 was designed primarily to increase the accurate and effective range of .30 caliber weapons. This was done by devising a boat tail or taper heel streamline-based projectile weighing approximately 172 grains. According to Technical Regulations #1350A prepared under the direction of the Chief of Ordnance, and dated Washington, May 18, 1934, the .30 M1 ammunition was adopted in the early part of 1926 as a result of development work undertaken primarily to gain increased range and superior accuracy over the wartime M1906 cartridge. At that time it was stated that this .30 M1 cartridge is the standard service ball ammunition and will supersede the M1906 when the supply of the latter is exhausted. It is also stated in that publication (page 30) that the .30 M1 is used in United States rifles caliber .30 M1903 and M1917 as well as in all caliber .30 automatic rifles, machine rifles, and machine guns.

The caliber .30 M1 ammunition gives a muzzle velocity of approximately 2600 feet per second, the chamber pressure is approximately 46,000 - 48,000 pounds per square inch. The extreme range at an angle of 30 degrees is approximately 5500 yards.

Ammunition caliber .30 M2, 1939, is in general similar to ammunition caliber .30 M1906 except for the fact that due to the nature of the powder which is the result of developments in the .30 M1 cartridge the chamber pressure of the 1939 type .30 M2 ammunition is approximately 38,000 - 40,000 pounds per square inch. The muzzle velocity, exterior ballistics, and the extreme range, are substantially identical with the ammunition caliber .30 M1906.

The exterior ballistics of caliber .30 M1 and M2 ammunition are substantially the same up to about 600 yards. However, the terminal or remaining velocity of the M2 flat-base bullet is increasingly less at a given range than that of the projectile M1. The table of comparisons on page 151 is given by way of illustration.

In the light of the data and other information it would appear undeniable that M1 ammunition is superior to 1939 M2 or M1906 ammunition at ranges beyond 600 yards. Up to 600 yards there is practically no measurable difference between the per-

COMPARISON OF M1 AND M2 AMMUNITION

Range—Yards	600		800		1000		1200	
Ammunition—Caliber .30	M1	M2	M1	M2	M1	M2	M1	M2
Angle of Departure—Minutes	20.2	20.2	30.6	31.6	43.7	46.9	60.3	66.5
Time of Flight—Seconds	.875	.887	1.275	1.320	1.745	1.838	2.285	2.430
Remaining Velocity—Foot-seconds	1634	1536	1382	1260	1185	1075	1051	965
Remaining Energy—Foot-pounds	1020	786	730	529	536	385	422	310
Maximum Ordinate Feet	3.1	3.17	6.6	7.08	12.4	14	21.5	28

formance of these types of ammunition. In view of the above figures it would appear certain that the penetration and striking energy of M1 bullets is distinctly superior to that of M2 bullets beyond 600 yards. The amount of lead required where it is necessary to shoot at moving bodies such as troops on the march at ranges in excess of 600 yards would be greater where M2 ammunition is fired than M1. Hostile troops protected by light covering, such as wood, logs, brush, dirt emplacements, gravel, etc., will be less likely to sustain casualties when fired upon by M2 ammunition than by M1 at ranges substantially beyond 600 yards.

Due to the increase in the angle of fall of M2 over M1 ammunition, M2 ammunition gives a lessened danger space at the longer ranges as compared with the M1.

It must be generally conceded that the accuracy of M1 ammunition at the longer ranges is greater than that of the M2. This is due partially to the extra weight of the projectile, which is 22 grains heavier than the M2 projectile, and also in some measure to the design of the base of the bullet.

The accuracy performances of caliber .30 M1 ammunition prepared for the 1925 National Matches are so well known as to require no further reference. This ammunition gave mean radii in the vicinity of 3 inches at 600 yards in National Match rifles fired from special machine rests. The extreme vertical deviation of this ammunition in those tests was superlative. It is not believed to have been approached by any other service ammunition to date.

One of the most distinct advantages of M1 ammunition over M2 lies in the fact that the M1 bullet, due to its weight and shape, and for those reasons due to its greater remaining velocity at given ranges, is much less affected by the wind and requires much less adjustment by the soldier when experiencing variations in wind or target or combat ranges. This ability to "buck the wind" is one of the most outstanding and important advantages of the M1 ammunition. It is understood that this characteristic is noticeable even at ranges of 300 to 600 yards in comparison with the M2 ammunition.

It must be observed that it is more difficult to manufacture the M1 bullet than the M2 bullet because of the difficulty of accurately fabricating the boat tail of the M1 bullet. Therefore, the M2 bullet is easier to manufacture.

One of the criticisms of M1 ammunition is the tendency of the M1 bullet to cause more erosion at the breech end of a rifle barrel than the flat-based M2. For example, British technical authorities have frequently brought out this point as a reason for not adopting the boat-tail type bullet in the British ammunition as compared with the flat-base type which is the standard of the British army in the .303 Mark VII cartridge. However, in this connection it would be well to call attention to the fact that the British use a 174-grain bullet instead of a 150-grain bullet, notwithstanding the fact that the British cartridge does not have quite so much potential power as the U.S. service cartridge. The heavier bullet gives much better performance in the wind and gives greater accuracy at longer ranges than the 150-grain bullet, regardless of the design of the base of the bullet.

Because of the design of the base of the M1 bullet, it is difficult to get an equal application of gas at the time of ignition. This sometimes results in unequal escape or pressure of the gas upon the projectile as it passes down the bore. In this respect the M2 bullet is superior to the M1.

Taking the two cartridges, M1 and 1939 M2, as a whole, the M2 type with the reduced chamber pressure of slightly less than 40,000 pounds per square inch causes much less wear and tear upon the gun, particularly on a semi-automatic rifle. This is true regardless of the design of the rifle mechanism itself. The basic reason is very obvious.

The greater the chamber pressure set up in a given cartridge case, the more difficult is the extraction of that cartridge case, especially in any automatic weapon. Greater chamber pressure in a given brass cartridge case in general causes the brass case to stick more tightly to the chamber walls of the barrel, and hence to extract with greater difficulty. Since the chamber pressure of the M1 cartridge is almost 10,000 pounds per square inch greater than that of the M2, it is inevitable that the M1 ammunition would be more difficult to handle than the M2 for the reason of extraction. This does not mean that weapons cannot fire any shots with M1 ammunition where they can fire with M2, but it does mean that in any automatic, regardless of its design, the mechanism is less likely to cause functional difficulty, especially as to extraction, if it is being fired with M2 ammunition. Given an automatic which performs perfectly with M1 ammunition, it is not possible to increase the performance beyond the 100 per cent perfection by firing M2.

On the other hand, it is not to be denied that such an automatic might have fewer broken parts over a period of thousands and thousands of rounds where it is fired almost exclusively with M2 ammunition. It is of course the duty of a designer of an automatic to construct the mechanism so that it can handle with perfect satisfaction the most powerful ammunition which it may ever be called upon to fire, such as, for example, higher pressured armor-piercing types of ammunition which may be and are available for .30 caliber weapons.

There is one peculiar feature of semi-automatic rifles which must be emphasized in conjunction with the discussion of M1 and M2 ammunition. Attention is called to the fact that all so-called semi-automatic rifles are cocked with the cartridge in the chamber and the bolt closed and locked. This is essential in order to get accurate rifle fire. Therefore, when a semi-automatic rifle has fired several dozen rounds, it is extremely hot. As is often the case in combat, or even in target firing, the operator may be required to leave a cartridge in the chamber with the breech closed and locked, with or without the safety on, a substantial period of time ranging anywhere from a few seconds to 3 or 4 minutes. The inevitable result is that the chamber pressure of that cartridge is increased extremely due to the heat which is generated in the chamber from previous firing.

By way of illustration, if a given semi-automatic rifle fires approximately 100 rounds at a rate of from 15 to 30 shots per minute, the pressure of a .30 M1 cartridge left in the chamber of that rifle after such firing for 3 to 4 minutes will be increased from the normal 48,000 pounds per square inch to something in the vicinity of 65,000 pounds per square inch. The result is that in firing that shot after such a period of "cooking," a great deal of difficulty will be encountered in the extraction of the empty cartridge case. In fact, this is not infrequently the cause of actual preignition, or the actual explosion of the cartridge without the aid of the firing pin. Accidental discharge of cooked ammunition, for the above reasons, together with extraction difficulties constitute a very undesirable situation.

Suppose, however, that in the same semi-automatic rifle above described, after firing a number of rounds, a cartridge having a normal chamber pressure of only 38,000 to 40,000 pounds per square inch were left in the chamber under the above conditions. The chamber pressure of this cartridge would be increased possibly to 50,000 pounds per square inch, but this would not be any more than the normal chamber pressure of the caliber .30 M1 ammunition. Consequently, the extraction difficulty resulting from the increased pressure would not be so marked.

In addition to this, the lighter the bullet, irrespective of chamber pressure, the less the kick caused in the firing. It is well known that heavy bullets in and of themselves will cause a rifle to kick more than lighter bullets. It is also true, of course, that reductions in chamber pressure tend in turn to reduce the amount of kick. The combination of a reduction in the weight of a bullet and the reduction in the chamber pressure definitely results in a reduction in the kick. This not only affects the shooter's shoulder, but it also saves a great deal of wear and tear on the whole structure of the weapon.

By way of a graphic example, a recent informal test was conducted with a machine rifle or light machine gun in which the extractor was so defective that the weapon would not fire consecutively 5 rounds of M1 ammunition. The same weapon fired 200 or 300 rounds of M2 ammunition without a single stoppage. This indicates the favorable effect which M2 ammunition has on extraction in a given automatic weapon.

The powder used in M1 ammunition is especially designed for the bullet weighing 172 grains. It is noted that M2 ammunition using the same powder but a lesser charge, gives, in conjunction with the lighter weight 150-grain flat-base bullet, more muzzle flash than is found with M1 ammunition. The slower burning powder designed for the M1 cartridge tends to be burning more noticeably after the projectile has left the muzzle than is the case when the same powder, although of a greater charge, is used in the M1 load.

It is believed by some authorities that perhaps the best way to avoid the difficulties of manufacture of the boat-tail bullet of the present M1 cartridge, while still retaining the advantages in general of the M1 load, would be to use the commercially available 170- or 180-grain flat-base bullet with exactly the same powder and powder charge that is used in the present standard M1 cartridge. It is believed that this would be much more beneficial all around than to use the M2 load with the 150-grain bullet. The 180- or 170-grain flat-base bullet is not nearly so much affected by wind, and requires less windage adjustment. This bullet will give much greater accuracy at longer ranges. It will give a greater terminal velocity although not so great a terminal velocity as the M1 bullet. It should be as easy to manufacture as the 150-grain bullet. The amount of weight saved by reducing the bullet weight 22 grains is hardly of sufficient importance when one considers the importance of accuracy at mid ranges, and above all the importance of reducing the effect of wind upon a rifle bullet. The heavier bullet will also give better penetration at mid-ranges and longer ranges. Where it becomes necessary —as may often be the case regardless of tactical conceptions which are previously laid down—for riflemen to fire at ranges beyond 600 yards under certain circumstances, the heavier bullet will be much more effective.

Up to 600 yards the accuracy of M1 and M2 ammunition is about the same. In fact, at 100 and 200 yards it is not improbable that M2 ammunition might give slightly better groups than M1.

Some authorities contend that it is a great loss to the efficiency of heavy machine-gun fire that the service should discontinue the fabrication of M1 ammunition, in view of the fact that with this ammunition heavy machine-gun organizations can deliver effective barrage fires up to ranges almost twice that of the effective fire of the same weapons with the flat-base M1906 or M2 loads.

Recently a great deal of attention has been paid to the application of the semi-automatic rifle as a combat rather than as a target weapon. Some attention is paid to the effectiveness of volume of fire put down upon areas by semi-automatic rifles, in counterdistinction to the importance to be placed upon the accuracy of single-aimed shots however rapidly or slowly delivered by trained riflemen. If so much attention is to be paid to the application of the semi-automatic rifle as a so-called combat weapon for the increase of the potential volume of the rifleman's fire, it would seem distinctly advantageous that such a weapon be capable of delivering barrage fires at ranges beyond those where it is possible for a rifleman with an average rifle to deliver effective aimed fire. For example, ten riflemen armed with semi-automatic rifles might under many conditions be capable of delivering the equivalent of a machine-gun barrage at ranges of 1200 to 1500 yards or more. This fire could very well be conducted by ten riflemen, each firing 30 rounds per minute, or a total volume of fire of 300 rounds per minute placed upon an area in the same manner as the fire of a heavy machine gun, very often not available at the time required in the circumstances which arise in combat. It might therefore be distinctly advantageous from the combat point of view to consider the maintenance of M1 ammunition with its greater extreme accurate range. This would be true even though it were accepted that a rifleman cannot fire accurately in combat at an individual target beyond 600 yards. It would seem to hamper the combat application of the semi-automatic rifle to deny the effectiveness of the M1 ammunition fired in barrage fires by groups of semi-automatic riflemen, where heavy machine-gun fire cannot be made available for lack of the guns, or where it is desired to lay down auxiliary fire to augment the effect of the machine-gun barrages.

Where troops are advancing, or where they are disposed in depth, as is frequently the case in modern warfare, rifle fire which is directed at front-line units may very often miss those units and yet cause innumerable casualties to support or reserve troops upon whom this long-range fire may have a very devastating effect.

Terrain conditions vary in different wars and even in the same war. It is hardly possible to determine accurately just what types of terrain will be the theater of wars in which the United States armed services will be engaged. There certainly can be no reasonable argument against maintaining the greatest possible danger space for small arms fire, regardless of questions of the accuracy of individuals armed with rifles firing individual shots.

Several European military authorities have placed greater emphasis upon velocities of small arms ammunition at ranges up to 400 or 500 yards than upon maintained velocities beyond that range. Accordingly, those authorities have attempted to increase muzzle velocities from around 2500 foot-seconds up to 3000 or more foot-seconds. Attention has been called to the fact that it would be reasonably practicable to load the M2 150-grain flat-base bullet into the M1 case with a greater powder charge, thus obtaining a muzzle velocity of nearly 3000 foot-seconds. Such a load is practically the equivalent of a commercial load which is advertised at 3000 foot-seconds with a 150-grain hunting bullet. The bullet is exactly the same as the M2 bullet except for the umbrella-point nose. Such a combination is readily available commercially, and has the advantage of greater muzzle velocity and flatter trajectory at ranges up to 500 yards. It also has greater penetration up to that range. Moreover, it retains the feature of reducing the weight per cartridge of 22 grains.

As regards the advantage of using M2 ammunition on rifle ranges in thickly settled communities, it is quite as practicable to use the higher velocity load mentioned above so far as safety is concerned. In fact, bullets having higher velocities at short ranges tend to fly apart upon impact against the ground, sand, gravel, etc., and are not so likely to ricochet and go off some distance from the point from where they first contact the ground. The extreme range of the higher velocity load with the 150-grain bullet is no greater than the extreme range of the M2 load. It is an advantage to have a cartridge which can be used on ranges in thickly settled communities for target practice, but it has been questioned by United States military authorities whether this advantage was of such importance that it was necessary to reduce the striking power, range and accuracy of .30 caliber ammunition which is primarily designed for use in warfare. In time of war it is felt that every possible means should be made use of to injure and destroy the enemy.

It is interesting to note that the muzzle energy of the former

1906 150-grain bullet is 2430 foot-pounds, and that of the 1929 M1 National Match bullet is 2920 foot-pounds, or 20 per cent increase; but at 1000 yards, the energy of the 1906 is only 382 foot-pounds, while that of the boat tail is 750 foot-pounds, or 96 per cent increase in striking energy.

The mean radius of National Match ammunition for 1929 at 600 yards in three different rifles averaged 3.18 inches, the extreme vertical 7.99, the extreme horizontal 8.02. At 1000 yards the average of the extreme vertical deviation was 21.33, 23.44, 19.97 inches for three different lots.

A table of elevation for M1 and M1906 ammunition shows that at 600 yards, 17.4 minutes is the elevation for M1 and 20.7 minutes for 1906. At 1000 yards it is 36.1 for M1 and 50.0 for M1906.

Attention is called to the fact that with a 10-mile per hour wind at 3 or 9 o'clock, the M1 and M1906 bullets are affected as follows:

Yards	M1 Bullets Inches on target	150-Grain M1906 Inches on target
200	2.22	3.0
300	5.85	8.0
400	10.80	15.0
500	17.00	24.0
600	25.20	36.0
800	45.60	69.0
1000	69.00	115.0
1200	98.00	172.0

Attention is called to the fact that as between .30 M1906, Remington 180-grain flat-base Olympic load and National Match 1929 M1, the M1 has a flatter trajectory than the 180-grain flat base from a range of about 500 or 600 yards on. For example, at 600 yards the elevation for M1906 is 21 minutes, for 180-grain Remington 18 minutes, for M1 17 minutes. At 1000 yards it is 49 minutes for M1906, 41 minutes for Remington 180-grain, 36 minutes for M1. (At 800 yards it is 33 minutes for M1906, 30 minutes for Remington 180-grain, and 26 minutes for M1.)

THE NEW 1941 CALIBER .30 M2

In 1941 the United States Ordnance Department brought out an improved M2 cartridge having increased muzzle velocity and greater chamber pressure. The exterior ballistics of this new load are substantially equivalent to the commercial 150-grain high-speed, having a muzzle velocity of 2800-2900 foot-seconds. The chamber pressure is about 45,000 pounds per square inch.

This ammunition gives a much flatter trajectory up to maximum rifle and light machine gun ranges of 600-700 yards than the old M2 or the M1. Muzzle flash has been reduced. Barrel erosion is decreased as compared with the M1 bullet. Penetration is improved up to 600-800 yards. For aircraft fire the time of flight is reduced.

CERTAIN TACTICAL CONSIDERATIONS

Bearing in mind the points brought out above respecting the characteristics, power, range, and accuracy of ammunition (accuracy is specifically discussed in Chapter 17, page 265), we shall now consider the tactical application of ammunition of various types when fired from automatic weapons.

Savage beasts invariably fight each other "tooth and nail." Primitive man probably began his own forays against his fellows on the same basis. Thereafter he learned to throw rocks, and to use crude daggers, spears, and eventually the bow and arrow.

From then on as man has become more civilized, so to speak, he has developed more elaborate protective methods of projecting death-dealing media with increasing accuracy over greater spaces. There have been periods in our history when it was found that the long bow and even the crossbow were very effective. All sorts of preliminary artillery weapons were developed, including the ballista and other forms of catapult.

Then came gun powder, and we find various forms of weapons, culminating with the muzzle-loading rifle, the breechloader, the repeater, then various forms of automatic weapons.

We find, in particular, that in the field of small arms there has been a definite and vigorous tendency to increase the power which can be placed in the hands of one man capable of walking on his two feet.

To quote from an article entitled, "The Problem of Arming the Individual Soldier," appearing in the *Marine Corps Gazette,* June, 1939:

Fundamentally, the solution of the problem of arming the individual soldier should be found by examining the objective, which is: To place in the hands of the individual the maximum power or force which can be easily operated, controlled, and transported by one man on his two feet.

We find that in the process of seeking the above-expressed objective it has been attempted to increase the following:

1. The extreme effective range.
2. The extreme effective terminal velocity.
3. The extreme effective terminal energy.
4. To reduce the effect of gravity and atmospheric conditions upon the flight of the projectile.
5. To increase the speed and penetration of the projectile.
6. To increase the accuracy of the projectile.
7. To increase the volume of projectiles which the operator can deliver in a given time with maximum effect.

It has been inevitable that with the development of more effective ammunition there has been a tendency to develop protective means such as semi- and full-armor plate and other types of protection, as well as trenches and other measures taken by troops to protect themselves from flat trajectory fire.

Whereas in the days of the muzzle loader it was customary for troops to move up to within a few yards before delivering murderous volleys at each other in closed ranks, it has gradually become the practice to engage hostile troops with rifle and machinegun fire at ranges of from 300 yards to several thousand, depending upon the terrain, visibility, and other conditions.

More recently it has become necessary for the individual armed with rifles, machine guns, etc., to protect himself against the attack of low-flying airplanes. This, in turn, has made it essential that the soldier or the gun crew be equipped with weapons having ammunition capable of coping with modern airplanes. This, in effect, means that the ammunition must have high velocity, accuracy, terminal energy, and extreme effective range.

Of all the factors which influence the conduct of warfare, it is generally agreed that the most influential factor of all is terrain. It is undeniable that to date the most able generals in history have capitalized upon the conditions of the terrain upon which they fought. However, it is far from being practicable for an army to select just exactly the type of terrain which is most desired. Try as we will, mankind has not yet succeeded in making terrain to suit the requirements of armies. There are so many other civilian requirements to be met, such as the comfortable housing of individuals, the raising of crops, the construction of roads, etc.

With the exception of those nations which are certain to fight in their own backyards, the nature of which backyard is very readily ascertainable, most nations can never be sure just exactly what will be the conditions of the terrain upon which their armies must fight.

The larger nations cover so much area that their armies must plan on fighting to some extent in open country such as is found in Flanders or on the agricultural plains of France, or in rocky areas such as abound in Abyssinia, or in cold, wooded, and swampy areas such as Finland, or on desert plains such as those of Africa, or in jungles such as those of South America, or in forests such as may be found in many countries. Moreover, a great deal of fighting may be conducted in the vicinities of cities and towns where there are many buildings.

Perhaps the army, or a portion of the army, may be called upon to execute a large-scale landing such as that at Gallipoli during the first World War. Here again different terrain conditions must be faced.

If all wars were to be fought in jungle wildernesses such as those of South America, where it is impossible to see more than one or two hundred yards at any time, it would be quite practicable, no doubt, to issue weapons of the so-called submachine gun type exclusively, as the range would never be sufficient to require the power of higher-powered rifle ammunition.

On the other hand, should the fighting occur on open plains such as those of the western or midwestern part of the United

States, or other similar localities, soldiers would be capable of observing each other at ranges up to several thousand yards. Under such conditions soldiers armed with limited range weapons might be severely handicapped, as they would be subjected to barrages and bursts fired from an enemy in many cases 1000 or more yards away.

Under certain circumstances, as for example in fighting in cities and towns, soldiers may have opportunities to fire at the enemy from buildings at ranges of from a few feet up to 1000 or more yards. Under many conditions it may be desirable to have as much penetration and terminal energy as possible to penetrate the protective covering which may be resorted to by opposing troops. Against fire of low-powered small arms, a stump or a healthy log is very often sufficient to protect the enemy, when one shot from a high-powered rifle or machine gun would put an end to the operation.

A great deal has been written on the question of the need for accuracy in weapons issued to individual soldiers. It is often argued that the individual soldier is bound to be a very poor marksman, and that therefore there is no need of giving him a very accurate or powerful weapon. It is argued that the individual soldier is not capable of hitting anything beyond 300 yards at the very best. It is therefore argued that it is unnecessary to give him a weapon which has much accuracy or range beyond 200 or 300 yards. It is also argued that it is a waste of good ammunition to give the average soldier high-powered cartridges or high-powered accurate weapons because the average soldier will merely burn up the ammunition. Some have argued that every soldier could just as well have a submachine gun instead of a high-powered rifle, and a few have even argued that it might be well merely to issue edged weapons and leave the problem of laying down fire to expert machine gun crews.

Having discussed above the question of terrain conditions, it is quite relevant to consider the variations in troops themselves. For example, within the United States we find that the troops enlisted or drafted from various sections of the country represent very much of a cross-section of troops found throughout the world. For example, troops coming from some sections of the

United States are excellently trained by their everyday life to the handling of weapons. Like most of the Finnish troops, certain sections of the United States offer to our National Army a very high percentage of skilled riflemen.

In the United States it has always been more or less of a tradition that our manpower was generally familiar with firearms, and the first World War showed that this tradition had not died. Through the strenuous efforts of such organizations as the National Rifle Association, the National Board for the Promotion of Rifle Practice, the Junior Rifle Training Organzations, the multitude of rifle clubs in the United States, and many public-spirited citizens, this country has a very high percentage of potential rifle marksmen.

In such countries as China it is not possible to count upon very many experts in the art of rifle shooting. On the other hand, Switzerland is an outstanding example of a nearly 100 per cent rifle expert nation, where rifle shooting is on a par with baseball in the public eye. And in this respect, as well as others, Russia has surprised the Germans.

Suppose, however, that a large percentage of troops in an army are not particularly expert with small arms. Nevertheless, the factor of morale and the confidence which any soldier must feel when he knows that he has a very powerful, accurate, and effective weapon, must not be overlooked.[3]

[3] For further discussion see Chapter 13, Combat Efficiency.

CHAPTER ELEVEN

Combat Notes

COMBAT FIRING

THE writers fervently pray that there will never be any combat firing, and if that prayer is answered, this section can be eliminated.

However, it is our duty to learn what to do if war comes. There is nothing more ghastly or more futile than to die because of one's own willful ignorance, unless it be to allow or cause others under one's command to die uselessly because of ignorance.

The lives, safety, and success of comrades will often depend upon the intelligence and ingenuity of machine gunners and automatic riflemen, individually or as squads, sections, platoons, and companies. Every effort must be made to keep the guns functioning. The following is a list of preliminary measures which should be taken to insure reliable operation.

1. Clean all operating parts (i.e., the barrel, bolt or breechblock, receiver, ignition parts, etc.). In particular, be sure the *chamber* is clean.

2. Never leave the gun with any springs under tension, if possible (i.e., the mainspring, hammer spring, etc.).

3. Inspect the extractor frequently to be sure it is in good condition. If in doubt, replace it.

4. With gas-operated guns, such as the light Browning, be sure the gas port, piston, and cylinder are clean and in good working order.

5. Keep all parts lightly oiled or graphited. Be sure to carry plenty of oil or graphite. Never oil a dirty gun if you can possibly clean it first. Do not, however, use any lubricants in freezing temperatures.

6. Check all screws, bolts, nuts, etc., to make sure they are tight, and keep them tight.

7. On the heavy Browning be sure the headspace is correctly adjusted. If the breechblock does not support the cartridge snugly in the chamber, you may regret it.

8. Inspect the lips of magazines and their retaining notches (Browning light) to be sure they will function. Also check magazine springs.

9. In loading belts or magazines be sure the cartridges are properly seated.

10. Check the condition of the firing pin. If in doubt, replace it.

11. Be sure the barrel of a recoil-operated gun is free to slide.

12. If the barrel or chamber is badly worn or scarred, replace the barrel.

13. Be sure the sights are left at "battle range" (usually 500 yards). You may otherwise forget where your sights are set, and fail to register in an emergency.

The following is a list of ordinary measures which should be taken to insure reliable operation during fire.

1. As soon as you suspend firing, see that your gun is fully loaded and ready to resume firing. Otherwise, you may forget your gun is empty and lose time when new targets suddenly appear.

2. Do not fire aimlessly without checking your bursts. Bullets planted haphazardly in the landscape are of no profit.

3. Always put on the safety when you stop firing, especially if you expect to change your position.

4. Never let your ammunition get dirty if you can possibly help it. If it is dirty, *clean* it off.

5. If sand, etc., is blowing about, cover the breech and muzzle of your gun with any covering you can spare. Or carry the breech of the gun under your arm, coat, shirt-tail, etc.

6. Always be sure there is no obstruction in the bore before firing. If in any doubt, use your "pull-through."

7. Whenever you can, clean the chamber and lightly oil it. Keep all working parts, gas parts especially, lubricated during fire. Keep the gas port open.

8. Check your sight settings frequently, especially if you cannot locate your bursts.

9. Do not hold your machine gun like grim death. The harder

you grip it, the greater your dispersion. Just be sure your mounts are properly placed on the ground.

10. In firing a machine rifle, always lie down directly back of the gun, not at an angle as when shooting the repeating rifle.

11. Never fail to collect all the loose ammunition you can find.

12. Do not set up your guns in positions which expose your flanks.

13. Always try to screen your flash when firing machine guns at night. You can shoot the enemy in front of you if he sees your flashes; but the enemy on your flank is looking for set-ups.

14. After you have inflicted material losses upon the enemy, do not linger in the same position to gloat. It may not be healthy.

15. If you are issued a new and untried lot of ammunition, if possible try out a few single rounds to make sure it works in your gun before committing yourself to action. You never can tell about wartime ammunition.

16. Do not waste the fire power of automatics by placing them where they have no field of fire.

17. As a general rule, do not shoot to the direct battle-front. Sandbag or otherwise protect your position to the direct front, and shoot to the flank. That is, your normal fire should be directed against the enemy's *flank*. Remember the shape of your cone of fire, *long and narrow*.

18. Always remember that machine gunners are mutually dependent. You can protect the gunner to your left or right more effectively than he can protect himself, and vice versa.

The following measures can be taken *only* under circumstances of great stress, as where you have a much-worn gun, are virtually surrounded by the enemy, have no time to clean anything, and your gun is showing signs of developing stoppages.

1. If you have oil or graphite, smear as much of your ammunition as possible with the lubricant. Soak the chamber with lubricant, as well as the working parts. Oiling cartridges is not justifiable in peacetime, but an oiled shell will extract much easier than a dry one. In fact, if a gun is too far gone to eject shells, oiling the chamber or cartridges will often make enough difference to produce normal functioning. Moreover, lubricant on the bullets will help the bore to some extent.

2. If you are out of oil, water on the cartridges will help considerably. If it is raining, so much the better. A wet shell will extract more easily than a dry one. So dip your ammunition in water if possible.

3. If you have no water but there is an available mud puddle, or at least the mud is moist, soft and gritless, use the mud in lieu of grease on the cartridges. The mud should be rubbed lightly over the part with the hand, not plastered on. It must not be applied in chunks.

4. Failing the above, saliva on the cartridges will help measurably.

5. The imagination can readily conjure up other substitutes for the above which soldiers under the strain of mortal combat quite often find available.

6. When every remedy has failed, the authors suggest dispatching a runner to headquarters with your resignation.

The reader is assured that the above remedies—excepting 6— are entirely practicable.

Mud puddles, brick walls, or other objects against which the strike of a bullet produces a visible splash, are excellent targets for sighting in automatics. Having established by trial shots the exact sight settings required, more hits can be scored on enemy troops exposing themselves in the vicinity of such "splash" targets.

PART FOUR

How They May Be Employed in Combat

CHAPTER TWELVE

Fire Effect

Factors Affecting the Composition of the Elements;
Bayonet; Selection of Semi-Automatic Rifle; Selection of
Light Mortar; Hand Grenades; The Pistol; Submachine
Gun; The Rifle; Versatility; Economy of Ammunition

"AND we ought always, when referring to infantry, to speak of fire effect, not fire power. Because fire effect is intimately allied with movement while fire power is a static conception." So writes Major General George A. Lynch, Chief of Infantry, in *Infantry Journal,* November-December, 1939. He also writes in another article of the "marriage of fire and movement in that moving fire which is alone decisive."

Fundamentally, fire effect is composed of fire power coupled with mobility. Included in these two basic elements are several important sub-ingredients. A complete list is here submitted.

Fire power

1. Powerful, versatile, one-man weapons having high potential rates of sustained, deliverable fire.

2. Accuracy and range of delivered fire.

3. Intelligent control of delivered fire.

4. Timely application of fire.

5. Adequate supply of ammunition to maintain fire.

6. Comparative invulnerability to destruction by hostile counterfires.

Mobility

1. Weight of weapon—one load not to exceed 10-15 pounds.

2. Weight of ammunition—load not to exceed about 20 pounds. (NOTE: Two full Mills belts plus two full bandoleers equal 320 rounds, weighing 20 pounds.)

3. Uniform rate of march. The rate of march of all rifle units, including light machine gun and light mortar squads should be based upon and maintained at the rate of march of the fully-equipped, rifle-armed soldier. Two rates of march are not compatible with mobility.

The integration of the above elements will result in the attainment of fire effect. Since this is our objective, an examintaion of the above list is in order. In conducting this examination constant consideration must be paid to the application of the factors to the more extreme conditions of combat. Combat conditions are never "average."

FACTORS AFFECTING THE COMPOSITION OF THE ELEMENTS

The quasi-professional golfer appears on the links with a heavy bag full of clubs. He uses at least five woods and a dozen irons. The player carries one club at a time, his caddy carries the bag.

The golfer has clubs for long range, short range, medium range, high-angle, and flat shots. The green is his area of fire, the cup is his target. Like the commander of the larger echelons he has his g.p.f.'s (drivers). His number two, three, four, and five woods are his howitzers. His niblicks are his mortars. His midirons are his 75's. His mashies are his rifles and machine guns. And his putter is his rifle at short range, his pistol, and his bayonet.

Alas, the poor platoon commander, and even battalion commanders, cannot indulge in such an awesome array. They, like the mediocre public links amateur, must get along with a brassie or midiron, a mashie, and a putter. They, too, must carry their few clubs under their arm.

In a word, the types of weapons of the smaller units must be few in kind and versatile in scope. Moreover, to follow the analogy of airplane engine design requirements, the weapons selected must offer the maximum horsepower per pound, horsepower in terms of fire effect meaning maximum deliverable fire, range, accuracy, and penetration.

The following is a list of the types of weapons from which a selection can be made:

Bayonet
Pistol
Hand grenades
Submachine gun
Bolt-action Rifle plus bayonet
Semi-automatic Rifle (plus bayonet)
Automatic or Machine Rifle (bipod)
Light Machine Gun (tripod)
Light Mortar (60 mm.)

Having all the combat requirements in mind, what should be selected from this list if:

(a) Only one weapon can be chosen.
(b) Only two weapons can be chosen.
(c) Only three weapons can be chosen.

The following answer is submitted:

(a) The semi-automatic rifle.
(b) The semi-automatic rifle plus the light mortar.
(c) The semi-automatic rifle plus the light mortar plus the machine rifle, bipod mounted.

If four were included, add hand grenades; if five, add tripod-mounted light machine gun; if six, add the pistol; if seven, add the submachine gun.

BAYONET

With regard to the bayonet, this instrument is rarely used; so rarely that it does not justify its normal weight of one pound. A dagger of half the length and half the weight of the conventional bayonet would be fully as deadly. Such a bayonet can be used on the rifle without subordinating that rifle's fire effect to the bayonet.

The bayonet is essential for night attacks, guarding prisoners, and "threatening the enemy." An example of the latter application of the bayonet is submitted.

During World War I the Americans attacked a town. One battle-maddened doughboy chased a German several blocks. The

Yank finally won the race, thrust home with his bayonet, and then had difficulty in withdrawing the blade. A passing officer, seeing the trouble, advised discharging the piece. Whereupon the soldier pulled the trigger.

Comment: The average velocity of a bullet is in excess of 2000 feet per second. The average velocity of a doughboy-propelled bayonet is less than 30 feet per second. Training time has been spent teaching soldiers to fire their rifles to loosen a bayonet stuck in an enemy.

SELECTION OF SEMI-AUTOMATIC RIFLE

This type of weapon combines more of the essential characteristics desired to produce fire effect than any other.

1. It weighs about 9-10 pounds.
2. It may be used with a bayonet.
3. It can fire in bursts of 8-10 shots in two seconds.
4. It can fire 8-10 aimed shots in 8-15 seconds, and 20-40 aimed shots in one minute.
5. It can fire accurate single shots, slow-fire.
6. It uses the same ammunition as the heavier machine guns and has the same range and penetration.
7. One soldier can, if necessary, carry this rifle and 320 rounds of ammunition without altering the normal rate of march.
8. By suitable squad organization, fire control and discipline can be insured.
9. The rifle-armed soldier is much less vulnerable to hostile fire than a machine rifle or light machine-gun crew.
10. At close range the semi-automatic is almost as deadly as the submachine gun because of its high rate of fire.
11. At medium ranges single aimed shots can be fired rapidly and accurately.
12. At ranges beyond 600-800 yards the semi-automatic rifle can be fired effectively in bursts. A fully air-cooled semi-automatic rifle once fired bursts at a rate of 25-80 shots per minute continuously for 90 minutes, a total of 2400 rounds.
13. Because of its potential volume of fire plus its portability,

the semi-automatic makes possible the timely application of intense fire.

14. It is excellently adapted for anti-aircraft fire against strafing airplanes.

15. The following table of accuracy, slow and rapid fire, based upon extensive tests witnessed by, conducted by, or reported to the authors is submitted.

TABLE OF ACCURACY

Semi-automatic Rifle—Slow and Rapid Fire

Rifle: Caliber .30.
Position: Prone with rest, or bench rest.
Sights: Iron. Peep hole, .050 inches average.
Ammunition: Assorted makes, M1, F.A. M2.

Range 100 Yards

1. Number of shots per group.............   5
   Number of groups.....................   11
   Average diameter of groups ....   2 inches
   Total shots   55
2. Number of shots per group.............   5
   Number of groups.....................   10
   Average diameter of groups ....   1.975 inches
   Total shots   50
3. Number of shots per group.............   10
   Percentage of shots in normal spread   85
   Number of groups.....................   10
   Normal spread, average ....   2.81 inches
   Total shots   100

Range 200 Yards

4. Number of shots per group.............   10
   Percentage of shots in normal spread   80
   Number of groups.....................   18
   Normal spread, average ....   4.5 inches
   Extreme spread, all shots, average ....   7.53 inches
   Total shots   180

Range 600 Yards

5. Number of consecutive bullseyes 14
   Diameter of bullseyes .... 20 inches

Range 1000 Yards

6. Number of consecutive bullseyes 10
   Diameter of bullseyes .... 36 inches

Rapid Fire

7. Target: "D" target, reduced to half size.
   Dimensions of target: 13 x 9.5 inches.
   Range: 100 yards.

No. of shots	No. of seconds	Score value	Bullseyes	Diameter of group (inches) [1]
10	11	100/100	10	$4\frac{7}{8}$
10	15	100/100	10	3
30	70	145/150	25	9
35	60	173/175	33	10
40	66	197/200	37	9

Range 200 Yards

Rapid Fire

Target: Standard "A" and "D."
Dimensions: "A," 10 inches; "D," 26 x 19 inches.

No. of shots	No. of seconds	Score value	Bullseyes	Diameter of group (inches)
5	5	25/25 (D)	5	12
5	5	25/25 (D)	5	1
5	8	25/25 (A)	5	2
5	5	25/25 (A)	5	8
5	6	25/25 (A)	5	5.5
5	9	25/25 (A)	5	5.5
5	9	25/25 (A)	5	5

Average—200 yards—35 shots.
5 shots in 6.71 seconds. Perfect score, all bulls. 5.57 inches.

[1] 35 out of 40 shots grouped in 6 inches.

Range 600 Yards

Rapid Fire

Target: Standard "B."
Dimensions: 20-inch bullseye; 36-inch 4-ring.

No. of shots	No. of seconds	Score value	Bullseyes	Diameter of group (inches)
20	60	94/100	14	26
10	18	46/50	6	22
10	15	47/50	8	26

SELECTION OF LIGHT MORTAR

A highly portable type of high-angle fire weapon is essential to combat those elements of the defense whose positions are inevitably defiladed from flat-trajectory fires. Moreover, the light mortar is essential as a means of covering indefinitely located targets, as well as defiladed areas through which an attack may be launched. While many of these missions might be properly left to the heavy weapons echelons, small unit commanders are too frequently without liaison. The problem of helping the squad rests with the platoon and company commanders in a majority of cases.

The rifle grenade was a makeshift weapon at best, limited in range, accuracy, and bursting radius. The new 60 mm. mortar combines unusual long-range, effective bursts with accuracy and reasonable portability. No load exceeds about 12 pounds.

The chief weakness of the light mortar is its comparative vulnerability to hostile fire where suitable protective terrain is lacking. Moreover, it cannot be put into action as rapidly as the semiautomatic rifle.

SELECTION OF THE MACHINE RIFLE, BIPOD-MOUNTED

The choice of this weapon over the tripod-mounted light machine gun may be questioned. Attention will therefore be directed to these two types of weapons.

In general, the bipod-mounted gun is magazine or possibly drum fed. The tripod-mounted gun is belt fed. All guns in these classes are necessarily air cooled.

Guns of the tripod-mounted class weigh in excess of 20 pounds without mount. The mount weighs at least 10 pounds or more. An air-cooled barrel is not too well adapted to belt feed. Belt feed is not entirely well adapted to practical mobility. Such guns require a small squad to attend each, which results in a distinct increase in the vulnerability of the weapon to hostile fire.

Accordingly, the tripod-mounted gun lacks several of the most essential elements required to produce fire effect.

The bipod-mounted machine rifle weighs, with bipod, from 13 to 24 pounds. The British Bren is an example, weighing 21 pounds. This weapon is fed from 30-round, top-side mounted, detachable magazines, is gas operated, and has an auxiliary folding tripod.

The modified Browning Machine Rifle (B.A.R.) weighs about 21 pounds with bipod. This weapon is fed from 20-round detachable magazines, and has a butt-stock rest for fixed fires. The removable barrel of the Bren constitutes its most distinct advantage over the Browning.

The German M34 recoil-operated gun is convertible, having belt or drum feed, and tripod or bipod mounts. This weapon weighs 24 pounds without any mounts.

Even the bipod-mounted guns are too heavy to conform strictly to the requirements. According to General Rowan-Robinson in his book, *Imperial Defense,* the British made the mistake in adopting the Bren of not insisting sufficiently upon lightness.

An illuminating commentary on such weapons as the 22-pound Bren is quoted from a condensed British article appearing in the *Infantry Mailing List,* Vol. XVI, 1938, pp. 174, 175.

In tests to determine the handling of the Bren light machine gun during the infantry attack, certain points were brought out. Originally, this gun was regarded as an integral part of the section, never to be taken away. It was found, however, that the gun rarely could be fired when so used unless the section or platoon to which it belonged was working entirely on its own, or had ample room for maneuver. Further, the action of seeking and occupying good firing positions—usually on the flank—disorganized the sub-units concerned. Riflemen of the section tended to become mere servants of the light machine gun, or else were inclined to forge ahead and leave the L.M.G. and its crew far behind, thus weakening and disorganizing the section. If the riflemen waited for the L.M.G., the advance was slowed down; and in the final phase of the attack, the number of bayonet men was considerably reduced through the consequent disorganization.

In consequence, it was often found that much of the automatic firepower of a rifle battalion was inoperative or could not be employed for covering fire.

A weapon having the general characteristics of the Bren, but weighing not over 13-14 pounds with bipod, would conform to the essentials needed to insure fire effect.

In the last analysis the so-called light machine gun, tripod-mounted, belt fed, may prove too light for heavy work and definitely too heavy for light work. Even the Bren and the modified B.A.R. with heavy air-cooled barrel are almost too heavy to be fired as rifles, semi-automatically, from the shoulder without mounts or supports.

HAND GRENADES

These are excellent for very short-range purposes. Further comment is superfluous.

THE LIGHT MACHINE GUN

This weapon has already been discussed. (See Chapters 4 and 15.)

THE PISTOL

Essentially this is an officers' and non-coms' sidearm. It would be more useful if it were designed to be used optionally with a stock and larger magazine, in which case it would also serve a major part of the function of a submachine gun. The United States Army is at present developing such a weapon, the S.R.M1.

SUBMACHINE GUN

Most of these weapons weigh 9-11 pounds. An arm having the limited range, accuracy, and penetration of a pistol cannot justify this weight except for special uses. Such a weapon is useless against low-flying airplanes. It is effective only up to 100-300 yards, and lacks effective penetration except against personnel almost entirely exposed to fire.

The submachine gun is a highly specialized, limited-purpose type of weapon. It may be compared to the professional golfer's "sand wedge" niblick. But within its field it is a very deadly arm, as has been shown by recent developments in Europe.

THE RIFLE

The familiar bolt-action repeating rifle was not included in the list because of the semi-automatic rifle. Unless a machine rifle of not more than 12-15 pounds were available, the rifle would be our first choice in the absence of the semi-automatic rifle. The following table on page 183 gives a tabular comparison of the rifle, semi-automatic, and submachine gun.

VERSATILITY

The soldier never knows what terrain he may be required to operate on. In flat, open country with rolling hills he may be fired upon by hostile infantry at 600-1000 yards. Moreover, the soldier may need to defend himself against airplanes and armored or semi-armored vehicles, or may be called upon to fire upon a partially protected enemy under cover behind logs, brush, etc.

The Ordnance Department of the United States Army has developed the finest military rifle and machine-gun cartridge in the world. No other army can match its accuracy, trajectory, range, and penetration. This achievement is due in large measure to improved powder and well-designed bullets skillfully combined.

The so-called M2 ammunition was originally developed to provide a lower-powered, lower-pressured load for target practice on restricted ranges. The breech pressure of M2 ammunition is about 38,000 pounds per square inch, as compared with 48,000-50,000 pounds per square inch in the M1 boat-tail ammunition.

The new 1941 M2 ammunition is fully as accurate as M1 ammunition at 600-800 yards. Moreover, its trajectory is flatter up to 600 yards.

In addition to the new standard 1941 M2 ammunition, the Ordnance Department has developed an excellent armor-piercing load, as well as a tracer load, which is effective up to 1000-1200 yards. Armed with a semi-automatic rifle and a beltful of new .30 M2 ammunition, the soldier has a combination capable of performing the widest variety of missions. So equipped he is less likely to waste his shots, yet, when targets are presented, he is well prepared to hit a maximum number from 5 yards up to 1000 yards.

ECONOMY OF AMMUNITION

Well-controlled riflemen are less likely to exhaust ammunition than machine gunners. Uncontrolled troops are a total loss in any army. The fact that they are capable of burning up more ammunition in a semi-automatic rifle is of less significance. Either troops are under control or they are not. Armament does not affect control. Controlled riflemen will fire generally on observed targets. The percentage of hits per minute, no shots wasted, is quite amazing. Economy of ammunition does not justify failure to take full advantage of exposed targets.

In the last analysis, timing is economy. If the infantry can move quickly to the point of vantage, a few minutes of sudden, intense, accurate, paralyzing fire, may determine the issue conclusively. Surely five or ten, or even twenty pounds of rifle ammunition per man is not too high a price to pay for the attainment of the tactical objective.

Infantry targets are fleeting. A brief high rate of aimed fire is more economical and more efficient up to 500-600 yards than prolonged slow bursts from heavier machine guns. The semi-automatic can deliver a 10-shot burst in two seconds at longer ranges.

CONCLUSION

By way of summary, a table is presented giving condensed data relative to the fire effect of semi-automatic rifles and machine guns.

Military development, like all other development, is a series of adaptations to existing limitations, followed by concepts applied to and culled from those existing limitations, followed by the overthrow of prior limitations unrealized because of the tenacity of prior concepts, followed by a gradual comprehension of the innovation, followed by the formulation of new concepts based upon the new and slightly diminished limitations.

Hiram Maxim was told in 1885 that a machine gun was of no military value. Airplanes were at first used only for reconnaissance. Some confusion still exists even today regarding the correct missions, if any, for tanks.

Our general concept of automatic fire is predicated chiefly upon the concepts which have resulted from long years of employment of machine guns of limited design, weighing over fifty to one hundred pounds with mounts.

Why must tripods be used? Because the heavy guns could be fired no other way.

Why must belts be used? The heavy gun could only justify its lack of mobility by an increased capacity to deliver sustained fire. Hence, the water jacket.

Why do heavy M.G.'s fire by indirect laying? Because they are often too vulnerable when fired by direct laying.

Conservatism congealed is catalepsy. Radicalism rampant leads to ruin. For some the task lies in maintaining the present to insure a safe, secure foundation for the transition into the future. For others the task lies in blazing the trail. Often the pathfinders go astray. Often their blaze leads nowhere. But still they try, and inevitably the trail reaches the next limited objective. Thus the history of the search by military men for the ultimate in fire effect.

And still the search goes on. Though ours is but a passing phase, it is no less important, most especially to us. The unsolved problems of today may be merely burned-out embers at the fire-side of tomorrow's historians, but upon us they may inflict third-degree burns.

TABLE OF FIRE EFFECT

SEMI-AUTOMATIC RIFLE, MACHINE RIFLE OR LIGHT MACHINE GUN, HEAVY MACHINE GUN

	Semi-Automatic Rifle	Machine, Rifle or L.M.G.	Heavy M.G.
Ammunition	.30 M1 (or M2)	Same	Same
Weight................	9½-10 lbs.	Usually 20 lbs.	About 35 lbs.
Weight of mount.......	None needed	2½ lbs.	About 45 lbs.
Range for effective aimed fire	600-1000 yds.	600-1000 yds.	Bursts only
Range for burst fire....	1000-2000 yds.	1000-2000 yds.	2500 yds.
No. of shots per second, 100% man hits—			
at 100 yds.	1 per sec.	100% man hits only by semi-automatic fire	100% man hits not possible by bursts
at 200 yds.	1 per sec.		
at 300 yds.	1 per 2 sec.		
at 500-600 yds.	1 per 3-4 secs.		
No. of shots per minute, 100% man hits, deliverable, aimed fire—			
at 100 yds.	40-45 per min.	Same only by semi-automatic fire	100% man hits not possible by bursts
at 200 yds.	30-35 per min.		
at 300 yds.	20-25 per min.		
at 500 yds.	15 per min.		
No. of effective "burst" shots—			
per second	4-5	10	10
per minute	50-65	150-300	250-400
No. of men used per gun	1	2-5	6-10
Average volume of burst fire per 10 men per minute..............	500-650	600-750	400-800
Vulnerability of gun to hostile fires..........	Slight	Quite vulnerable	Extreme

CHAPTER THIRTEEN

Combat Efficiency of the Rifle

Target Dimensions; Time Factors in Relation to Combat Efficiency

"THE infantry must be strengthened in its attacking power. That is and will remain the most urgent requirement at the moment. To make technical progress reach this end will continue the most immediate problem. To imagine that the limits have been reached, however, is to misunderstand the essence of technology and to underrate the fundamental importance of the infantry as a part of the army organization." [1]

It is proposed to examine this subject in the light of recent discussion concerning the relative importance of the semi-automatic rifle to the efficiency and accuracy of rifle fire in actual battle. Moreover, the relative efficiency of indiscriminate volume fire will be analyzed.

TARGET DIMENSIONS, ACCURACY, AND PROBABLE HITS

First should be considered target dimensions, average group accuracy, and probable hits at combat ranges. The following data on combat accuracy are submitted as representing reasonably average conditions.

TABLE I

COMBAT ACCURACY DATA

Height of prone man: 18-20 inches
Width of man: 18-24 inches
Height of kneeling man: 48 inches
Height of standing man: 66 inches

---

[1] Colonel Hermann Foertsch, German General Staff, in *The Art of Modern Warfare* (Kriegskunst Heute und Morgen).

Maximum combat rifle range: 600 yards

Table of errors—

1. Rifle and ammunition error if fired by the most expert rifleman, using service ammunition in a good .30 rifle, based upon firing 10 shots at a perfect target under perfect conditions.

Range	Diameter of error (3 in. for each 100 yds.)
200 yards	6 inches
300 yards	9 inches
400 yards	12 inches
500 yards	15 inches
600 yards	18 inches
1000 yards	30 inches

2. Amount of error to be allowed for combat, condition of rifle, visibility of target, etc.:

2 inches for each 100 yards of range

3. Error of average military rifleman of average training under good target conditions from prone position:

2 inches for each 100 yards of range

4. Allowance for nervousness, excitement, incorrect sight adjustment:

3 inches for each 100 yards of range

Result: Dispersion of 10 inches for each 100 yards of range.

Range	Diameter of dispersion
200 yards	20 inches
300 yards	30 inches
400 yards	40 inches
500 yards	50 inches
600 yards	60 inches (5 feet)
1000 yards	100 inches (8-9 feet)

From the table figures it would appear that a reasonably well-trained rifleman is quite certain of hitting a prone man-target consistently up to 200 yards, with an even better certainty of hitting a kneeling or standing man every shot up to 200 yards.

Suppose the rifleman is 50 per cent efficient, as suggested above. Thus, out of 10 shots, he hits a prone man-target five times. In other words, every time he fires a 5-shot clip, he will obtain two or three hits up to 200 yards. This is not exactly *probability;* it is more nearly *certainty.*

The fire of supporting weapons cannot be maintained within 200 yards. Hence, riflemen are very much on their own at 200 yards, if not 300 yards. Since supporting weapons have a bad habit of not supporting, rifle fire at longer ranges may be very essential.

Consider the efficiency of a poorly trained rifleman who delivers fire in the direction of the target. Suppose his 10 shots are kept inside a 6-foot square, or 36 square feet, the target representing 2.25-3 square feet. There is less than one chance in twelve that he will hit the target. And it is not healthy to wait too long before you hit a target that is shooting back at you at 200 yards.

Returning to the above data, longer ranges may be considered. The prone man-target represents about 2.25-3 square feet. At 300 yards the rifleman will fire within 30 inches or 6.25 square feet. The chances of a hit are about one in each two or three shots. In other words, out of every clip of 5 shots—even assuming 50 per cent efficiency—the rifleman is quite sure to get one hit and possibly two hits per 5 shots at 300 yards.

At 400 yards, the group is 40 inches, or rather, theoretically, 40x40 inches (3.3x3.3 feet). This is 10.89 square feet, and the target is 2.25-3 square feet. Therefore the chance of hitting the target is about one in four. Even if the rifleman is 50 per cent efficient, he is quite sure to get one and possibly two hits out of 8-10 shots.

However, at 400 yards the target may kneel or stand. The area of the target will then amount to 1.5x4 feet if kneeling, and 1.5x5.5 feet if standing. Or 6 square feet kneeling and 8.25 square feet standing. Add to this the fact that elevation error is more likely than windage error, which further improves the rifleman's chances.

Thus, the chances of hitting a kneeling target are better than one out of two, and of the standing target roughly three out of four. Roughly, at 50 per cent efficiency, the rifleman will hit these targets once or twice out of every 5-shot clip at 400 yards.

At 500 yards the grouping is about 16 square feet; at 600 yards, 25 square feet.

The targets are as follows:

		Group Size
Prone	2.25-3 sq. ft.	16 sq. ft.—500 yds.
Kneel	6 sq. ft.	25 sq. ft.—600 yds.
Stand	8.25 sq. ft.	

	Probability at 500 yards	600 yards
Prone target...............	About 1 in 6	1 in 10
Kneeling target............	About 1 in 3	1 in 4
Standing target...........	About 1 in 2	1 in 3

In other words, if the rifleman is only 50 per cent efficient, he will nevertheless hit a prone target once in 12 shots at 500 yards, once in 20 shots at 600 yards.

But combat targets at these ranges are more likely to be standing. Thus, the rifleman's chances if 50 per cent efficient are one in four at 500 yards, and one in six at 600 yards.

Suppose an untrained rifleman succeeds in keeping his shots in a 12-foot square at 600 yards. His chances of hitting a standing man are 144 ÷ 8.25 or 1 in 17. He, too, may be 50 per cent efficient, or he may obtain only one hit in 34 shots, against the trained rifleman's one hit in 6 shots at 50 per cent efficiency. Here, at 600 yards, the trained rifleman will obtain about six hits to the untrained rifleman's one.

At 1000 yards the trained rifleman will shoot generally within a 100-inch square, or about 70 square feet. The standing man represents 8.25 square feet. The chance of hitting the target is about one in nine, or one in twenty if the rifleman is only 50 per cent efficient.

Untrained riflemen, having no knowledge of wind allowance and elevation setting, would be unlikely to accomplish anything at 1000 yards. They would do well to shoot into a 24-36 foot square at 1000 yards. Their chance of hitting a standing man would be less than 1 in 70 if they were 100 per cent efficient.

To check the accuracy of the above figures on average trained riflemen, the following test was actually conducted, firing on water at 1000 yards. The target was a cylindrical can, 18 inches in diameter, 24 inches long. It lay flat in the water, and due to the wind drifted end toward the rifleman. Thus, the target represented about 2-3 square feet.

The rifleman had shot several 10-shot groups of 3-4 inches at 100 yards with the .30 rifle used. Ammunition was of M1 type. Now 100 rounds were fired. Sight adjustment based on observing the splash required 6 shots. The can was hit on either the sixth or seventh shot. Two holes were found in the can after 10 shots. Firing was deliberate throughout, loading by clips.

After firing 100 rounds, 21 entrance holes were counted (42 holes total). Thus the prone man-target was hit better than once out of every 5 shots at 1000 yards.

Apply a combat deduction of 50 per cent and these would have been one hit out of every 10 shots.

According to the above accuracy data, the *combat* rifleman was credited with 70 square feet at 100 yards, which, divided by the prone target of 2-3 square feet would give roughly one chance in twenty-three to thirty-five, or, say, one in thirty.

The factors favoring the test which would tend to account for the actual 1 to 5 ratio, experienced in the above firing may be found from Table I, Combat Accuracy Data.

At 1000 yards the rifle gives 30 inches. The error of the rifleman is 2x10 or 20 inches. Total, 50 inches. But there are combat factors under paragraphs 2 and 4 of Table I. These are combat itself, condition of rifle, visibility of target, nervousness, excitement, sight adjustment, etc. Total, $2 + 3 \times 10$ or 50 inches.

On the basis of the test conditions, Table I indicates a figure of about 16 square feet at 1000 yards. The target is 2-3 square feet, or the probability is one hit in 5 to 8 shots. Thus, based on this test at 1000 yards, the combat accuracy data appear substantially correct.

A considerable number of firing tests at 600 yards may be compared. The "B" target bullseye of 20 inches is practically identical with the prone man-target, or, roughly, 2.5 square feet. An expert rifleman will hit this bullseye from five to ten times in 10 shots. Less expert riflemen (marksmen, sharpshooters) will get at least one to three hits out of 10 shots.

According to the combat accuracy data, the rifleman would get about one hit in ten at 600 yards. However, 30 inches out of the 60 inches computed for 600 yards consist of combat factors. On the target range the data indicate one in five hits. This would mean two bulls at 600 yards out of ten, which an average rifleman will usually obtain (for example, a score of 40-42).

The very best experts apparently average six to eight bullseyes or prone man-target hits out of 10 shots on the 600-yard target range. For example, the 1940 United States Marine Corps Rifle Team averaged 47.6 at 600 yards in the National Team Match.

At 200 yards an average well-trained rifleman will not often miss a 10-inch bullseye prone, slow fire. Double this bullseye and you have the probable group-diameter under combat conditions.

TIME FACTORS IN RELATION TO COMBAT EFFICIENCY

The second topic to be considered is time factors. Combat efficiency demands not only accuracy but an equal consideration of time. Combat targets are not static. Targets move rapidly and take cover. They are exposed as little as possible and for as brief a time as possible.

It is customary to consider rapid fire in terms of how many shots are fired in one minute. This is unreal and very misleading. The true criterion and measure of efficiency are expressed in terms of how many seconds are required to fire the necessary number of *effective* shots. Thus if 10 shots are required to obtain one casualty at 600 yards, the test is: How many seconds are required to fire those ten effective shots?

This is where the somewhat controversial subject of semi-automatic rifles must be considered. The true and ultimate worth of the semi-automatic is not so much its ability to fire more shots per minute than other guns, but rather its ability to get the same number of hits for the same number of shots in less time.

Again a table is submitted to show the amount of time needed by the average well-trained rifleman to operate with the maximum hitting efficiency as expressed in Table I.

Speed ratio about 2 to 1 (3-1). In some cases it might be 1.5 to 1. This means that the semi-automatic requires one-half the time required by the M1903.

Table II can be checked with the facts by referring to target firing. At 200 yards on a 10-inch bullseye the average rifleman can fire barely

TABLE II

TIME REQUIREMENTS IN COMBAT

Range (yds.)	Group (in.)	Seconds per shot, M1903 rifle	Seconds per shot, semi-automatic rifle
100	10	6	2-3
200	20	6	2-3
300	30	10	5
400	40	12	6
500	50	15	6-8
600	60	20	7-10
1000	100	30	10-15

5 shots in 30 seconds. This figure is probably too low; 10 seconds per shot is more likely to prove the rule.

At 300 yards the Marine Team (1940) averaged 47.9 rapid fire. Probably all men shot within about 15 inches or one-half the combat figure, and they needed 6 seconds per shot. But to maintain that accuracy the average rifleman would require at least 10 seconds per shot.

At 600 yards an average expert has made 44, and once 45 was made, with an M1903 rifle in 60 seconds. In one case there were four bulls. To shoot into 30 inches on a target (60 inches is stated for combat) would require pretty careful holding, good position, etc., and 20 seconds is a pretty short time for such accuracy.

Comparisons may now be submitted with the semi-automatic rifle, caliber .30. The actual ratio of firing speed of both types of rifles in expert hands proves the following:

1. 5 shots in 3 seconds, M1903, unaimed.
   10 shots in 1.5 seconds, semi-automatic, unaimed.
   Ratio 4 to 1 for semi-automatic.
2. 5 shots in 20 seconds, M1903, 100 yards, aimed.
   5 shots in 10 seconds, semi-automatic, 100 yards, aimed.
   Ratio 2 to 1 (group sizes almost identical).
3. 10 shots in 13-15 seconds, semi-automatic at 200 yards, 8-inch group (all bullseyes).
   10 shots in 1 minute, M1903, same range, same group.
   Ratio 4 to 1.
4. At 500 yards 16 shots were fired in 70 seconds from a semi-automatic, all in 25 inches. The M1903 requires 80 seconds for 10 shots, at least.
   Ratio about 2 to 1.

5. At 600 yards several semi-automatic performances may be noted.
   20 shots in 60 seconds with 14 bullseyes on 20-inch bull, score 94.
   10 shots in 15 seconds with 8 bullseyes, score 47.
   28 shots in 60 seconds with 16 bullseyes, average 90 per cent score.
   (All but two within 36-inch four-ring.)
   The M1903 gave a 44 in one minute, or 88 per cent against 90
   and 94 per cent. A score of 45 for 10 shots in 40 seconds was
   fired in comparison with a 47 for 10 shots in 15 seconds.
   Ratio about 2 to 1.
6. At 1000 yards 10 shots fired in 30 seconds from a semi-automatic
   gave 25-inch vertical, less than 50-inch extreme spread. No actual figures are available on the M1903 but at best 1 shot in
   6-10 seconds might be expected.
   Ratio about 2 or 3 to 1.

Further miscellaneous data are available to support the firing
efficiency of the semi-automatic rifle.

For example, at 500 yards, two 10-shot groups fired at 1.4 seconds per shot gave extreme spreads of 26 and 28 inches. Visibility
was very poor due to rain and fog. The combat figure at 500
yards is 50 inches in Table I.

At 600 yards 10 rounds were fired in 12 seconds, and 10 in 15
seconds, both giving a 26-inch group. In the latter group 9 were
in 16 inches.

At 300 yards comparative tests were conducted on combat targets consisting of a prone man silhouette painted brown, exposed
on a stick for 5-second intervals for 10 exposures. The bolt-action
rifle in expert hands scored once frequently but rarely two hits
out of 2 shots in 5 seconds. The semi-automatic scored four hits
out of 4 shots in 5 seconds.

The semi-automatic was tested to determine the maximum
number of shots which could be fired in 10 exposures. The following results were noted:

RANGE 300 YARDS

Total shots fired in total of 50 seconds, or ten
5-second exposures 44
Total hits....................................... 24
Maximum shots per 5 seconds................. 6

Minimum shots per 5 seconds 3
Maximum 100 per cent efficient shots 4
Minimum 100 per cent efficient shots 3
Number of shots required per hit 1.8
Number of seconds required per shot 1.13
Number of seconds required per hit 2.08
Number of hits per exposure 2.4
Number of shots per exposure 4.4

The above data bring out a number of interesting points. At 300 yards the combat time-chart allowed 5 seconds per shot. Under target conditions this may be halved, so that we may allow for 2.5 shots per 5 seconds. The rifleman in question was an expert, so he may be allowed 3 shots for maximum efficiency per 5 seconds. Thus, he may be allowed 30 shots in 50 seconds. It may be inferred that at this rate he will obtain about 25 hits out of 30 shots.

In 50 seconds he obtains 25 hits, or one hit every 2 seconds. Let us take 1 second per shot as 100 per cent perfect. Thus his speed efficiency is 50.

His accuracy efficiency is 25 ÷ 30, or 83.3 per cent.

It is submitted that his true combat efficiency may be found relatively by averaging 83.3 with 50, or 66.6, the figure of efficiency. The formula is:

$$\frac{(\text{hits} \div \text{rounds}) \text{ plus } (\text{hits} \div \text{seconds})}{2}$$

Thus, 10 hits ÷ 10 shots plus 1 hit per second equals 100 per cent.

Suppose we assume that with an M1903 rifle the man behind the gun would have fired 1 shot each 5 seconds, with 10 hits out of 10 shots. Then his efficiency would be 100 averaged with 20 or 60.

Suppose with the M1903 he fired 15 shots, obtaining 10 hits in 50 seconds. Then the average would be 10 ÷ 15 with 1 ÷ 5, or 66 with 20, or 43 the figure of efficiency.

In the actual test the figure of efficiency at 300 yards was as follows: 24 ÷ 44 with 1.0 ÷ 1.8 or 54.5 with 55.5, equalling a figure of efficiency of 55. This indicates that the rate of fire was too high, and, as indicated above, 2 or 3 shots per 5 seconds would have been more efficient than 1.13 seconds per shot.

Another similar test was conducted at 200 yards with a similar target, 20 inches wide, 20 inches high. However, this target was exposed 5 seconds, and masked for only 5 to 10 seconds. The rifle was not put to the shoulder till the target was seen.

From 3 to 5 shots were fired on each exposure. Four shots appeared to be the efficient maximum. Forty shots were fired in the 50 seconds of exposure, or 1.25 seconds per shot.

Percentage of hits 87.5
Hits per second 70
Figure of efficiency . . . . 78.7 per cent

On the D target at 200 yards the following data were obtained:

Rifle	No. of shots	Hits	Time	Percentage of hit efficiency	Hits per second	Figure of efficiency
Spec. M1903	5	5	10 sec.	100	.50	75
Semi-automatic . .	5	5	5 sec.	100	1.00	100
Semi-automatic . .	10	7 [2]	9 sec.	70	1.00	85

At the 1940 National Matches, the M1903 was fired at 200 yards rapid-fire with 10 bullseyes out of 10. The M1 Garand rifle at the same range had 16 bullseyes. Both had an accuracy efficiency of 100. The M1903 speed efficiency was 16.6. The M1 Garand was 26.6. Thus the figure of efficiency for the Garand was 63.3, and for the M1903 was 58.3.

But since both rifles made 100 per cent hits in this case, the true relative efficiency is found in the figure of speed efficiency, 16.6 for the M1903, 26.6 for the Garand.

Previously reference was made to 600-yard firing with two semi-automatic rifles. One gave 16 bulls in 60 seconds, 28 shots; the other gave 14 bulls in 60 seconds, 20 shots. The first obtained an efficiency figure of 41.8; the second, 46.6.

The M1903 gave 4 bulls at 6 seconds per shot for 10 shots. The figure is 20.8. Suppose the M1903 fired 10 bulls at 12 seconds per shot, 10 hits. Its efficiency figure would then be 54.

In one test at 600 yards with a semi-automatic, 9 out of 10 shots

[2] Three shots were just out due to error in windage, a combat reality.

fired in 20 seconds hit a 20-inch circle. Here the figure of efficiency is 70. Where in the same time 6 bulls were made, the figure of efficiency was 55.

A comparative test of sustained fire at 100 yards on a 6-inch bullseye is submitted for consideration.

> M1903 rifle—
> 55 hits out of 80 shots
> 6 seconds per shot
> 0.13 hits per second
> Figure of efficiency, 40.8
>
> Semi-automatic rifle—
> 71 hits out of 80 shots
> 3 seconds per shot
> 0.29 hits per second
> Figure of efficiency, 58.5

In another 100-yard test between both M1903 and semi-automatic rifles the following results were found (on the same target).

> M1903 rifle—
> 15 hits out of 15 shots (100 per cent)
> 4 seconds per shot
> 0.25 hits per second
> Figure of efficiency, 62.5
>
> Semi-automatic rifle—
> 28 hits out of 30 shots (93 per cent)
> 2 seconds per shot
> 0.46 hits per second
> Figure of efficiency, 69.5

In Table I a prone man was represented roughly by a 20-inch target. Under target conditions at 100 yards this may be computed as a 10-inch target. Frequently from a semi-automatic rifle 10 shots have been fired in 10 seconds at 100 yards, all shots well within 10 inches.

Thus, at 100 yards in combat a semi-automatic can have a figure of efficiency of 100.

Moreover, 5 shots have been fired in 5 seconds at 200 yards, all within 10 inches. Again the figure is 100.

It is because of these proofs that the above system of computing efficiency is offered.

It will be noted that full weight is allowed for accuracy. Thus, if a rifleman took one hour per shot and made 100 per cent hits, his figure of efficiency would be at least 50.

At a distance of perhaps 10-20 yards a rifleman using the M1903 might fire 5 times in 5 seconds and obtain 5 hits on a 20-inch target. It is possible.

At 12 yards a semi-automatic delivered over 60 shots in 60 seconds, with all shots inside a 10-inch bullseye.

To summarize this part of the study, it has been submitted that the semi-automatic is capable of combat efficiency materially greater than the bolt-action repeating rifle, chiefly because it can deliver the same number of hits in half the time.

The question arises whether the semi-automatic rifle is equal in accuracy to the M1903.

In the 1940 National Matches the Marine Corps Reserve Team averaged 46.8 at 600 yards with the M1 Garand rifle. The Marine Corps Team was second, averaging 46.7.

The best men in the Marine Corps—and certainly better shots than the above—using the M1903 rifle at 600 yards averaged 47.6. Garand rifles in Wakefield practice in 1940 gave several 10-shot possibles at 600 yards, with up to 6 and 7 Vs.

A semi-automatic rifle gave a 6-inch vertical at 600 yards. A 9-inch vertical was noted at 500 yards, and again there were numerous 10-shot possible groups at 600 yards.

It is rather doubtful that the superb accuracy of the M1903 can be surpassed or even actually duplicated in any automatic weapon. Loading and chambering the rounds may influence the accuracy. Bullet points may be battered slightly by comparison. Barrel bedding may not be quite so good.

On the other hand, the M1903 National Match rifle is a tinkered rifle. Service rifles in the hands of troops will never deliver such accuracy. They do not get such expert adjustment and care. The average service M1903 today shows a number of defects.

Another factor must be considered. The M1903 has been fired

by a host of experts who have trained with it over many years. Many records are established with it.

Quite frequently the statement is made that no army but the United States has adopted a semi-automatic rifle despite the allegation that there have been plenty of various types offered for adoption.[8]

Actually, these statements are not true. Of course, there have been many inventions offered. The Germans actually issued the Mondragon semi-automatic rifle in 1914 but withdrew it because of mechanical unreliability. Not long after World War I the British nearly took a "self-loader" but found it required greased cartridges, so nothing doing.

The inference that the semi-automatics offered, all lacked accuracy, and were therefore rejected, is not correct. Most of the inventions offered had too many serious defects in design.

In favor of the semi-automatic rifle are several undeniable factors. The kick is used in some measure to operate the mechanism, and the shoulder kick is measurably reduced. This very decidedly increases the rifleman's efficiency. Most obvious of all is the fact that the rifleman is firing a self-operated weapon. The fatigue which undeniably results from operating a bolt is eliminated.

Loading is a common factor. It is certainly no more difficult in the semi-automatic. Moreover, this weapon holds from 8 to 10 rounds, against 5 for the M1903.

It has frequently been alleged that more time is required to teach a man to *shoot* the semi-automatic rifle. This is not supported either by the facts or by logic.

Instruction is similar on holding, aiming, trigger squeeze, positions, sight adjustment, loading. But on M1903 bolt manipulation considerable time must be spent which is *not* required for the semi-automatic. Bolt manipulation is boring, tiresome, but essential if any appreciable fire is to be delivered from the M1903.

Inefficiency in manipulation is covered up by *wild, inaccurate* shooting. The poorly trained man will pump off his shots anywhere to get in ten a minute. The moment he succeeds in closing his bolt, he grabs for the trigger.

[8] Recent news reports indicate that another semi-automatic rifle has been ordered by certain "friendly foreign governments."

With the semi-automatic the same man has nothing to do but release the trigger, aim, and release it again. He has a feeling of security that his piece is always ready.

Arguments relating to such items as cleaning, care, malfunctions, and unreliability need not be discussed here. It is assumed as a basis for this study that any rifles used are in good working order.

In order to improve potential combat efficiency, as set forth in Tables I and II (pages 184 and 190), it would be appropriate to consider the factors which bear most heavily on the problem of getting rapid hits with a minimum number of rounds.

It is submitted that given reasonable holding, position, sight alignment, trigger squeeze, and automatic reloading, the most important factor is sight setting. For if the sights are not properly set, an expert can put a small group of shots far enough out to preclude even an accidental hit at any range.

The most important of the two sight factors is the lateral adjustment. An examination of the target makes this obvious, for the body is not over 18-20 inches wide, whereas it may be from 20-72 inches high. Moreover, a "short" shot may ricochet forward into the target.

The influence of the wind must be carefully studied at ranges of over 300 yards. Moreover, every rifle should be very accurately zeroed for windage and frequently checked. This can be done quite readily at short ranges of 10-25 yards if necessary, using an aiming point having a vertical line drawn through it. A very few shots will suffice to check the windage setting. At very long ranges some slight allowance may be required to correct for drift.

Suppose a carelessly sighted rifle is off on windage one point or four minutes of an angle. This means an error of 8 inches at 200 yards, and an error of 20 inches at 500 yards. This latter, 20 inches, equals the breadth of the whole target.

A consideration of elevation adjustments brings up several points. Using .30 ammunition, if a rifle is accurately sighted in at 200 yards, it will require about a two-minute drop in elevation for 100 yards, and a two-minute raise for 300 yards. Thus it will be about 4-5 inches high at 100 yards, and 6-8 inches low at 300 yards. Sighted for 300 yards, it will strike about 1 foot high at

100 yards, and about 1 foot to 15 inches low at 400 yards. The deviations added to the combat deviations in Table I do not exceed the height of a standing man, but they amount to more than the height of a prone man.

It will be noted in Table I that a deviation of 3 inches per 100 yards is allowed for combat excitement and errors in sight adjustment. In other words, the error is allowed for amounts to 3 minutes of angle. This may be compared with the following elevation tables for .30 ammunition.

TABLE III

Yards	.30 M1 EL. — Change		.30 M2 EL. — Change	
100	2 mins.	3 mins.	2 mins.	3 mins.
200	5 mins.	3 mins.	5 mins.	3 mins.
300	8 mins.	3 mins.	8 mins.	4 mins.
400	11 mins.	3 mins.	12 mins.	4 mins.
500	14 mins.	4 mins.	16 mins.	4 mins.
600	18 mins.	4 mins.	20 mins.	6 mins.
700	22 mins.	4 mins.	26 mins.	7 mins.
800	26 mins.	6 mins.	33 mins.	7 mins.
900	32 mins.	6 mins.	40 mins.	9 mins.
1000	38 mins.	6 mins.	49 mins.	

It will be noted that the differential for each 100 yards amounts to 3 minutes up to 500 yards inclusive, and not over 4 minutes up to 800 yards inclusive, using M1 ammunition. It does not exceed 4 minutes up to 500 yards inclusive with M2 ammunition.

Assume a prone man-target at 500 yards. The range is incorrectly estimated to be 600 yards. This means 4 (M1) or 6 (M2) minutes too much at 500 yards. That means shooting 20 (M1) or 24 (M2) inches too high, or the height of the target.

Assume an incorrect setting of 400 yards on a 500-yard target. This error being 3-4 minutes too little or a center of impact 15-20 inches too low.

At 500 yards a combat group diameter of 50 inches was computed (Table I), of which 15 inches was allowed for sight error at this range.

Obviously it is desirable to diminish this error whenever possible. It is in part a mechanically correctable error, whereas other

errors are not. But unfortunately the human error of range estimation is involved. A great many people would estimate a true
500-yard target to be 300 or 700 yards.

Consider a standing man at 700 yards, this range being suggested by the fact that an estimated 600 yards is taken to be the
maximum effective combat range. Assume the man is 5 feet 6
inches tall. The range is estimated to be 500 yards. The foresight
is aimed at the middle of the man-target. The error then is 8 (M1)
or 13 (M2) minutes—56 (M1) or 91 (M2) inches. The combat
group diameter is 70 inches less 21 inches for sight error, which
may appear too little here. With M1 ammunition the error is
not quite so great as the height of the target.

Suppose on the same target the estimate is 900 yards. Error:
10 (M1), 14 (M2) minutes; 70 (M1), 98 (M2) inches.

But, it is argued, one never shoots at 700 yards in combat.
Therefore consider a prone target actually at 250 yards, but estimated at 400 yards, which is quite probable in the case of poorly
trained personnel. Error: 4.5 (M1), 5.5 (M2) minutes; 11.25 (M1),
13.75 (M2) inches. Height of target, 20 inches. The combat group
diameter is 25 inches. The sight error allowance is 7.5 inches.

In other words, this error in sight setting will result in a serious loss of hitting efficiency at any battle range. The center of
impact of a 25-inch pattern or group of shots is raised about 12
inches above the center of a 20-inch target. Thus, only the upper
half of the target is in theory exposed to fire. Twice the number
of shots will be required to hit the target.

Remedies may be found to reduce this error, as follows:

1. Devote time in training to range estimation.

2. Use sights which are accurately zeroed at a basic range (100
or 200 yards) and which have accurate battle adjustments in 100-
yard movements.

3. Reduce the height of the trajectory of the ammunition, and
at the same time try to reduce the amount of drift caused by the
wind. For example, the M2 bullet with the 1941 normal maximum powder charge develops up to 2800-2900 foot-seconds. (M2
1939 service load gives 2600-2700 foot-seconds maximum.) At
600 yards the 150-grain high-speed bullet strikes 48-54 inches
higher than the M2, or requires 8-9 minutes less elevation. The

old M2 requires about 20 minutes for 600 yards, the 150 high-speed about 12 minutes. Thus the range differential is less for the high-speed. Therefore, errors in range estimation would result in less error on the target.

Thus, suppose the ammunition required the following elevations up to 600 yards as compared with .30 M1 and old .30 M2:

Yards	M2 '41—2900	M1	M2 '39	180-grain flat-base
200	4	5	5	5
300	6	8	8	8
400	8	11	12	11
500	10	14	16	14.5
600	12	18	20	18

An error of 200 yards short in range estimation of a target at 600 yards, would mean a center of impact 24 inches low with the high-speed, 42 inches with M1, 48 inches with M2.

Attention is called to the similarity of the 180-grain flat-base bullet figures to those of the M1.

Errors in windage have already been discussed (page 197). However, consideration of the effect of the wind itself upon combat efficiency and how it may be reduced should be mentioned here.

Bearing in mind that the target is only 20 inches wide, Table IV indicates the importance for combat efficiency of accurate wind calculation, and of the influence of bullets in reducing the deviation.

It will be observed from this table that if the wind were blowing at 20 mph, then these figures would be doubled. Thus, with M2 at 400 yards the deviation would be 30 inches; with M1, 21 inches. At 500 yards it would be 48 inches with M2; and 34 inches with M1.

The wind error can be reduced by simplified methods of instruction in wind doping. Fast, well-balanced bullets will reduce the wind drift.

Errors both in wind and elevation can be reduced in combat by firing a tracer and accurately judging its strike. Beyond 400 yards tracers actually strike one foot lower per hundred yards than they appear to do; i.e., four feet low at 800 yards.

TABLE IV

Wind: 10 mph from 3 or 9 o'clock.

Yards	Minutes of Deflection .30 M1	Inches on target .30 M1	Inches on target .30 M2—1939	Combat Group Diameter
200	1.1	2.22	3.	20 inches
300	1.9	5.85	8.	30 inches
400	2.6	10.80	15.	40 inches
500	3.2	17.00	24.	50 inches
600	4.0	25.20	36.	60 inches
700	4.7	34.90	51.	70 inches
800	5.4	45.60	69.	80 inches
900	6.0	56.80	91.	90 inches
1000	6.6	69.00	115.	100 inches
1100	7.3	84.40	143.	
1200	7.8	98.00	172.	

Returning again to the question of accuracy, the above discussion of combat group diameters has assumed that the rifleman fired from the prone position; or from the sitting position with rest. Pure offhand firing without rest is likely to be rare at ranges of over 100 yards.

If the rifleman is actually on his feet, he will probably be in a position to rest his rifle and partially support his body; as, for example, in a trench, behind a wall or a tree or the corner of a house.

However, in the event that the firing is conducted from an offhand or kneeling position, the group diameters should be increased by ten inches for each hundred yards; i.e., at 500 yards 50 inches plus 10 times 5, or 50 plus 50, total 100 inches.

Bearing in mind that a trained rifleman might not shoot better than 20 inches per 100 yards, the question arises whether, after all, "scatteration fire" is not more practical in the last analysis.

Consider a problem at 400 yards. There are 10 enemy targets advancing through a field. They are in skirmish line about 5 yards (15 feet) apart. They present a mass target 150 feet wide. Each target represents about 8.25 square feet in area, a breadth of 0.5 yards (1.5 feet), and a height of 5.5 feet (66 inches). Two riflemen with practically no training oppose them. What might happen?

For reference, an expert will shoot 40-inch groups. (80-inch from standing or kneeling.) The untrained men will shoot no better than 12-foot groups, or about twice the size of the expert's worst.

The untrained men aim into the middle of the skirmish line.

(a) Suppose their windage was off. Then their 144-inch groups might be located between files, 180 inches apart, and no hits would be scored.

(b) Suppose they are correctly located as to windage but they are too low on elevation and hold too low in addition. All the shots go into the ground too far short.

(c) But suppose their groups are perfectly centered. Then they will require from 16 to 18 rounds for one hit.

(d) Suppose they shoot larger groups (18-foot groups), and suppose they are centered. Then they will have two targets within their group area. They will then require about 10 shots per hit.

(e) Suppose they shoot 34-foot groups. Then they will have three targets within their group area. They will require about 15 shots per hit.

Thus their efficiency in hits runs from about 10 shots per hit up to 15. To give them the benefit of the doubt assume that they average 10. Then the two riflemen each require 50 rounds to hit five men.

Compare these performances with those of two expert riflemen. Based upon Table I, the experts will obtain 3 hits per 4 shots. Suppose they are standing. Then they will do better than 1 hit per 3 shots. Thus, the two experts will require 15 shots each to hit their 5 targets. But suppose they make additional errors. Say they require 20 shots per man to hit 5 targets. By comparison, the untrained men required 2.5 times as many shots, or 50 per man.

A comparison may now be made of semi-automatics versus hand-operated rifles, based upon hits per minute efficiency. It is assumed that the rates of fire are as follows:

Rifle	Shots per minute
M1903	10
Semi-automatic	20

Thus the untrained men will obtain 1 hit per minute with the M1903, and 2 hits per minute with the semi-automatic.

The trained riflemen will obtain better than 2 hits per minute, actually 2.5 hits per minute with the M1903; but they will obtain 5 hits per minute with the semi-automatic.

Thus, the two experts with semi-automatics would account for the 10 enemy targets in 1 minute, requiring 2 minutes to accomplish this with the M1903.

The two untrained riflemen would require 5 minutes with the M1903, and 2.5 minutes with semi-automatic rifles.

In other words, time is saved by semi-automatic rifles and by expert riflemen. It seems hardly necessary to bring in comparisons between the single-loader and the repeating rifle.

Query, how long would those 10 targets remain exposed under fire?

Writers occasionally speak of the "fog of war." This fog is sometimes very real. Also there is darkness, and there may be smoke screens, and other such hindrances. Under many conditions accurate shooting beyond a few yards may be impossible. Yet to prevent enemy movements, fire may be essential.

Even this possibility cannot justify the doctrine of the untrained rifleman, for the next day may be bright and clear. Whatever volume of area-fire an untrained man can deliver on a clear day, a trained man can deliver the same volume with greater effect on dark days or in fog or smoke.

In the discussion of comparative hitting efficiency between trained and untrained men, an example was used of 10 enemy targets 15 feet apart.

Suppose the targets are as follows:

(a) Five men grouped around one heavy machine gun.

(b) Three men grouped around one light machine gun.

(c) Four officers standing at an observation post.

(d) A column of infantry in threes, 100 yards in length.

(e) A field artillery piece served by seven men.

Roughly speaking, these examples offer the following area for effective hits:

a. 15 square feet.
b. 8 square feet.

  c. 33 square feet.

  d. 25 square feet (note also depth).

  e. 56 square feet.

The trained rifleman will shoot within 16 square feet at 500 yards, 25 square feet at 600 yards, 36 square feet at 700 yards, and 70 square feet at 1000 yards.

It is obvious that on these targets the efficiency of the trained rifleman will be far greater than that of the "scatteration" shooter.

The following table is presented to indicate the ranges up to which the trained rifleman will obtain percentage hits as stated, operating at full efficiency as established in Table I, and with reference to the above combat targets, a to e inclusive.

TABLE V

	(a)	(b)	(c)	(d)	(e)
Target areas	15 sq. ft.	8 sq. ft.	33 sq. ft.	25 sq. ft.	56 sq. ft.
Maximum range for 100 per cent hits....	400 to 500 yds.	About 300 yds.	About 650 yds.	About 600 yds.	Over 700 yds.
Maximum range for 50 per cent hits.....	600 to 700 yds.	About 500 yds.	About 900 yds.	About 800 yds.	Over 1100 yds.
Maximum range for 25 per cent hits.....	About 900 yds.	600 to 700 yds.	About 1200 yds.	About 1100 yds.	Over 1200 yds.

On the above as upon any targets, correct adjustment of the sights is essential. An untrained man firing upon the column of threes could very easily miss the whole target by incorrect windage adjustment, although a tremendous group dispersion might accomplish an occasional stray hit.

A further study of the above Table indicates that on many potential battle targets a trained rifleman could reasonably obtain practically 100 per cent hitting efficiency up to 500 yards.

A comparison of the combat efficiency of the semi-automatic rifle versus the M1903 or SMLE indicates that the semi-automatic can maintain the same hitting efficiency in about one-half the time, or twice the hitting efficiency in the same time.

On the targets indicated above, the semi-automatic would be more efficient because it could deliver the necessary number of hits required for each target (i.e., one bullet would not necessarily silence a gun crew) in half the time.

Correcting for range and wind errors is simpler and quicker with the semi-automatic because of the facility with which the operator can deliver effective aimed shots, provided the bullet strike can be observed, or where tracers are used.

In the final analysis, all rifle and machine-gun fire consists of groups or patterns of bullets which are placed as nearly as possible on the target. The smaller the groups and the more accurate the adjustment on the target, the fewer the shots required for a given number of hits.

The process of bracketing a target in artillery fire, as in small-arms fire, is expedited by accurately delivered rounds. The bracket having been narrowed, fire for effect is then delivered until the target has been destroyed.

No one seriously contends that accuracy in the delivered fire is not essential in artillery. Machine-gun fire proceeds on the same basis. The machine gun is adjusted on targets or on an area, and the controlled bursts are scientifically placed to obtain the maximum effect.

For example, a machine-gun crew is ordered to fire on a road junction at 1500 yards. Enemy troops are using this junction. The machine gun is carefully sighted and all possible corrections for wind and elevation are applied. The machine-gun crew seeks a small, compact cone of fire. For distribution they traverse and search. But they do not loosen up the clamps and spatter bullets all over the landscape on the theory that a few shots are bound to hit the road junction.

The same is true where a machine gun fires upon personnel; as, for example, on a column of troops on a road. The cone or pattern of fire is adjusted to coincide with the target.

Thus, a rifleman firing upon an opposing enemy soldier follows the same process. Under certain conditions one shot may be enough per target. But for the most part the rifle makes a pattern or group which the rifleman endeavors to place upon the target. Out of so many shots, one will score a hit. The smaller the group, the greater the chance of a hit.

In other words, for each rifleman there is an imaginary circle around his target. He shoots into that circle almost every shot. The rifleman's combat efficiency may be measured by the size of his circle or group and by the speed with which he can deliver the necessary shots required for a hit.

Under some conditions of combat, rifle targets are difficult to locate and the situation may demand an intense volume of fire on an area, chiefly to immobilize enemy troops or, as it has been often described "pinning them to the ground." For such missions trained riflemen are obviously more efficient. Moreover, the semi-automatic is definitely better suited for such quasi machine-gun missions. Unfortunately, because of World War I experience, too many people have concluded that this area fire in a general direction is sufficient. They espouse the semi-automatic rifle as an "area squirter."

Others, who favor the doctrine of the accurate individual shot, object to the semi-automatic rifle as an inaccurate weapon. (There are others who view with alarm the potential ammunition consumption of the semi-automatic.)

For super-supreme accuracy in the international matches, a single shot Martini action was generally used. Next to this ranks the M1903 action, but fired by single-loading. Feeding rounds through the M1903 magazine is not conducive to the highest accuracy due to bullet battering and irregular chambering.

Therefore, why did we ever adopt a repeating rifle? The famous Martini action was originated by H. L. Peabody, of Boston, in 1862, and manufactured in Providence, Rhode Island, and adopted by many foreign nations, though not by the United States Army. The British used it successfully for some years—till 1885—and have always favored this action.

Of course the Mauser action offered rapid-fire possibilities in an accurate, powerful, modern cartridge. The Boers used Mauser magazine fire with surprising effect against the British, while at the same time building up many records for highly accurate rifle fire up to 800 yards.

In World War I the accuracy and intensity of British SMLE rapid fire caused the Germans to believe they were opposed by many machine guns.

Since World War I there has been a distinct trend toward light machine guns. Many European armies are organized with the LMG crew as the basic unit of fire, instead of the rifle. Thus it is sought to obtain a volume of fire from a controlled source. The apparent inability of certain nationalities to shoot a rifle effectively may have contributed to this doctrine, as well as the fact that inventors flooded the market with numerous 20-pound light machine guns after World War I.

It is undeniably true that some armies simply cannot obtain men capable of hitting anything with a rifle. However, average Americans, Britishers, Canadians, Anzacs, and other Colonials appear quite capable of developing this ability. The Marine Corps once developed a prize winning international rifle team in Haiti. It can be done, as the record shows.

The submachine gun has been widely used during the past few years by some armies and some civilian defense units. England has had little time and less ammunition for training individuals of these defense units. Pistol ammunition is cheaper and more readily obtainable.

The submachine gun spatters bullets up to 150-200 yards. Buckshot is also effective at short range.

Large enemy groups at very close range are, no doubt, best combated by intense volleys of shots on the "mow-'em-down" theory. But that sort of fire does not help much if the enemy lies out 400 to 500 yards away and picks off submachine gunners who cannot possibly reach back.

Then, too, there is the question of the hitting power of the bullet, its penetration, and its effectiveness against light vehicles, airplanes, etc. For example, troops are generally somewhat demoralized to find that bullets are coming right through what appeared to be an impregnable tree trunk. The M1 bullet will penetrate up to 1.5 feet of solid oak, and 6 inches of brick masonry.

The fact is that modern infantry really needs a more effective armor-piercing rifle cartridge for use against light tanks. Such a cartridge would only be practicable if adapted to a high-powered rifle, preferably of the automatic type.

The history of firearms betrays a marked tendency to cling to established methods, often at grave cost.

History shows that Colt was forced to fight for eleven years to get his revolver adopted for military use. Resistance to the single-shot breechloader as a replacement for the muzzle-loader was encountered on the ground that the breechloader would "too soon exhaust the soldier's supply of ammunition."

If the Boers were deadly with their magazine Mausers, they would have been more deadly with semi-automatic rifles. A single bullet is the cheapest battle instrument to inflict one casualty. Its accuracy was improved by rifling, its velocity, power, trajectory, and accuracy improved by powder and bullet design. The efficiency and speed of its delivery was improved by the cartridge case with primer, first in the breechloader, then in the repeater, and now in the semi-automatic rifle.

Any system for a pure individual rifle which called exclusively for the projection of bullets in bursts would result in a definitely certain loss of efficiency. But so long as each bullet is controlled and directed effectively toward its target, then the potential rate of delivery cannot be too fast, one second per shot being close to the peak of the human machine.

Select a super-accurate muzzle-loader—and there are such. Select also an 1873 Springfield—and amazing records were made with it. Select a Springfield and finally a semi-automatic rifle. Consider the amount of training time which would be required to teach a recruit to fire these arms at 200 yards with sufficient accuracy and rapidity to obtain 100 per cent hits at from 2 to 30 seconds per hit, using a standing or kneeling man-target. Consider the time required to train a man to load the muzzle-loader rapidly; the breechloader; then the M1903; and finally the semi-automatic.

It is expected that a soldier should fire 10 shots in 1 minute on the D target at 200 yards, and obtain a high percentage of hits with the M1903. Obviously, the recruit could reach this rate of fire with much less training if the semi-automatic rifle were issued. Obviously, an equal amount of training would result in a much higher degree of efficiency, especially since much of the period could be devoted to improving the accuracy of the single aimed shots.

The final conclusion is inescapable. Combat efficiency with the rifle depends upon the accuracy of delivery and speed of delivery of individual bullets. It depends upon the efficiency of the fire in terms of the average of shots per hit with hits per second. It depends upon flat-shooting, wind-bucking bullets directed by careful aim through correctly adjusted sights.

Since the repeating rifle was obviously far more efficient in battle than the single-shot arm, it seems logical—and the facts support the proposition—that a semi-automatic rifle is correspondingly more efficient than the repeater, provided of course that it retains the essential characteristics of the repeater but with the addition of a reliable self-loading action.

The following quotation, from *The Art of Modern Warfare* by Colonel Hermann Foertsch of the German General Staff is of unusual significance:

The effectiveness of equipment has steadily increased. The means employed have steadily become more complicated in their structure and their manufacture, but their service has mostly become easier. Performances that used to require a Manual of Arms are today done mechanically.

A man who sees nothing more in a machine than some new kind of strange instrument, who yearns for the "good old times," when there were no motors, radios, armored vehicles, or quick-firing guns, has not correctly read the signs of the times.

The fact that fighting after all does not consist of uninterrupted, continuous fire, but rather of moments of great fire intensity, following after long periods of comparative quiet, and of comparatively short duration as against the time consumed in the entire action, speaks rather in favor of the employment of still more quick-firing weapons. It is just these high spots that demand a maximum of fire concentration.

CHAPTER FOURTEEN

Automatics in the Squad

*Types of Arms; Mobility of Arms; Foreign Trends;
Considerations*

"IT is the duty of infantry in attack to bring fire to bear on the enemy, to overwhelm him by means of fire and shock effect, and to carry his position; on the defense, its duty is to destroy the enemy by fire effect and counterattack, and to hold its own position. . . . For this reason the infantry is everywhere equipped, down to its smallest units, with all the various types of weapons, each different in effect, but all of them supplementing one another. . . . They must be so organized that the quickest possible kind of co-operation is assured."[1]

The squad or group of about one dozen men is the basic infantry unit. It is proposed to analyze the types of arms and their distribution within the infantry squad. In view of current arguments over the relative merits of various classes of weapons, such as rifles, submachine guns, L.M.G.'s, etc., the actual merits of any one of these weapons as complete cure-alls will be studied. This analysis need not include discussion of particular weapons by name. Hence the first part of the study includes a tabulation of the various classes of weapons to form the basis for a uniform standard of terminology upon which to proceed.

TYPES OF ARMS

The two elements of force required in the infantry squad are *fire power* and *shock power*. There are three main classes of infantry squad weapons designed to provide those elements. They are as follows:

[1] Colonel Hermann Foertsch, German General Staff, in *The Art of Modern Warfare.*

FLAT TRAJECTORY WEAPONS

1. Long-range weapons; i.e., machine guns
2. Medium-range weapons; i.e., rifles
3. Short-range weapons; i.e., submachine guns
4. Close-combat weapons; i.e., pistols

HIGH-ANGLE FIRE WEAPONS

1. Long-range weapons; i.e., mortars
2. Medium-range weapons; i. e., light mortars
3. Short-range weapons; i.e., rifle grenades
4. Close-combat weapons; i.e., hand grenades

HAND-TO-HAND WEAPONS

1. Heavy bayonets fixed to rifles
2. Light bayonets fixed to rifles
3. Broad swords, machetes
4. Trench knives, daggers

The characteristics of weapons of the flat-trajectory type, together with a descriptive title, are presented briefly in the table on page 214.

The following special characteristics of some of these weapons should be noted:

Heavy machine gun: This weapon can be fired over the heads of friendly troops. It can be fired by indirect laying. It can fire several hundred rounds in one-half minute.

Medium light machine gun: This gun can perform some of the missions of the heavy M.G. With a belt it can fire 100 rounds in less than 20 seconds.

Light machine gun: This gun can perform some of the missions of the heavy M.G.

Light machine rifle: This gun can perform some of the missions of the medium M.G. It can also perform missions of the semi-automatic rifle and can be handled as such. Like the L.M.G., it can deliver 20-40 rounds in from 3-6 seconds. It can deliver 100

Class	Heavy M.G.	Medium L.M.G.	L.M.G.	Light machine Rifle	Semi-auto Rifle	Hand-operated Rifle	Sub-machine gun	Auto pistol	Revolver
Weight plus mount, if required.	35 lbs. 80 lbs.	25 lbs. 35 lbs.	20 lbs. 22 lbs.	14 lbs. 16 lbs.	9.5 lbs.	9 lbs.	7-8 lbs.	2.5 lbs.	2 lbs.
How fired.	Tripod only	Tripod or bipod	Tripod or bipod	Tripod or bipod or shoulder	Shoulder	Shoulder	Shoulder	Hand	Hand
How loaded.	Belt or strip	Belt, strip, drum	Detach-able Magazine	Detach-able Magazine	Clip	Clip	Detach-able Magazine or drum	Detach-able Magazine	Singly in cyclinder
Limits of effective burst range, flat-base bullets.	1800 yds.	1200 to 1400 yds.	1200 to 1400 yds.	1200 to 1400 yds.			300 yds.		
Accuracy limits, single shots.	Not so fired	600 to 800 yds.	600 to 800 yds.	600 to 800 yds.	600 to 800 yds.	600 to 800 yds. (1000 yds. with telescope)	100 to 200 yds.	50 yds.	50 to 75 yds.
Rates of effective fire.	150 to 300 per min.	100 to 250 per min.	100 to 200 or 60 semi-auto	100 to 150 or 60 semi-auto	15 to 25 per min.	5 to 10 per min.	100 to 200 or 50 to 60 semi-auto	20 per min.	12 per min.

rounds in one-half minute. The term "Light machine rifle" is used here chiefly to distinguish this class of weapon from the L.M.G. which might also be called "Heavy machine rifle." In semi-automatic fire the L.M.R. can deliver 20-30 aimed shots in 20-30 seconds.

Semi-automatic rifle: In one aspect this arm can fire short bursts of 8-10 shots in 3-4 seconds. It can fire 8-10 aimed shots in 8-10 seconds.

Submachine gun: Models of this gun weigh from 6-10 pounds. Various types of pistol ammunition are used. In some of these guns the ammunition is capable of accurate shooting at a man-target up to 300 yards. However, it must be noted that with the same amount of skill an average rifleman could shoot at a corresponding target 800-1000 yards away just as well. This matter will be discussed further below.

Pistol: This weapon usually holds from 7-10 rounds which can be fired at short range in from 10-20 seconds.

Revolver: This is a most reliable hand weapon. It can fire 6 shots in 10-12 seconds.

The second main class of high-angle fire weapons is presented in brief, condensed form as follows:

Mortar: This is a light smooth-bore cannon about 81 mm., weighing, without mount, about 40 pounds. The mount, base plate, and mortar total 134 pounds in three equal loads. The light shell weighs 7 pounds, with a range of 100-3000 yards. The heavy shell weighs 15 pounds with a range of 100-1200 yards. The rate of fire is normally 10-15 per minute, but for short strings can be raised to 1 round every 2 seconds.

Light mortar: In general this is a smaller edition of the mortar, about 60 mm., weighing about 15-20 pounds, without mount. Total weight is about 30-40 pounds. Several types of shell are used, giving ranges up to 500-1500 yards.

Rifle grenade: This is a fragmentation bomb which is propelled from a rifle grenade discharger by firing a special rifle cartridge. It has a range of 50-300 yards.

Hand grenade: This is a small, hand fragmentation bomb, sometimes attached to a stick or strap for throwing. Maximum range is about 30+ yards.

The types of hand-to-hand weapons are self-descriptive. The average heavy bayonet weighs about 1 pound, with a 16- to 20-inch blade. The light bayonet, fast gaining in popularity, weighs about one-half pound or less, with an 8- to 10-inch blade. The only modern army using the sword as a real weapon is the Japanese. Trench knives, daggers, etc., have been in part absorbed into the light bayonet.

MOBILITY OF ARMS

"Weapons, to be effective, must be brought to bear on the enemy. They must be mobile." [2]

As we are concerned with the twelve-man squad, primary stress must be laid upon mobility. "The infantry marches under its own power, on foot . . ." [3] This applies most of all to the squad. Therefore we must confine ourselves to weapons which may be readily carried by the individual soldier on foot for a reasonable distance. An examination of the weight statistics tends to eliminate the heavy M.G. and the mortar from the squad. These weapons clearly must be assigned to a special weapons squad.

We are now ready to examine several alternative proposals as regards arming the squad.

A. Give them all one type of weapon.

B. Give part of the squad one type of flat-trajectory weapon and part one type of high-angle fire weapon.

C. Scramble all the weapons together and issue one of each.

D. Study the actual, probable, and possible requirements of the squad on the offense and defense, and issue weapons best suited to the requirements disclosed.

E. In following the above proposal (d), issue as few types as possible, in order to simplify the squad armament, but enough to insure sufficient versatility of fire.

The proposals may now be analyzed in detail.

[2] Colonel Foertsch.
[3] Ibid.

Proposal A

1. Historically the infantry squad carried a rifle with bayonet, two venerable, inseparable, conservative, and time-honored weapons. Supporting fire comes from heavy machine guns and artillery.

2. Train every man to be a sniper. Give him a match rifle with telescope and teach him to get a hit every time he pulls the trigger. Teach him to sneak forward and stalk targets.

3. Give every man a semi-automatic rifle. Teach him to shoot as accurately as training time will permit.

4. Give every man a submachine gun. He cannot hit anything over 200 yards anyway, even if he had a rifle. The submachine gunner can carry more rounds so that he can spray more lead. The real job of the squad is to fight at close quarters.

5. Give every man in the squad a light machine rifle which he can operate as a machine gun at longer ranges, as a rifle or M.G. at medium ranges, and as a rifle or as a submachine gun at short ranges.

6. Assign an L.M.G. to each pair in the squad, one to operate the gun and the other to carry ammunition and act as an assistant.

7. Of what use is flat-trajectory fire when everyone is usually under cover, out of sight? By using light mortars or rifle grenades the entire squad can plaster the enemy in their holes as well as out in the open.

Considerable argument, in favor of the one-weapon squad proceeds upon the propositions that the infantry cannot move without supporting weapons; that the squad is of value only at close range. Therefore, give the squad a rifle or even a submachine gun. If the enemy are really dug in, only heavy mortar and howitzer fire will move or neutralize them, without which support the squad will be useless.

The submachine-gun argument proceeds along the same ground, except that it generally presupposes a poorly trained, somewhat inefficient squad whose members cannot hit anything with a rifle, but who can spray pistol lead at short range. The allegedly realistic concept of the poorly trained squad composed of people who cannot hit anything anyway, is exemplified by a recent cartoon depicting a private soldier in the act of striking a large, docile "Ferdinand" squarely on the stern with a large fiddle, said soldier remarking the while: "The sergeant said I couldn't do it."

The efficacy of accurately aimed, deliberate rifle fire, either from rifles or from semi-automatic rifles has been historically exemplified by the Boers, as well as by the United States Marine Corps and other famous rifle organizations. The tradition in this country of the American Rifleman cannot be ignored. As a regiment, Morgan's Riflemen were inhuman. There are many other similarly famous units.

The view which obtains in some circles that a semi-automatic rifle is not to be used to deliver accurate single shots but rather to blast off generally directed volleys is not founded either upon clear reasoning or upon fact. Those semi-automatic rifles which have been adopted are capable of normal rifle accuracy. However, if rapidity of fire is such a serious disadvantage, then we should return to the single-shot arm and give up the magazine weapon.

The light machine rifle proceeds in a different direction. Provided such an arm can be fired easily and accurately as a semi-automatic, and provided it can be controlled reasonably in automatic bursts, it offers a more versatile weapon than any on the list. A weapon which weighs substantially more than the average rifle (9 to 10 pounds), is not, however, entirely mobile. Nevertheless, for some years the United States Army and Marine Corps have issued one 16-pound Browning Machine Rifle to each 8-man squad, and the B.A.R. man has managed to keep up with the others. The standard British musket of 1775 weighed 15 pounds. The redcoats who lugged those guns plus their packs out to Concord and back to Boston in almost a single stretch were rugged, to say the least.

The question of the mortar and grenade as an exclusive weapon can best be discussed by again quoting Colonel Foertsch:

"It is true that these weapons, whose projectiles act by means of their explosive effect, are not able by themselves to destroy the enemy or to put him out of action except by a lucky hit, nor have they sufficient penetrative power to pierce even relatively light protection."

Proposal B

The proposal to give some of squad members one flat-trajectory type of weapon and the others one high-angle fire type of weapon can be disposed of by re-examining proposal A as to the best flat-trajectory weapon to choose.

The high-angle fire weapons include the light mortar and the grenade discharger. The choice narrows to the problems of relative effectiveness versus relative mobility. The light mortar is a more effective weapon and gives the squad more independence. The grenade discharger is a short-range weapon which presupposes adequate supporting barrages from heavier mortars.

Proposal C

This proposal calls for a scramble of all the weapons. This is not quite so simple as would appear. Some analysis is essential.

1. We rule out those weapons which weigh above 25 pounds on the ground of mobility.

2. We have twelve men to whom the following weapons must be distributed: Medium L.M.G., L.M.G., L.M.R., semi-automatic rifle, sniping rifle, rifle, submachine gun, pistol (or revolver), bayonet, light mortar, grenade discharger, hand grenade.

Actually there are ten main weapons plus the auxiliary bayonets and hand grenades.

The medium L.M.G. and the L.M.G. require two men each. The squad leader carries the pistol. The rifleman, mortar men, grenadier, and submachine gunner carry grenades. The rifleman uses a heavy bayonet; the semi-automatic rifleman, a light or heavy bayonet. The gunners carry daggers.

This would seem a most imposing array. The chief drawback is this: suppose the short-range personnel were casualties at long range and the heavier long-range weapons proved too clumsy for quick shoulder shooting at short range. For example, the medium L.M.G. and the L.M.G. are not adapted for snap shooting at 50-100 yards. The light mortar is limited to a minimum range of 100-150 yards.

Another objection is the fact that within one squad there would
be a great diversity of ammunition and ammunition loading, as
well as weapons. Of course the antidote for this is simple: make
up uniform squads, each one of which has weapons of the same
kind. Again there exists a serious objection, as expressed in the
quotation from Colonel Foertsch at the beginning of this chapter: the infantry must have versatile weapons, so organized that
the quickest possible co-operation is assured.

Proposal D

This proposal calls for an examination of actual, probable, and
possible requirements of the squad. To do this we must have
in mind not only a general picture of the squad in normal action
but also a brief picture of the squad in less likely though none
the less important engagements.

First we should consider the general picture of the squad in
attack.

1. The squad moves swiftly by truck or automobile to a designated point, from which they move forward on foot with full
ammunition allowances. As they proceed toward the enemy positions (strong points disposed in depth), they are protected by
the supporting fires of the heavier weapons echelons.

2. Hostile fire, however, soon forces deployment, and the squad
proceeds in skirmish line.

3. As the squad comes within 600-1200 yards of the enemy
infantry positions, heavy machine gun, light artillery, and mortar fires are added, while gradually the heavier weapons' barrages
diminish. Supporting tanks may appear, hunting out machine
gun, light artillery, A.T., and mortar crews, firing upon hostile
infantry rifle groups and light machine-gun crews.

4. Now the squad is forced to cover. Hostile strong points are
within 300-900 yards. Hostile machine-gun fire is coming from
both flanks. A light mortar is ranging the position. Several of
the squad rise and slink forward. They take cover in a ravine.
They observe a light machine-gun crew, range 500-800 yards.
They fire on this target while several more of the squad move
forward and engage the mortar. Gradually all of the members
of the squad work their way forward. The movements of some

are covered by those others who have reached favorable positions from which to deliver covering fire.

5. The squad is now generally within 300-500 yards of the enemy positions. Supporting fires of the heavy machine guns, mortars, and light artillery have partially lifted and begin to cover enemy reserve positions. Enemy tanks and A.T. guns have neutralized supporting tanks. The squad is now entirely on its own.

6. Hostile rifle, light machine gun, and light mortar fires are intense. Taking advantage of every bit of cover, crawling, slinking, and by short, irregular rushes, the squad closes within 50-150 yards of a hostile strong point. Hostile resistance is reduced to rifle, light machine gun, and rifle grenade fires. Occasionally bursts from submachine guns may be delivered.

7. Members of the squad have closed in on a hostile L.M.G. crew under cover of supporting fire from other members of the squad. As they are about to rush the last twenty yards they are met with hand grenades. While the enemy crew are thus engaged, others of the squad put the L.M.G. out of action with fire at close range.

8. Having forced a local withdrawal, the squad proceeds further into the enemy positions, being met with additional rifle, machine gun, and mortar fire. As they push on, members of the squad observe a light howitzer crew, a mortar crew, and a heavy machine-gun section firing upon other units of the attacking force. These targets are 800, 500, and 300 yards off, respectively. Due to the general confusion and intermingling of forces, heavy weapons' fires are impossible. The problem rests with the squad.

9. At length the squad reaches the objective, a designated ridge. Here the attacking units re-form.

10. Suddenly the enemy launches a counterattack. The squad takes positions and prepares to stop the attack.

11. The squad is heavily shelled and stays under cover. When the barrage lifts, enemy infantry can be seen fleetingly as they move forward. The squad leader observes an L.M.G. crew moving forward at 400-700 yards. A mortar is firing from a gully 500 yards away.

12. To the left flank an accompanying gun is being moved into position 600 yards off.

13. The enemy move in closer. Here and there riflemen and gunners may be seen briefly as they move from cover to cover. The supporting fires of both sides have lifted.

14. As the enemy infantry close within several hundred yards, the defensive fires become intense. A few of the attackers reach within several dozen yards of the defense, but these are stopped by hand grenades and point-blank rifle fire. As the attackers fall back in confusion, the squad pours in a heavy fire, followed by pursuit of the enemy.

Although the above may be described as a general picture of the operations of a squad, nevertheless there are many minor variations. The squad may perform special missions. Moreover, the operations may be on islands, along beaches, in tropical jungles, in northern forests, along rivers, in snow-clad mountains, or on deserts, rolling plains, pampas, in the middle of cities and towns, in places where the road bed is heavy, in places where there are no roads at all.

The squad may be carried within close sight of the enemy in automobiles. Tanks may predominate in one action, be entirely helpless in another. If the German attack on France was any indication, an infantry squad may find itself miles inside the enemy lines, or rather, to be more exact, deep within enemy defensive combat groups. Our nice, orderly concept of even, orderly lines of units, with each class of weapons in just the right place, is dangerously misleading.

German artillery carried rifles in France because often the artillery was firing with French infantry close by. For that matter, German infantry had plenty of accompanying artillery, some of the guns being mounted on tank chassis.

The French lacked the most vital element of a successful defense, a strong offense. When the Germans seized France by the throat, the French tried to protect their throat. Instead, they should have been prepared to punch the Nazi midriff.

As a graphic picture of the end of a French infantry position, the following extracts are taken from a recent story by the well-known George Surdez, portraying a local action in France in the year 1940.[4]

"Sights, seven hundred, seven hundred—" Franchard called.

"Seven hundred—" the group commanders repeated.

An armored car had appeared, followed by several larger vehicles, troop-lorries. The remaining thirty-seven went into action, with swift, deep, barking explosions. This time, the shells took effect, for the car lurched, seemed to spin, and ended with its nose in the ditch. Courton yelled his satisfaction with the others. This was the first cheering sight they had seen in quite some time.

The fire of the automatics, even at that range, proved good. Many men, alighting from the lorries, were caught by it and dropped. The survivors ran swiftly into the fields, fell prone, became invisible. They used their own rapid-fire small arms, a new sound started, which would not end for a long time, the pattering and chipping of bullets on stones and bricks.

More infantry appeared three hundred yards behind the first, probably come from lorries stopped out of sight. At first, there were long lines of men stringing across the plain, then those lines dissolved into small groups that came forward.

That was the beginning of a new phase of combat, a patient, dogged approach. The enemy's combat groups functioned smoothly, progressing without haste, alternating like the pistons of a machine, coming nearer, nearer.

Six hundred—five hundred—"

And at five hundred, the Legionnaires had another moment of pleasure: The enemy was nailed to that limit. There were fifteen to twenty French automatics available, handled by men who were recovering their combat calm rapidly, men taught in the best school in the world. Here was one thing in which the defenders matched their efficient foes—combat group firing. And they made the most of it.

Anything that attempted to walk, run or crawl beyond that fatal five hundred meter limit was at once caught in a curtain of bullets, dispersed, shattered.

Two men refilled the metal magazines for each gun. The long clips of twenty-five clattered on and off in seconds. And the barrels started to smoke, each group was clustered around one of the little monsters, as they trepidated and shook.

Another long line of Germans, very far off, doubled over the fields, came within extreme range, dispersed and advanced in groups, to reinforce the front. Estimates of the number of men facing them went from group to group.

The storm of explosions ended, the infantry appeared again. Supporting groups fired so furiously that the air seemed a solid sheet of humming death. Warped lead and stone chips screamed everywhere. But the automatics hammered again, the advancing knots of men melted, gray-clad bodies strung out for fifteen, twenty, twenty-five yards. A whistle stopped the attack.

Clouds of steam rose as canteens were emptied over the barrels. The faint glowing vanished. Captain Franchard touched Courton's shoulder.

"At least forty went down this time. They're paying for this company, at any rate. Next time they advance, try this gun on the supports—they were crowding up in bunches."

"Understood, Captain."

Courton gave him a hand rolling a big barrel before a vent, an opening fourteen inches wide, protected by iron bars an inch thick. He panted and perspired, but followed instructions. Franchard hoisted himself to the top of the barrel, crouched there, half-kneeling, half-squatting. He held an automatic rifle, and there were a dozen full magazines handy.

"They'll be coming in—in a minute—hand me the stuff as I need it—that's the lad—" the Captain laughed: "They're four minutes late already. Doesn't mean much, but any little helps, eh, my big friend?"

The automatic hammered quickly, filling the vault with fumes and sounds. Some men had placed barrels beneath the second vent, and were using rifles.

"Cartridges—"

Courton passed up a full magazine. The shooting resumed.

"That's startled them," Franchard said, resting the butt of the gun on the barrel-head, keeping his eyes directed outside. "They were all in a bunch." He laughed: "They're behind the trough now. Allah! How they can use shelter. Must be twelve or more of them, and you can't see a helmet, not one. Say, it's no joke firing this way. I've got a kink in my side—eh—eh—"

Meanwhile, only one gun was being fired now, clips of three: One, two and three, pause, one, two and three—adjusted, deliberate shooting. The two struggling soldiers suddenly froze, looking upward.

A black object had rolled to the brink of the vent, was poised as if about to halt. Instinctively, their heads sank between their shoulders. It was stopping, it would—no, its momentum had lasted a tenth of a second too long, it quivered on the edge, started to drop . . .

The grenade exploded between the vent and the barrel's head.

Proposal E

Under section Proposal D a brief study of the squad in action was considered. In this section we are to issue to the squad the widest possible variety of weapons to give the squad versatility of fire.

As a general proposition we may commence with the medium L.M.G. Experience indicates that four men must be assigned to this gun. However, the crew members may be armed as follows:

Number 1—L.M.G.
Number 2—Rifle or a semi-automatic rifle
Number 3—Submachine gun and extra ammunition for the L.M.G.
Number 4—Crew leader—pistol or a submachine gun

Eight men are left in the squad. One may be armed with the light mortar. If so, he requires an assistant, probably rifle-armed. Or these two men may carry rifles with grenade dischargers.

Six men remain. Of these, one may be armed with a sniper's rifle, having a detachable telescope. With the sniper may be the second-in-command, armed with a rifle or semi-automatic rifle.

Of the four remaining, one is the squad leader who may carry a submachine gun or a pistol. The other three may be armed as follows:

A. Three rifles
B. Three semi-automatic rifles
C. One L.M.R., one semi-automatic rifle, one submachine gun
D. One sniper rifle, two rifles (or semi-automatic rifles)
E. One sniper rifle, one rifle (or semi-automatic rifle), one submachine gun

All the riflemen and submachine gunners carry grenades, and the rifles may be equipped with a bayonet if needed (night attacks, heavy fog, etc.).

Specific recommendation is impossible at this stage. Proposal F may serve to clarify our thoughts.

Proposal F

Here we take the view that we desire to simplify the squad armament without seriously impairing versatility. Specifically we desire to accomplish the following:

1. Uniform loading
2. Accurate rifle fire
3. Rapid, accurate rifle fire
4. Volume fire, or bursts at long range
5. Effective enfilading fire
6. Effective high-angle fire
7. Close combat high-angle fire
8. Maximum mobility
9. Rapid application of fire

Therefore we must make reductions to common denominators, so to speak. First of all, we need two light mortars or two grenade dischargers.

Next we must consider what weapons are the most versatile. Regardless of our personal predilections we must all admit that the light machine rifle leads the rest, with the less mobile L.M.G. a close second, and the more mobile semi-automatic rifle a close third. The dangerous limitation on the submachine gun is its short range.

We have, then, the following possible solutions:

1. Squad leader with rifle (or semi-automatic rifle), two rifle grenade dischargers, two L.M.G.'s, seven rifles (or semi-automatic rifles). Of the latter seven riflemen, two are assigned to the L.M.G.'s as assistants, and two more may be used as assistants in emergency.

2. Squad leader with rifle (or semi-automatic rifle), two rifle grenade dischargers, three L.M.R.'s, three semi-automatic riflemen assisting the L.M.R.'s, three semi-automatic riflemen.

3. Squad leader with rifle, two grenadiers (as usual), four L.M.R.'s, four rifles (may act as assistant L.M.G.'s), one sniper rifle.

4. Squad leader with submachine gun, two light mortars, four L.M.G.'s, four L.M.G. assistants with submachine guns, one sniper.

5. Same as above, except three L.M.G.'s, three assistants with submachine guns, and three extra submachine guns (emergency L.M.G. assistants).

However, several of the above proposals are not consistent with the requirement of simplification. We must rule out some weapons. Also, we must face some realities.

For the basic squad the submachine gun appears dubious, though it certainly has many uses elsewhere.[5]

The medium L.M.G. may serve excellently as a special squad weapon of the platoon or company. But that is another story. The L.M.G.—but preferably the L.M.R.—belongs definitely in the squad. The light mortar is not too light. The rifle grenade discharger or an equivalent 50-350 yard weapon is essential if there is lacking a light mortar effective at 50-150 yards, as well as up to 300-500 yards. The average light mortar seems better suited to the platoon's special mortar squad. It is not easy to lay the high-angle fire weapon accurately for ranges over 300 yards without more elaborate mounts than the squad is adapted to employ.

The rifle or the semi-automatic rifle—one or the other—is essential to the squad. The trend is toward the semi-automatic arm. The L.M.R., as well as the L.M.G., may be fired semi-automatically. The L.M.R. can be handled from the shoulder as a rifle. The L.M.G. is not well adapted for this purpose.

Sniping can be carried out with a semi-automatic having special sights, and possibly a telescope.

Suppose we consider a squad as follows:

Squad leader: Semi-automatic rifle
Second-in-command: Semi-automatic rifle
Scout: Semi-automatic rifle
Scout: Semi-automatic rifle with scope, special sight
Gunner: L.M.R.
Ass't: Semi-automatic rifle

[5] The new United States Army Short Rifle M1 (SR M1), weighing 5 pounds, eliminates some of the disadvantages of the submachine gun here.

Emergency Ass't: Semi-automatic rifle
Gunner: L.M.R.
Ass't: Semi-automatic rifle
Emergency Ass't: Semi-automatic rifle
Grenadier: Rifle grenade discharger
Grenadier: Rifle grenade discharger

This squad may be grouped as follows:

Squad leader
Sniper scout
Gunner
Rifleman (ass't)
Rifleman (emergency ass't)
Grenadier
Sub-leader rifleman
Rifleman scout
Gunner
Rifleman (ass't)
Rifleman (emergency ass't)
Grenadier

Riflemen are issued hand grenades. The emergency assistant gunners are used for the L.M.R. chiefly on the defense. The grenadiers may also serve as riflemen at ranges over 400-500 yards if required. (Example: Beach defense, delivering fire on troops landing. Or fire on flat, entirely open terrain where high-angle fire is useless.)

The squad armament chiefly consists of:

Light machine rifles................   2
Semi-automatic rifles 9 (10)
Sniper semi-automatics   1
Grenade dischargers   2
Hand grenades—Yes (optional issue)
Bayonets—or light bayonets.........   10

In certain situations the squad may be rearranged into two teams, as follows:

Squad leader—four riflemen—two grenadiers
Sub-leader—two gunners—two assistants

Where more intense automatic gun fire of some duration is to be required, as in an extreme defensive situation, another arrangement is as follows:

Squad leader—two gunners—four riflemen (as assistants)
Sub-leader—two riflemen—two grenadiers

In this combination the sub-leader and four men act as ammunition carriers. The three-man gun crews on the L.M.R.'s serve as gunner, loader, and magazine re-loader (i.e., refilling empty magazines for insertion by the loader). Barrel-changing or cooling is also accomplished by the third member. The squad leader directs the fire of the L.M.R. crews. The sub-leader's group is responsible for the flanks and protects the L.M.R.'s from hostile grenadiers, hand grenades, etc. (Example: A withdrawal, defense of a key position, and other special missions, such as a final protective line mission at night using aiming stakes, etc.)

Attention is called to the fact that the combined effective fire of two L.M.R.'s will nearly equal that of one heavy, water-cooled machine gun.

In another aspect, however, the L.M.R.'s are operated purely as semi-automatic rifles. Automatic fire may not be desired or required. Thus the squad has the fire effect of twelve semi-automatic rifles (two grenade dischargers). Actually, the L.M.R.'s have a somewhat greater capacity for semi-automatic fire than the semi-automatic rifle itself.

The sniper should have a specially selected rifle with the best ammunition available. He should be chosen on the basis of marksmanship and scouting qualifications. His telescope should be suited for firing in bad light, as well as for its magnification. The sniper's problem is rather to distinguish targets than to magnify them. The telescope should be easily detachable, iron sights being normally affixed.

The same organization is adaptable to an armament consisting of repeating rifles and L.M.G.'s. As stated above, the medium L.M.G. is believed insufficiently mobile for the squad.

Weapons of the medium L.M.G. type are best suited for a separate echelon of the rifle company, or for special units. Mounted on a tripod, this weapon furnishes a base of fire for the rifle platoons. More mobile than the heavy water-cooled gun, it has, nevertheless, a capacity for sustained fire greater than that of the L.M.G. or L.M.R.

FOREIGN TRENDS

Having analyzed the various possible choices of weapons for the squad, it is proposed to compare the foregoing conclusions with actual modern trends.

The German squad or *gruppe* consists of two teams. Four men compose the medium L.M.G. crew, seven the rifle team, and the group leader makes the thirteenth. The sub-leader is with the rifle team.

Of the L.M.G. team, #1 is gunner, #2 is assistant, #3 is rifle-armed, and #4 is probably armed with a submachine gun. Numbers 2 and 4 at least carry pistols. The two teams are separated in deployment, the interval rarely exceeding 80 yards. The German medium L.M.G. weighs about 24 pounds.

An examination of recent German thought indicates the following significant points:

1. Speed of attack depends chiefly upon the individual soldier's mobility. He must be given the lightest weapons practicable. The heavy pack is out. Infantry organization is in a state of flux.

2. The closest concentration of fire, both as to time and space, is characteristic of modern fire tactics.

3. Surprise effect is a decisive factor in gaining fire superiority, and such surprise effect can and should be achieved by all units, including the squad.

4. Fire superiority is gained chiefly by automatic weapons.

5. The squad moves forward as close as possible before opening fire, but since heavy-weapon support in practice fails to cover the squads at ranges closer than 300-700 yards, the squads must have their own independent, self-supporting fires.

6. The riflemen of the squad "cover the enemy with well-aimed rifle fire, in order to break completely his will to resist." [6]

7. The squad fire from cover and seek surprise effect. They

---

[6] Quoting Colonel Altrichter, Director of the German Kriegschulo.

prepare under cover, suddenly bob up and quickly deliver their fire.

"The calm fire action with the rifle is a thing of the past. The modern rifleman must be trained systematically in rapid fire."[7]

8. Teamwork between the L.M.G. crew and rifle team of the German *gruppe* is admitted to present a difficult problem. Since the L.M.G. is limited to fire between gaps, it must not be as far in rear as the width of the gap.

Thus it appears that the German group with its separate L.M.G. team and medium L.M.G. is not entirely satisfactory. Twenty odd years ago the heavy M.G. frequently failed to keep close enough to the rifle units to help them. The medium L.M.G. today, as a squad weapon to be found in the rifle platoon organization, seems lacking in mobility.

In this connection the British experience with their 21-pound L.M.G. indicates that although the Bren was orginally regarded as a "section" (same as squad) weapon, its lack of mobility as an individual infantryman's weapon caused it to slow down the movements of the riflemen, or else to be left too far behind to be of use.

It is significant to note that the British sought a squad weapon; that the 21-pound L.M.G. is too heavy as a squad weapon; that the German medium L.M.G. is too heavy also as a squad weapon; that the tendency with such weapons is to develop a separate echelon; that such echelons take on a supporting role; that the final outcome is to leave the squads to support themselves with rifle fire only, the very situation it was hoped to avoid.

The Austrian squad consisted of ten men and a leader. There were two men on the L.M.G., one submachine gunner, one sniper, six riflemen.

The Russians have one L.M.G. in each eight-man squad, a separate high-angle fire squad in each platoon.

The Swiss have a thirteen-man squad of two teams, six men in the L.M.G. team, six in the rifle team, and a leader. The French army had practically the same squad organization—six in the L.M.G. team, five in the rifle team including one grenadier, and the squad leader, total twelve.

[7] Ibid.

The United States had an eight-man squad, consisting of the squad leader (rifle-armed), one automatic-rifleman, a rifle-armed assistant, one rifle grenadier, and four riflemen. The Marine Corps at one time included one submachine gunner in place of one rifleman.

The new war-strength United States squad is composed of twelve men; peace-strength, of nine. The L.M.R. (automatic-rifle) is found in a separate squad composed of eight men; two L.M.R. teams of three men each, a leader and assistant leader. Thus, there are two (three in defense) L.M.R.'s per platoon of 35-40 men.

A medium L.M.G. (tripod-mounted, belt-fed, air-cooled machine gun weighing about 24 pounds, mount about 18 pounds) is contemplated for the rifle company. This weapon is not designed for shoulder fire.

As regards the rifle squad, the United States has for some years looked toward the semi-automatic rifle to increase the fire effect of the individual infantryman while not adding unduly to his armament burdens. The current United States squad is armed with the semi-automatic rifle, M1. At least one other government has since followed the United States in adopting a semi-automatic rifle for general issue to troops. At the same time its forces will also be equipped with a light machine rifle some eight pounds lighter than its earlier model L.M.G. Details of the infantry organization contemplated are not available at this time.

Finnish forces in 1939-40 fought close-swarming Russian infantry with submachine guns, rifles, and L.M.G.'s.

The Japanese emphasize the L.M.G., which supports the bayonet-armed riflemen, being the source of most of the platoon fire power. Japanese emphasize the bayonet and sword. Rifle fire is incidental, little emphasized. One reason for this is that the Japanese are not very good riflemen. Another reason is, too many Chinese and too little Japanese ammunition.

The Japanese platoon consists of five eight-man squads, three of which are armed with one L.M.G. (22½ pounds) each, the other two with one 11-pound, 56 mm., grenade thrower each. Riflemen make up the balance of each squad.

In general, it appears that the trend is toward versatile weapons in the squad. The Germans, British, and French in particular sought to obtain an all-round light automatic for the squad. The United States had a light automatic more of the rifle type at the close of the war. The European object was defeated in part by mobility's arch enemy, weight. To obtain weapons comparable to the continental types, the United States has added mounts to the auto-rifle, recently reduced the weight of the heavy M.G., and developed the semi-automatic rifle.

From the viewpoint of the foreign military and technical critics, and purely in the spirit of academic criticism, the United States weakness is, in substance, that the semi-automatic may prove unreliable even for manual reloading under severe combat conditions; that it may unprofitably exhaust the individual's ammunition; that the United States auto-rifle as modified lacks the removable barrel and convenience of re-loading needed in an L.M.G. or L.M.R.; that the medium L.M.G. (or lightened heavy M.G., which it really is) is not suited for semi-automatic fire, lacks the speed of fire application of the European L.M.G. or medium L.M.G. since it is not adapted for shoulder firing (as is the German medium L.M.G., for example).

European weaknesses have already been indicated in other connections. In comparison, the United States auto-rifle can be quite readily fired from the shoulder, operates accurately from the bipod; the United States medium L.M.G. is modified from a very reliable heavy M.G.

Under some conditions, semi-automatic riflemen can fire intense barrages—about 40-50 accurate burst-rounds in a minute. Yanks usually make good shots and are good mechanics.

CONSIDERATIONS

Having examined the United States and foreign trends, it would seem adequate merely to select the best of those systems, or to obtain an average and then copy the most prevalent system.

Nothing could be more inappropriate or ill-advised. While certain useful features may be indicated by these systems, there are a multitude of other factors to be taken into account. Chief among the factors to be dealt with are the following:

1. The characteristics of the people of the nation; their temperament, education, etc.

2. The nature of the terrain, climate, and general conditions where they may fight.

3. The weapons which are available currently in numbers, types, etc.

4. Weapons which can be procured.

5. Whether the nation can procure the best weapons available from other nations or whether it depends upon its own facilities.

6. The military policies of the nation.

7. The attitude of the authorities toward innovations.

8. The condition of the army.

Thus, the Japanese temperament and the type of people found in their army differ widely from those of the United States. The British, though like us in part, have widely scattered colonial and native forces to consider. Germans are more inclined to discipline and group co-ordination than the independent, individualistic American who, like the English, Swiss, and Finns can usually develop into an expert rifleman, whereas the Japanese and Chinese are not well adapted to precision rifle fire.

The Finns fight only in Finland and vicinity. Germany designed an army primarily to defeat France and the Low Countries. The Japanese army is designed primarily for operations in China. Britain fights in extreme climates and on widely assorted terrain. But most of these nations know the probable fields of their operations. The United States forces can never be quite sure of the specific conditions they may face. Here we have on our continent a wide variety of conditions. Then there is South America, Oceania, the Caribbean, possibly Europe, etc., etc.

In the Spanish Civil War a great many weapons left over from the first World War were used. Thus, many old, decrepit L.M.G.'s showed up badly mechanically. The British are fighting with what they have and can get. For example, they have a rifle in production and can get it. The United States has a semiautomatic rifle in production, but no more rifle production. In this case that satisfies both governments, fortunately, but results in different squad equipment.

Many small nations—and some not so small—depend upon foreign-made arms. Thus, the famous German Mauser, as made in Germany, was sold all through South America, as well as to many nations in Europe. Today South America can obtain no German-made weapons. The anti-axis nations seek arms from America.

Some nations, such as Germany, plan ahead, set a general date, and attack at their own pleasure. Others, by being disarmed hope to be left alone. When attack becomes imminent, they try desperately to obtain anything they can get. Others, like the Swiss, remain well armed and hope for the best. Others, like the United States and England, hide their heads in the sand until the smell of their own tail feathers burning causes them to run about clucking and squawking, fluttering one way and then another. During this process a lot of ostrich eggs are broken and the bird loses many of its feathers. When the peace dove's interlude comes again, the ostrich vows that burning tail feathers would have been a far, far better fate, and digs another hole.

The attitude of the authorities towards innovations is a factor of considerable importance. The Germans appear to lead the rest in looking ahead. They foresaw the importance of the machine gun, the magazine repeating rifle, and many other now common weapons. They capitalized on the tank, on the airplane, on parachute troops, on gas, on the use of aircraft to support an attack. They have led the rest of the world in developing anti-tank weapons, aircraft cannon, armored plane cockpits, non-inflammable petrol tanks. Yet the United States is supposed to be the greatest manufacturing nation in the world. The British and ourselves have controlled most of the world's sources of materials. Worst of all, the Germans have adapted many Yankee inventions to their own ends, for we really started the tractor, the machine gun, and the airplane over here.

Logically, one would suppose that weapons should develop because of specific demand for them. While this is often the case, it is more often the fact that the new-type weapon beats on the door for many years. This was true of the single-shot breech-loading rifle, of the military repeating rifle, of the machine gun, of the airplane, the submarine, of the recoiling-barrel light artillery cannon, and many other innovations. For every one that was worth while, there were many crack-brained, useless devices, of course.

If we copy anything from the Germans, it could well be their comparative attitude of alertness toward new and often radical concepts. Colonel Hermann Foertsch has observed that the vanquished always studies hard to improve, whereas the victor is often complacent and static.

It is easy to blame the military attitude in a democracy for any military shortcomings, but the fact is that the public enforces its all-pervading will upon the military policies of our nation. During the piping periods of peace, the United States armed forces are regarded as dangerous, barely necessary, burdensome, though highly ornamental martinets. Public funds are saved by chopping off army-navy money. Comes war, and John Q. Public wants a universe-smashing military-naval machine pronto.

At a recent lecture, the speaker stoutly defended the military power of the country. Said he:

"Indeed, the minuteman of America has never died. A million men can spring to arms over night." Pausing for effect, a voice from the back of the room cried:

"To what arms?"

And another voice answered: "A million men spring to arms in this country every night."

CONCLUSIONS

Gazing into the future through the medium of numerous authorities, including Colonel Foertsch and Colonel Altrichter of Germany, and General Lynch and Lt. Colonel Phillips of the United States, it appears almost certain that the squad, as well as the larger units of which it is a part, will possess more versatile and more powerful armament, and will be designed to operate as independent teams. Moreover, every effort will be made to improve the mobility of the squad on their feet.

In the interests of simplicity, the squad needs weapons of the fewest types consistent with versatility of fires. The trend will be toward versatility of fire followed by uniformity of equipment, because it is always quicker and easier to get a variety of special-purpose weapons than to get more uniform, all-purpose or multi-purpose weapons. Evolution in one aspect consists of integration. Consider the newest howitzers, the history of the machine gun, for example. Or consider the handgun in military history. Today, our War Department is leading the way in seeking a five-pound submachine rifle (S.R.M1.), a weapon seeking to combine the characteristics of the pistol, the European pistol-carbine, holster-stock automatic (i.e., Luger, Mauser pistols), the submachine gun, and a short-range rifle.

Suppose, following this analogy, there were effectively combined the characteristics of the high-powered light machine gun, rifle, and semi-automatic rifle, together with an optional adapter for projecting rifle grenades. If such a weapon weighed little more than the rifle, we might find in it the answer of the future.

A further feature badly needed is a rifle cartridge capable of piercing light tank armor. The ability of the above squad weapon to fire bullets through an inch of armor up to 300-350 yards would result in giving the squad an ever-ready selection, versatile yet at the same time entirely uniform.

Barring this, it is believed that the more immediate future will show a trend gradually to the semi-automatic rifle and light machine rifle or gun in the squad. Those who are able to obtain submachine guns more readily are naturally going to resort to that weapon which will also prove valuable for special purposes. However, the War Department's new submachine rifle with its weight reduction of nearly 50 per cent is likely to shorten the future of the pure submachine gun, especially as a squad weapon.

In the last analysis, the individual infantryman seeks a weapon giving him the maximum fire efficiency consistent with operation and transportation by one of his potential mental and physical ability.

But what he gets when he goes marching off or riding off to war depends upon many things—some of which have been discussed herein.

CHAPTER FIFTEEN

Considerations Affecting the L.M.G.

*The German M34 L.M.G.; The British Bren Gun; The
French Light Hotchkiss; The Japanese Nambu; The
Mendoza L.M.G.; The United States L.M.G.; Conclusion*

THE modern infantry squad, group, or section, consisting
generally of about one dozen men led by a corporal or sergeant, is equipped with some form of automatic weapon, generally known as the L.M.G. or light machine gun.

This gun is customarily served by a crew of from two to four
men. Beyond that lies a chasm of contradiction, for there are
numerous conflicting ideas as to the characteristics, employment,
and utility of the L.M.G. Moreover, some authorities discredit
the term "L.M.G." on the ground that most of the weapons placed
in the light machine gun category are merely "automatic rifles"
or "machine rifles."

Some argue that the clumsy, heavy M.G. is rendered obsolete
by the L.M.G. Others contend that the L.M.G. even in its best
form is too unreliable, cannot deliver sustained fire, and cannot
deliver supporting fires over the heads of friendly troops. In rebut-
tal it is alleged that the L.M.G. can go along with the troops,
hence need not fire overhead. And the opposition replies that 20-
pound L.M.G.'s are not "light" and cannot be kept up with the
riflemen. And so the argument runs on.

It is proposed, therefore, to examine the various factors involved and attempt to present some solutions.

Men are invariably influenced by previously formulated conceptions when studying a new problem. Our conception of the
machine gun is very firmly fixed in our minds. It is a heavy firearm set on a heavy tripod mount. It has a belt and perhaps a

water jacket. Someone sits behind it, grasps the handle, and fires long bursts. Five or ten men are required to take care of it.

This "concept" gun is the backbone of the infantry defensive. You set up numerous crossfires, final protective lines, etc. You mow down the enemy when he attacks. Set up enough heavy machine guns and get enough ammunition and the attack must be stalled.

We conceive of the light machine gun as exemplified by a magazine-fed weapon having a shoulder stock and a two-legged mount. It is air cooled. There is usually an assistant or two beside the gunner.

In an attack the gunner directs assault-fire bursts at the enemy positions from the hip. He does not hit anything but he is "pinning them to the ground." On the defense the gunner shoots at gaps in the final protective line. This completes the picture, except that all machine guns fire from the flanks. You do not shoot to the front. Apparently you go quietly and very circumspectly to the front, and then you shoot almost parallel to the front or at a slight angle and catch the enemy on their flank with enfilading fire.

To eliminate any undue confusion, the L.M.G. is described by some authorities as a "weapon of opportunity." You just carry the L.M.G. around and if anything pops up, you pop it down. All of which prompts an inquiry into the subject of the L.M.G., as of 1941.

In the beginning, machine guns were regarded as artillery and handled as such. Mechanically they were somewhat complicated, unduly heavy, and not entirely reliable. The military mind was dimly aware of the value of sudden applications of intense small-arms fire from a single source upon personnel in close formations. The Germans were especially quick to grasp the importance of the machine gun, but many other countries viewed with alarm the tendency of M.G.'s to exhaust ammunition. Volume of fire from small arms could be obtained from rifles in crashing volleys, not unlike the belly-tearing blasts of eighteenth-century muzzle loaders fired by well-drilled automatons in close ranks. As a concession to radicalism, however, two heavy machine guns were assigned to a regiment, these to be employed as little as possible.

The three outstanding heavy machine guns of the period 1890-1918 were the Maxim (also known as the Vickers Maxim), the Colt Browning, and the Hotchkiss.[1]

The Colt Browning was succeeded by the Model 1917 Browning, but neither weapon was used to any extent by the United States Army in 1917-18, although some Colts were used by the Canadians and Russians.

The Maxim (German), Vickers (British), and Hotchkiss (French) were heavy guns weighing a total of about 100 pounds each with suitable mounts. All three were originally developed, along with the early Colt Browning, prior to 1900.

Probably one of the earliest "light" machine guns was the Benet-Mercie, a modified model of the Hotchkiss, weighing about 30 pounds, with bipod mount. The Benet was used by the United States Army from 1909 to 1916. It appears to have been unpopular from a mechanical point of view and is understood to have failed badly in the war in Mexico of 1916. It is not improbable that the Benet created an unfavorable attitude in the United States toward guns of its class.

Probably the most outstanding L.M.G. in the first World War was the Lewis, a 28-pound, bipod-mounted, drum-fed, gas-operated weapon, resembling the Benet in some respects but differing from the Benet's strip-fed and breech-locking mechanism.

The Lewis was used extensively by the British from 1916 on. More portable than the Vickers and easier to produce, the British used the gun as a front-line automatic to equal the effective fire of several dozen riflemen. It seems generally to have been regarded as a source of concentrated rifle fire.

The Germans used a modified form of Maxim known as the "light" Maxim, a rather heavy gun, nevertheless. They also used the Madsen L.M.G., a magazine-fed, bipod- or tripod-mounted shoulder weapon weighing about 20 pounds.

The French had a light Hotchkiss and in addition the famous Chauchard, known as the "Chauchat" or "Chautchaut." This 19-pound weapon was of the machine rifle or "auto-rifle" category, having a detachable magazine and an auxiliary bipod. Clumsy

[1] A complete survey of the development of machine guns is included elsewhere in this book.

and mechanically unreliable, it nevertheless saw much service and was used considerably on the offense, fired semi-automatically from the hip as a source of intense "assault" fire. Fired full automatically from the hip or shoulder, its burst was very wild.

At the close of 1918 the Browning machine rifle made its appearance, a much more satisfactory shoulder automatic than the Chauchard though no more easily controlled. This 16-pound automatic was usually fired semi-automatically and was in one aspect a compromise for a semi-automatic rifle. Lacking a removable barrel and mount and having a distinct tendency to climb in automatic fire, the B.A.R. has served more as a squad semi-automatic rifle than as an L.M.G., though it has recently been modified by adding a bipod mount and reducing the cyclic rate of fire.

During the past twenty-two years the L.M.G. has made considerable advances, especially in Europe. In fact, the L.M.G. has nearly supplanted the common rifle as the basic infantry arm. So many factors have influenced the trend of various nations toward certain types of L.M.G.'s, that it is necessary to consider the guns of certain representative nations in turn. Because of a belated influence upon modern military thought in the democracies, the German L.M.G. may first be considered, followed by the British and French, the Japanese, and the United States.

THE GERMAN M34 L.M.G.

The current German L.M.G. is an excellent illustration of a military weapon designed under the influence of somewhat diverse considerations.

It should be recalled that after 1918 the German army were deprived of most of their weapons and reduced to a mere police force. In short, Germany started with a clean slate, having practically no Maxim or Madsen machine guns, no aircraft machine guns, and for some years a general restriction upon any rearmament.

In order to equip the army allowed them by the Versailles Treaty, the Germans were forced to make a very little armament go a very long way. Thus, in considering a suitable machine gun they were definitely under the influence of this restriction. The ideal solution to their problem was an all-purpose gun, one which could be employed like the Lewis, from a bipod, with a magazine or drum, yet one which could be fired from a tripod, with a belt. Such a gun should be air cooled and suitable for tank and aircraft use. Above all, it had to be cheap and easy to produce.

No doubt influenced by their experience with the Maxim and Madsen, the Germans adopted the recoil-operated, 26-pound Solothurn, known as the M34. This gun is air cooled, and may be fired semi-automatically as well as automatically, having two separate triggers. The Solothurn has three interchangeable types of feed: a 20-shot detachable box magazine mounted horizontally from the side, a 40- or 50-shot kidney-shaped drum, and an open-link belt-feed system. The shoulder stock is straight and in line with the bore, thus minimizing the climb. Due to the shape of the stock, the sights are high above the bore, thus avoiding heat waves. The barrel is detachable.

The Germans use this gun for many diverse missions, including parachute-troop service. One gun is assigned to each twelve-man group, of which four men serve the L.M.G. Riflemen of the group advance by rushes under cover of short, intense bursts from their L.M.G., as well as from short strings of quickly delivered aimed fire from individual Mausers. Defiladed positions are engaged by light mobile mortars, and at close range by familiar "potato-mashers" which German infantry habitually carry in their field boots.[2] On the defensive—when, as, and if the Germans are put on the defensive—the M34 is suited for fire on final protective lines from a tripod mount.

On the whole, the M34 appears to be a reliable weapon. However, it is not equal to the heavy water-cooled Browning for sustained fire, nor is it a truly mobile squad weapon. Provided motor transport is available, the M34 may be moved up within a short distance of the enemy. Such was the case in France in 1940. Under less convenient conditions the M34 will prove somewhat difficult to carry on foot, or to move very rapidly from one position to another. Fired from a tripod it is not likely to prove as stable for overhead fire as the heavier guns, yet due to its weight it cannot comfortably be fired as a one-man shoulder weapon.

[2] Tactical considerations are covered more specifically in Chapter 14.

It may be described as too light for heavy work and too heavy for light work. Perhaps to cover up the clumsiness of the M34 the Germans have gradually increased the number of submachine guns issued to their infantry. It is believed that one Schmeisser or Suomi 9 mm. gun is being issued to each four-man L.M.G. crew and possibly one or two per group. These weapons provide intense short-range fire in a 10-pound special-purpose shoulder weapon.

Further reference to the M34 will be made in other connections.

THE BRITISH BREN GUN

The British were definitely influenced by their experience with the Lewis gun in 1916-18. The following quotation from the British *Text Book of Small Arms* (1929), page 154, indicates the background of the now well-known Bren.

The conspicuous advantage in fire power obtained by the German Army in 1914 by the extensive use of the machine gun necessitated immediate steps being taken by the Allies to increase their own machine gun armament. In the British Army the number of guns of the Maxim type was increased as rapidly as possible, but their production could not keep pace with the expansion of the army. Consequently the Lewis gun was introduced, and the new units were armed with it in place of the Vickers, as through certain modifications and the lapse of the old patents the Maxim has now come to be called.

As the war progressed it was found that the mobility of the Vickers was insufficient to allow it to keep pace with infantry in the attack. and the need for a lighter form of automatic weapon which could be carried easily by a single man became evident. The purpose which such a gun was required to fulfil did not call for the capacity of the Vickers for sustained fire, nor ordinarily for use at long ranges, and the Lewis and Hotchkiss were adopted to fill the gap. The Lewis being the more accurate was adopted for infantry purposes, and the Hotchkiss, being more robust and better shaped for carrying in a bucket, for cavalry.

At the end of the war the bulk of the fire power of the infantry unit was supplied by automatic weapons, and the principle of fire with movement had been developed to make the greatest possible use of them.

With the increase in the number of light machine guns to 2 to a platoon, the tendency is now for them to be pushed forward when the enemy had been located in order to pin him down while the rifle sections maneuver. For this purpose the Lewis gun has two disadvantages, its weight is too great and it is too liable to stoppages. Consequently a new problem has arisen, that of the production of a weapon which shall be of lighter weight and increased reliability, and yet equal in accuracy and in volume of fire to the Lewis. In dealing with this problem the needs of all branches of the Service must be taken into account, since it is undesirable for many obvious reasons that a variety of weapons should be in use, each specially suitable for one particular branch.

The Bren gun was developed in Brno,[3] Czechoslovakia, after the first World War, in 7.92 mm. The British tested models of the Brno product, known as the Z.B., as well as modified Hotchkiss, Browning (B.A.R.), Farquhar, Madsen, and other guns. Apparently the contest narrowed down to the Brno and Madsen. About 1930 the British War Office decided to proceed with the Czech gun in .303 caliber. Since the Brno gun was made at the Royal Small Arms Arsenal, Enfield Lock, it was called the BR-EN, or Bren Gun.

The Bren is a gas-operated, magazine-fed, bipod-mounted, 21-pound L.M.G. The action was believed superior to the Lewis in that it avoided the somewhat troublesome Lewis turning bolt, gas-rod-actuated camming system. The Bren uses a wedge-type block, linked to the operating rod. The feed is of the conventional staggered vertical box type, holding 30 rounds, mounted on top of the gun. The sights are necessarily offset on the left side. The stock is straight. A folding bipod and hinged shoulder support are provided. The barrel is quickly removable, of the air-cooled type. The gun is cocked with the bolt open, may be fired fully- or semi-automatically. Cyclic rate of fire is about 450-500 per minute.

In general the action and feed are simpler than the Lewis, the gun weighs about five or six pounds less. The magazines can be shifted in about 3-4 seconds by the assistant gunner, so that the maximum deliverable fire is in excess of 200 rounds per minute.

[3] Present-day spelling is Brünn.

The British have had three main difficulties with the Bren. Due to their use of the rim-cased .303, magazine, feed trouble has been noted. Due to cordite powder in the .303, the Bren heats up rapidly, requiring frequent barrel changing. Due to the design of some of the parts, production of the Bren has not been easy.

The tactical employment of the Bren is similar to that of the German M34. It is the basic infantry weapon of the British army around which the riflemen cling in maneuver. British authorities have complained that the 21-pound Bren with its unusually heavy magazines either lags behind the riflemen it should support or slows down the movement of the entire unit.

The British have developed a small, light-armored vehicle known as the Bren carrier, which transports one Bren and one .55 caliber Boys AT rifle (34-pound bolt-action rifle). It is also used for radio communication to artillery posts.

The Bren is regarded as the all-round automatic, filling the role of a machine rifle, L.M.G., and heavy machine gun. Fired semi-automatically, it is reasonably accurate. Its normal maximum combat range is said to be 1000-1200 yards. It is not used for overhead fire although it may be mounted on a multi-legged folding tripod which also serves as an AA mount if required.

It is understood that one Bren gun is assigned to every seven men. There has been some confusion about the British organization in this respect, for until recently sufficient Bren guns for such a distribution were lacking.

THE FRENCH LIGHT HOTCHKISS

This 7.5 mm., 20-pound, gas-operated, magazine-fed, bipod-mounted L.M.G. was in general very much like the Bren. It was developed after the first World War. The magazine was the single-column, detachable-box type, holding 20 or 25 rounds, mounted on top of the gun like the Bren to facilitate feed, yet permitting the gun to be placed close to the ground.

THE MENDOZA L.M.G.

Developed by the Mexican inventor, Mendoza, this gas-operated, magazine-fed, 18.5-pound, bipod-mounted, 46-inch, light machine gun is the Mexican army model of 1937, caliber 7 mm.

The gas action of the Mendoza resembles that of the Lewis, in that the turning bolt is unlocked by a cam arm operating in a cam path cut in the body of the bolt.

Unlike many other gas-operated arms, the Mendoza barrel may be removed quite as quickly as the Bren. The barrel-locking arm is swung out to the right of the receiver, thus disengaging transverse lugs from slots in the barrel, which may then be removed from the front. The bipod is attached to the barrel.

The gun is cocked with the bolt open for full- and semi-automatic fire. The striker is actuated by the bolt closure and has the unique feature of being formed with double ends so that if one point should break, the unit may be reversed and the other point used.

The gas port is slightly to the rear of the center of the barrel and the short, tubular cylinder is attached to this unit. The piston enters this open-ended tube as the barrel is assembled. The travel of the piston inside the cylinder is about two inches. When cocked the piston is outside of the cylinder. The gas port is adjustable.

This weapon is fired with bipod and shoulder plate. The 20-shot single-column box magazine is located perpendicularly on the top right side of the receiver.

This weapon is unusually neat, simple, and easy to disassemble. It does credit to this American nation which developed the earlier Mondragon gas-operated, semi-automatic rifle of 1912-14 and which has manufactured the excellent Mexican army Mauser and 7 mm. ammunition, as well as the Mendoza itself.

THE JAPANESE NAMBU

The Nambu is really a modified Hotchkiss, weighing about 21 pounds. The feed consists of a hopper on the left side of the gun which holds six 5-shot clips. The reliability of this feed under all conditions of war is dubious. However, the advantage of continually dropping clips into the hopper while firing cannot be denied. The Nambu is the chief source of infantry fire power. The riflemen shoot rather slowly and only at occasional individual targets.

The Japanese rely very much upon the bayonet and broad-sword, close in under protection of supporting heavier weapons and Nambus. The nature and size of the Chinese army may have influenced the Japanese use of the sword and bayonet from a practical standpoint.

THE UNITED STATES L.M.G.

Strictly speaking, there "ain't no such animal" as the United States L.M.G. The United States Army has recently modernized the Browning Machine Rifle, M1918, by adding a bipod, shoulder support, stock rest, and cyclic rate regulator. One of these guns is assigned to each 12-man squad.

During the past twenty years several modified Brownings have been studied. The cavalry developed an air-cooled heavy Browning on a special tripod mount, gun weighing about 26 pounds, mount about 12 pounds. They also tried out a heavy-barreled, 19-pound B.A.R. with bipod mount. The design of a belt for the B.A.R. was attempted.

None of the heavy Browning modifications includes any shoulder stock. The gun is fired from a tripod only. The present air-cooled Browning is regarded as a highly satisfactory tripod-mounted, belt-fed weapon.

The War Department is at present studying the development of an L.M.G. of the air-cooled Browning type, tripod mounted, belt fed, to weigh 22 pounds, mount to weigh about 18 pounds.

The chief difference in the United States approach to the L.M.G. results from the American idea that the individual rifleman is the true basic fighting unit, whereas the European view regards the L.M.G. squad as the smallest basic unit, made up of several individuals grouped around one L.M.G. In a sense the

United States view regards the L.M.G. as the servant of the riflemen, whereas the European regards the riflemen as servants of the L.M.G.

Having examined the outstanding types of L.M.G.'s in current use, and having allowed our concept of the L.M.G. to be influenced by the developments of the past, we should pause to consider just what in modern combat is required of the L.M.G.

Infantry squads must be mobile and they must have the maximum potential fire power. No time should be lost in getting into action when the opportunity is afforded. The members of the squad must not be unduly exposed to hostile fire while operating or moving with their weapons. Crews serving clumsy, easily spotted guns are inevitably subject to intense hostile fire. L.M.G. crew casualties are necessarily high. It may be dangerous to concentrate such a large proportion of the squad's fire power in one small group. Unless nearly everyone in the squad has an equal amount of fire power the effectiveness of the entire squad may be destroyed.

Perhaps we are still tied down by our previously formulated concept of machine guns and L.M.G.'s. Perhaps we should analyze the role of infantry more broadly.

Primarily, infantry squads move, hit, occupy, hit, move, hit, occupy, hit, move, hit, occupy. In another aspect they move, hit, destroy, move, hit, destroy. They move by truck, airplane, and on foot. They hit with small-arms fire and grenades. They hit suddenly, fiercely, intensely, and for brief periods. They occupy and destroy, or vice versa. They may defend, hence they hit and then move and hit in counterattack. Their fire is of no use if they cannot rapidly reach positions from which to deliver it effectively. A few shots well placed from an advantageous position are worth much more than a volume of shots poorly placed from any other position. One cannot assume that 4 out of 12 men, grouped together to serve a clumsy M.G., are necessarily going to be in the right positions at the right times to deliver the necessary fires.

The trend during the first World War lay toward more automatic weapons of the more mobile types. The trend today is to-

ward more and more automatics. To quote Colonel Foertsch
again: [4]

The fact that fighting, after all, does not consist of uninterrupted,
continuous fire, but rather of moments of great fire intensity, following after long periods of comparative quiet, and of comparatively short
duration as against the time consumed in the entire action, speaks
rather in favor of the employment of still more quick-firing weapons.
It is just these high spots that demand a maximum of fire concentration.

In the extreme, suppose every member of the squad carried an
L.M.G. Impracticable? Of course it would not be possible to go
this far. How about one L.M.G. for each pair of infantrymen?
Burn up too much ammunition. Gun too heavy. But don't we
want intense fire? [5] How about a recent British theory of having
one L.M.G. per three men? Fantastic? Why depend upon sig-
naling for supporting fires? Why not give every squad of twelve
men several field guns and a flock of L.M.G.'s? Ridiculous, of
course, except that Nazi infantry had plenty of accompanying
artillery in France, mounted on tractors, fired at very short ranges.
And their regular artillerymen all carried rifles, too.

Any gun which can be fired automatically requires at least one
or two men to assist the gunner and particularly to carry spare
belts or magazines, as well as spare barrels, parts, mounts, etc.
However, such a gun should be easy for one man to load and
operate alone, at least semi-automatically. In many situations the
gunner may require the gun more as a shoulder rifle to deliver
a few single shots from the shoulder on short notice. Otherwise
the gunner would be quite useless and unprotected on the march
or during a movement between positions. The problem of arming
parachute troops is raising this problem squarely. [6]

---

[4] Col. Hermann Foertsch, *The Art of Modern Warfare,* (*Kriegskunst Heute und
Morgen*).

[5] See also Chapter 14.

[6] Jumping from a height of approximately nine hundred feet, a Marine Corps
parachute trooper carrying in special pockets arranged on his body a caliber
.30-'06 twelve-pound Light Machine Gun in five disassembled parts, reached the
ground and was prepared to fire semi-automatically or full automatically within
two minutes from the time he left the plane. Silhouette targets exposed at slightly
over two hundred yards were hit with semi-automatic fire from the shoulder in
the kneeling position immediately upon opening fire. This trooper together with
his assistant armed with a folding submachine pistol of .45 caliber, then moved

In general L.M.G. fire is delivered in bursts against personnel in groups, or on small areas in which personnel are located. Machine guns preferably deliver flanking rather than frontal fire because of the nature of the cone which is narrow and deep. But L.M.G.'s must of necessity often deliver frontal fire, or fire against individuals in open order. In many instances semi-automatic aimed shots are more effective than bursts. Such fire is much less extravagant, and against widely scattered individual targets it is generally more effective. For such fire the weapon is best operated as a shoulder rifle.

However, the gunner may suddenly observe a small unit of the enemy moving in column on a road; as, for example, a mortar crew, or a heavy M.G. crew, or an A.T. crew. His ability to take position instantly and deliver a few intense bursts may prove highly profitable.

Coming to a suitable gun position, he may nevertheless set up his gun mount, prepare his crew, and deliver barrage fires upon profitable targets requiring a higher degree of accuracy in the distribution of the bursts.

If one L.M.G. has proved helpful to the squad, why not more, provided they are truly mobile? Colonel Foertsch intimates the trend, and the British have indicated their intention of issuing one Bren for every seven men, possibly one per every four men.

The former Chief of Infantry, General Lynch, has pointed out the fact that increasing the fire power of the individual rifle from the B.L. rifle to the magazine arm, to the semi-automatic, does not result in any reduction of the number of infantry employed. Steadily the basic and supporting fire power of armies has been increased. Today infantry units are absorbing some of the types of supporting weapons which originally were too cumbersome and unwieldy for the foot soldier. Thus there has been a steady increase in hitting power per infantry soldier. The combat group has grown smaller in numbers, but there are more groups. Each group has greater hitting power than in the past. Compare a modern platoon with a Napoleonic regiment.

forward by alternate rushes, and fired bursts of full automatic fire at designated areas. This test indicated among other things that parachute troops may jump during cover of darkness fully armed with a powerful weapon, and not dependent upon locating cargo parachutes.

Since the trend is toward an increase in L.M.G.'s, and since the squad weapons must be entirely mobile, a re-examination of L.M.G. characteristics is in order.

In general, the squad L.M.G. should not weigh more than the M1918 Browning Machine Rifle, or 16 pounds, and preferably several pounds less, to allow for a 2-pound mount and loaded magazine.

Despite the need for air cooling, the barrel should not weigh too much as otherwise it destroys the balance of the piece for rapid shoulder firing. The B.A.R. is superior in this respect.

The mount, whether bipod or tripod, should be instantly removable. Otherwise it renders the gun difficult to handle from the shoulder as a rifle. Again the B.A.R. conforms.

The barrel should be instantly detachable for replacement during intense barrage fire. The Bren conforms excellently in this respect, whereas the B.A.R. does not. The Bren is superior to the Solothurn in the speed of barrel changing. Provided the barrel design is simple, it is easier to change barrels frequently, carrying several spares, and allowing a short life for each barrel. A new barrel is not worth over 200-400 rounds of ammunition at current prices. Any air-cooled barrel is doomed to short life as compared with a water-cooled barrel, and the excessive weight of some air-cooled L.M.G. barrels is hardly worth their gain in endurance. For parachute troops the weapon should be easily carried in take-down form, the length of the unit with magazine not to exceed two feet.

The squad weapon is generally limited in the amount of ammunition available at one time for its consumption. It may fire intensively for several hundred rounds at a sustained rate of 50-100 rounds per minute. Barrels can be changed frequently during sustained fire except under desperate circumstances. The average light air-cooled barrel will stand over 1200 rounds at 100 per minute. No L.M.G. is likely to have that much ammunition on hand. A new spare 3- to 5-pound barrel weighs no more than 50-80 rounds of ammunition and is easily carried. Ammunition is more profitably expended through a new bore than through one which is all burned out.

The feed should, if possible, be suitable for sustained fire, be simple, entirely reliable, compact, and permit the gun to be conveniently handled as a rifle if desired.

The Bren feed is very simple and, but for the rimcase .303, quite reliable. However, the French Light Hotchkiss, Bren, and Madsen are not too well adapted for rifle handling, and they interfere with the operator's field of vision. Moreover, they tend to disclose or expose the crew when changing magazines.

The B.A.R. magazine is on the bottom of the gun and prevents lowering the gun close to the ground. The Swiss and Germans use a horizontal box, inserted from the left side of the gun. This has only the objection of bad balance. However, tests indicate this does not seriously impair the handling of the gun.

The M34 has, in addition to the side-mounted box, a drum and a belt feed as well. The drum is heavy and quite complicated. The belt is of the open-link type, depending upon the power of the gun to pull it through the action. This necessitates in part a special means of increasing the barrel recoil to insure power, in turn adding to the complication of the mechanism and increasing the muzzle-heaviness of the gun. The belt tends to render the gun less mobile, and the feed is not likely to be so reliable as with the simpler magazine system. However, the M34 is a very heavy gun and a greater volume of fire is really demanded of it than would be required of the Bren or the B.A.R.

The Nambu hopper system is interesting but depends upon gravity. The Lewis drum proved too unreliable.

Delivered rates of fire depend upon the speed of changing magazines. A belt-fed gun with 100 rounds in a belt, firing at an average cyclic rate of 500 per minute, could deliver nearly 400 rounds in a minute. The heavy Browning will deliver 500 rounds in one minute. The Bren can deliver up to 275 rounds in a minute. The Light Hotchkiss could deliver up to 240 in a minute. The Solothurn with drum magazine can deliver about 300 rounds in a minute, with box magazine about 225 in a minute. The B.A.R. can deliver nearly as many. But such rates of fire can rarely be used in actual practice.

Firing profitable bursts of 3, 4, 5, and 6 shots, and laying the gun accurately for each burst, the normal delivered rate of fire from any L.M.G. is not over 100 rounds per minute and often less. Even the heavy Browning rarely fires over 150 per minute, often much less. This is due to the fleeting nature of targets, the need for shifting or re-laying the piece, and the time required to spot targets, adjust sights, etc.

One man alone can fire 60 rounds in less than 20 seconds from the Bren if necessary, or at a rate of over 180 rounds per minute.

The gun which can be instantly laid on the target and fired intensely for several bursts usually gets more hits than one which requires careful setting up. Even the bipod is not always easily positioned for effective shooting on a moment's notice. The ground is often very poorly suited for a mount. Usually the gun can be rested on the ground, on the edge of a ditch, on a stump, log, low fence rail, etc.

It has been the practice with heavy M.G.'s to site them in pairs, far enough apart to avoid the loss of both from one hit. Two L.M.G.'s instead of one per squad would have many advantages. Two highly mobile L.M.G.'s, each capable of an effective aimed fire of 100 rounds per minute, would substantially equal the effective fire of one heavier-type M.G., yet would be less vulnerable to hostile fire, offer better immediate fire distribution, and engage more targets in a shorter space of time.

The heavier M.G. is more accurate at long range—it must be because it is less mobile. It can deliver more fire over a longer period—it must because it requires more time to move and to prepare to fire. It can fire by indirect laying—it must be able to do so frequently to avoid being quickly silenced by hostile fire.

Infantry groups are forced more and more to operate independently on their own. More and more they require their own supporting weapons.

CONCLUSION

The squad automatic or L.M.G. is likely to be found in increasing numbers. It is also likely to become more of a shoulder weapon and less of a tripod gun.

For stable, accurate fire from a solid mount, such a gun as the water-cooled Browning has few equals. Either the gun can fire safely over friendly troops from positions in the rear—hence it is

Name of Gun	Nation	Weight in Pounds	Mount	Feed	Where Feed Is Located	Caliber	How Cooled	Barrel Detachable	Action	Remarks
Solothurn	Germany	26	Bipod and Tripod	Magazine, drum, Belt	Side magazine, drum, belt under bolt	7·92 mm.	Air	Yes	Recoil	The three feeds may be used interchangeably.
Bren	Britain	21	Bipod and Tripod	Magazine	On top	·303 in.	Air	Yes	Gas	30-shot magazine. Tripod also used for AA mount.
Light Hotchkiss	France	20	Bipod	Magazine	On top	7·5 mm.	Air	Yes	Gas	20- to 25-shot magazine.
Nambu	Japan	21	Bipod	Hopper	Top, side	·256 in.	Air	Yes	Gas	30-shot, clip-fed hopper.
B.A.R.	U.S.A.	16	Bipod	Magazine	Underneath	·30 in.	Air	No	Gas	Bipod recently added.
Browning	U.S.A.	26	Tripod	Belt	On top	·30 in.	Air	Yes	Recoil	Cavalry type.
Madsen	········	20	Bipod	Magazine	On top	Several (8 mm., 6.5 mm., 7.9 mm.)	Air	Yes	Recoil	Used by Denmark, Germany, Holland, and others.
Benet Mercie	········	28	Bipod	Strip	Side	·30 in.	Air	Yes	Gas	Obsolete, U.S.
Lewis	········	28	Bipod	Drum	On top	·303 in.	Air	Yes	Gas	Obsolete, Britain.
Mendoza	Mexico	18.5	Bipod	Box	On top	7 mm.	Air	Yes	Gas	Turning bolt, 20-shot detachable magazine.

a heavy gun; or it delivers fire from points along the skirmish line—hence it is a "light" M.G. and not a "heavy" M.G.

An air-cooled version of the heavy Browning on an equivalent mount could probably deliver nearly equal fire, eliminate the water jacket, and reduce the weight slightly. But for the squad and platoon a handy weapon which can be shoulder-fired is essential. The higher echelons can furnish the heavy M.G., A.T., artillery, heavy mortar, and A.A. support. But the squads need their own, instantly applied and ever-present small-arms fire, both in single shots and in bursts.

It is the function of the truly light mobile, squad automatic to deliver sudden bursts at targets beyond the range of normal rifle fire, though within the extreme range of supporting heavy M.G.'s, whose fires it supplements. Normally this would be from 1200 down to 600 yards.

From 600 yards in, the squad show their teeth. The fast-moving L.M.G. picks off lone targets with single shots, group targets with bursts. Enemy personnel are forced to cover and their small-arms fire is neutralized by L.M.G. and rifle fire. Under cover of its close-supporting L.M.G.'s, the squad reaches enemy groups with grenades.

The situation is well-expressed by Colonel Hermann Foertsch: [7]

The nearer the infantry can work its approach to the enemy, however, the more difficult becomes its safe support by the artillery and the infantry auxiliaries to the rear. The last two or three hundred meters before the enemy position are the hardest. Here, the infantry must help itself with what it has. . . . There are now only two possibilities—either the attack breaks down under the weight of defensive fire effect, or it finds in its own resources the power to carry the men forward to assault at close quarters.

An infantry that believes that it is no longer able to undertake a decisive attack by its own power has, to a great extent, lost its meaning. . . .

The infantry must be strengthened in its attacking power. That is and will remain the most urgent requirement of the moment. To imagine that the limits have been reached, however, is to misunderstand the essence of technology, and to under-rate the fundamental importance of the infantry as part of the army organization.

[7] *Op. cit.*

CHAPTER SIXTEEN

The Problem of Ammunition Supply

The Origin of the Problem; Potential Rate of Exhaustion of Ammunition; Fire Control and Discipline; Loading Technique—Capacity; How the Semi-Automatic Rifle Is Best Employed with Economy; Transporting Ammunition

T HE marked increase in automatic weapons since the first World War presents us with a very serious problem of small-arms ammunition supply.

This problem is especially grave when we consider the semi-automatic rifle, a weapon designed to replace the manually operated bolt-action repeater. Many authorities believe that due to the increased potential volume of semi-automatic rifle fire, the soldier will quickly exhaust all available ammunition. Therefore an analysis of this problem with reference to the characteristics, requirements, and tactical employment of the smaller infantry units in combat is presented.

THE ORIGIN OF THE PROBLEM

The following is quoted from an official test report.[1]

I have seen it stated that celerity of loading and firing might be found objectionable, as *the soldier would too soon expend his ammunition.* . . . I am fully convinced that there is no force to such an objection. The soldier in battle, possessed of a gun that can be instantly reloaded, keeping his eye on the foe, confident of his power

---

[1] From the report of J. Green, First Lieutenant, U. S. Marine Corps, addressed to Colonel John Harris, Commandant, Marine Corps, under date of 6 February, 1860.

and strength (that he is always ready), naturally is inspired with courage and self-possession which are valuable to the soldier. . . . I can see no reason to justify the idea that a soldier qualified with an arm possessing great celerity of fire is likely to waste his ammunition at the first sight of a distant enemy. . . .

It is significant to note that this report was made on the breech-loading Sharp's rifle vs. the muzzle-loader. In other words, some authorities had apparently argued that the breechloader was not suitable for the soldier because it burned up too much ammunition, *as compared with the muzzle-loader.*

The above report concludes: [2]

I . . . recommend its adoption to the Marine Corps, believing, as I do, that such action on the part of the Government will increase *the efficiency of that force more than double its present power.*

When we contemplate the history of weapons, we find that the problem of ammunition supply has bothered the soldier since the advent of projectiles. In fact, supply has often figured as a deciding factor in the outcome of many important wars. We can only touch here upon small-arms ammunition, and the problem of its supply to and within infantry units.

POTENTIAL RATE OF EXHAUSTION OF AMMUNITION

If we assume that a soldier is determined to exhaust his ammunition supply by firing wildly, then we find that the average soldier's ammunition-burning ability is as follows:

Armed with a common bow, the soldier can fire off 1 arrow every 3 to 5 seconds, or about 12 to 20 arrows a minute, or about 120-200 arrows in 10 minutes, or about 1200-2000 arrows in one hour. Of course he is not aiming the arrows. That must be assumed, because if the arrows were aimed, casualties should result, in which case the ammunition could hardly be deemed to have been wasted.

Armed with a muzzle-loading rifle, an expert can fire about 3 shots per minute, or, roughly, about 30 shots in 10 minutes, or

[2] See *The Rifle in America,* by Philip B. Sharpe, pages 188-189.

about 180 shots per hour. Those who are familiar with muzzle-loaders may criticize these figures, yet we venture to assert that the average soldier probably could fire about 2 shots a minute from a rifled muzzle-loader, and 3 to 5 a minute from a smooth-bore musket.

Armed with a single-shot breechloader, the average soldier could probably fire about 10 or 15 shots per minute, or about 100 shots in 10 minutes. In one hour he could fire about 600 rounds.

Armed with the Springfield 1903 (or Mauser 1898, or SMLE, etc.), and *firing by single loading,* the average soldier can probably fire 15 or 20 shots in a minute, unaimed, or 100 shots in from 5 to 7 minutes, or inside of 15 minutes he can fire off 200 rounds, single loading.

The average soldier can discharge from 20 to 30 unaimed shots in 1 minute from a bolt-action repeating rifle, clip loaded. In 10 minutes he can burn up 200 rounds. In one hour he can burn up 1200 rounds, one whole case of ammunition.

Armed with a conventional semi-automatic rifle, the average soldier can discharge about 50-60 shots per minute, or in less than 5 minutes he can consume 200-250 rounds.

The soldier can more seriously damage the supply system by throwing away burdensome items in his pack. He can drop his extra shoes in the ditch, as well as his ammunition belts, etc.

If the soldier is inclined to exhaust his ammunition fruitlessly, he can do so with the bow and the earlier rifles as well as with the semi-automatic.

How long does it take to burn up 200 rounds?

Weapon	Approximate time	No. of rounds
Bow	10-12 minutes	200 Arrows
Muzzle-loader (rifle)	60-80 minutes	200 Loads
Muzzle-loader (smooth bore)	50 minutes	200 Loads
S. S. Breechloader	20 minutes	200 Rounds
Springfield '03 (Single loading)	10-12 minutes	200 Rounds
Springfield '03 (Clip)	6-10 minutes	200 Rounds
Semi-automatic rifle	4-5 minutes	200 Rounds

If we rule out the muzzle-loader, then it appears that in less than half an hour a soldier can burn up 200 rounds, regardless of the arm he is shooting.

Since we expect the soldier to "carry on" for several hours, or even several days, with 100-200 rounds, then, if he is inclined to burn up his ammunition wastefully, it will matter little what weapon he has. Once he is permitted to fire, then away go the arrows, bullets, or cartridges.

So far as the actual prevention of fruitless firing of ammunition is concerned, the answer is found in the next topic.

FIRE CONTROL AND DISCIPLINE

Generally speaking, a semi-automatic rifleman can score at least *twice* as many *hits per minute* as an ordinary rifleman. One leader is essential for every seven or eight riflemen, in order to insure fire control and discipline. *Therefore, one leader is essential for every four or five semi-automatic riflemen.* The new infantry squad provides a sergeant and a corporal for twelve men.

Not only is it necessary to group fewer men per leader because of the semi-automatic rifle, but also because of the fact that the men must be deployed with greater intervals between files due to the increased intensity of the fire brought to bear against them. Such increased deployment in turn reduces the influence which one leader can exert over an eight-man squad.

In this connection we should consider the two basic types of infantry rifle fire—aimed and volley. We may call these the American (aimed) and the European (volley).

As the reader well knows, the French, for example, did not emphasize individual marksmanship. French rifle units actually fire upon *areas* "infested" by the enemy, rather than upon individual targets in such areas.

In direct contrast the American soldier is trained to hit individual targets by aimed fire.

It is not within the scope of this work to discuss the merits and defects in these systems. With respect to ammunition supply we wish to emphasize the fact that *tactical results* must be considered with relation to ammunition consumption.

If, under the American system, the soldier is well trained as a marksman, then, as already stated, he will score at least twice or three times as many hits in the same interval of time, or the same hits in less time, armed with the semi-automatic rifle.

If, under the European system, the soldier is required to cover an area with fire, he can cover at least twice or three times the area in the same time, or cover the same area in less than half the time, armed with the semi-automatic.

To conclude this phase of the discussion, it is submitted that by organization, by practical disciplinary drills, and by marksmanship (target and/or combat firing) practice, the problem of ammunition supply can be solved in this aspect.

LOADING TECHNIQUE-CAPACITY

One means of guarding against profitless ammunition consumption is found in the methods of loading the magazine, as well as in the capacity of the magazine itself.

For example, troops can be ordered to fire by single loading at long range. The semi-automatic can be used very well as a single-loader (about 5-10 *aimed* shots per minute).

Another method is to reduce the magazine capacity, or to use a magazine cut-off, thus preventing the firing of too many quick shots in one "burst."

HOW THE SEMI-AUTOMATIC RIFLE IS BEST EMPLOYED WITH ECONOMY

Primarily, the soldier holds the rifle on his shoulder, and, having adjusted the sights, aims, then squeezes the trigger; aims at the next target, squeezes the trigger; aims at the third target, squeezes the trigger; and so on until there are no targets to shoot at, or until his magazine is empty.

Let us suppose the soldier shoots just short of the target, and has no time to correct his sights. He merely aims higher while squeezing the trigger for the second shot which he can thus deliver instantly.

It seems hardly necessary to call attention to the importance of the semi-automatic for use against strafing airplanes. At such times a sudden, intense volume of fire—5 or 10 aimed rounds in a few seconds—is mandatory.

In another aspect, semi-automatic rifles can be employed as light machine guns, especially in defensive positions where a larger supply of ammunition is available. In such cases, or where the tactical situation presents opportunities, a few riflemen can actually lay down a barrage.

For example, suppose we expect to fire a heavy Browning on a given area. The Browning requires a nine-man squad. It can normally fire about 200-400 shots per minute for a number of minutes. However, the Browning squad is hit by H.E. and is no longer available. One semi-automatic rifleman can fire at least 50-60 shots per minute for several minutes. Nine riflemen can deliver 450-540 rounds per minute. Subtract the fire of two leaders, one for three men, the other for four men. Nevertheless, the seven rifles, now amply controlled, can deliver 330-440 rounds per minute if needed.

Nine ordinary riflemen could deliver from 90-180 rounds a minute, all firing. To use the boxing analogy so ably applied to battalion combat tactics by Colonel Walter Wheeler in his *Infantry Battalion in War*, when the fighter has found an opening in his opponent's guard, he must deliver a paralyzing blow. The opening is only momentary. The boxer with the most powerful right arm can best deliver such a blow. The semi-automatic rifle doubles and even triples the soldier's knock-out power.

Thus, we feel justified in concluding that in actual combat the semi-automatic rifle may be called upon to fire more shots in a minute, but not more, if as many, shots in an hour or day.

Why have the great leaders of history employed the offensive so often at such great day-by-day cost in men and ammunition? Because, in many instances, they sought a quick, relatively economical decision. Trench warfare was extravagant because it tended to prolong the conflict before reaching a decision, exhausting all supply in the process.

On a small scale, infantry units, fighting locally, gain or lose decisions on the same basis. For example, if one squad is prevented from advancing by superior hostile fire, it is common practice to maneuver another squad, but perhaps much more frequently, a machine rifle (B.A.R.) to a flanking position from which a few profitable bursts can be delivered and the hostile resistance is broken. This procedure being so undeniably more economical and effective than for the stalled squad to fire their rifles ineffectively for a much longer period of time, how ridiculous it would sound were we to condemn the machine rifle because it can "burn up" 60-100 shots per minute. Actually, the bolt-action rifles might require many more rounds to gain the same decision, if any.

To repeat, the problem of ammunition consumption and supply cannot be divorced from the problem of obtaining tactical results. The two are inseparable. We learn the nine principles of war, of which two are at first blush inconsistent; namely, MASS and ECONOMY OF FORCE.

Applied to the semi-automatic rifle ammunition supply problem, these mean that we should and can use the same or a less number of rounds to achieve a desired result, yet with greater intensity and more paralyzing effect at the moment of delivery.

Not infrequently we may catch an enemy column off guard. As soon as a few shots are fired, the column scatters for cover. But for a few brief moments they present a nice, compact target. Our mission is to destroy this unit. The successful accomplishment of this mission with an intense burst of fire lasting but a few seconds is far more economical, both in the matter of men and ammunition, than a prolonged skirmish, requiring many minutes, if not hours, and many casualties.

Proper timing saves a boxer's strength and wins fights with a minimum of effort, permitting the maximum power to be applied at the crucial moment. By this means also can infantry win battles with a minimum expenditure of ammunition.

Within the Unit

There is a definite tendency in the latest tactical organizations to include "ammunition carriers," whose duty it is to transport as much ammunition as possible within the section, platoon, or company. Usually the A.C. also functions as an emergency member of the light M.G. or machine rifle crew.

To the Unit

It is interesting to consider the fact that while there has been an increase in ammunition-requiring agencies, there has also been a distinct increase in ammunition-supplying agencies since the first World War.

Attention is called to the fact that the road nets of the world are many times greater, wider, longer, smoother, straighter; that there are many times more trucks, cars, and similar transportation agencies.

Also we have the tremendous growth of air transport. Add to these the improved media of communication (telephone, telegraph, and radio) and one must confess the picture is not so black as regards supply of ammunition to rifle units, as well as for all other supply not specifically covered herein.

The idea of supply from the air is not new. The "Lost Battalion" received some aid, however misdirected, from aircraft. The Marine Corps used this agency in Nicaragua. The Italians used air transport for supply in Abyssinia. It is understood that the Second Division has successfully used this medium.

The sum total of these supply agencies is impressive. In one aspect, as regards the problem of ammunition supply, the effectiveness of these supply media is two-fold. First, they can directly supply ammunition. Second, because they can keep the soldier reasonably supplied with emergency rations and other needs, he can be freed to some extent from the old-fashioned heavy pack. Thus it may be possible for the soldier to increase his ammunition load at the outset.

CONCLUSION

To summarize:

1. The problem of ammunition supply is not new.

2. Semi-automatic and automatic weapons have not initiated the alarm over cartridge supply.

3. Earlier weapons burned up ammunition very successfully.

4. We must have fire control and discipline with any weapons.

5. We should have about 4-5 men per leader to insure fire control.

6. The magazine capacity can be reduced and single-shot loading can be required where advisable.

7. The automatics can be more effectively employed and, if so, may actually use less ammunition to gain a decision.

8. The tactical objective, rather than units of time, must be the measuring rod of ammunition consumption.

9. The tactical objective is best gained by the sudden, intense application of paralyzing fire at the crucial moment, which is usually of short duration.

10. Supply within and to the units is expedited by:

   (a) Ammunition carriers.
   (b) Improved road nets (as of 1941).
   (c) Increased number of trucks, cars, etc.
   (d) Advances in air transport.
   (e) Consequent possible reductions of soldier's pack, permitting some increase, if necessary, in ammunition load.

It is therefore submitted that the ammunition problem is far from being insurmountable, and that the price to be paid for the latest increases in the potential fire power of infantry is very cheap in terms of tactical success (attainment of objective), which is the only medium of exchange (measuring rod) on the combat front.

PART FIVE

Miscellaneous Considerations

CHAPTER SEVENTEEN

Accuracy

Accuracy at 100 Meters; Tuning Machine Guns; Muzzle Gland Adjustment; Headspace Adjustment; Loose Elevating Screws; Play in Elevating Screw Housing; Loose Traversing Screws, Play in Traversing Screw Housing; Vibration Due to Looseness in the Cradle; The Cyclic Rate; Mounting of the Tripod; Riding the Gun; Friction in the Recoiling Parts and the Feeding Mechanism; Worn Parts; Heavy Oil

WITH reference to automatic weapons, accuracy can be divided into two parts; namely, accuracy in semi-automatic arms which fire one shot for each manipulation of the trigger, and accuracy in full-automatic weapons which are habitually fired by bursts.

Accuracy in semi-automatic weapons has been discussed in other connections elsewhere in this book to a considerable extent. Inasmuch as the semi-automatic rifle is regarded as a weapon suitable to replace the conventional repeating rifle, it is inevitable that the accuracy of semi-automatic rifles and repeating rifles will be compared, and that the semi-automatic arm will be expected to deliver practically the same potential accuracy as the conventional bolt-action rifle.

Unfortunately, there exists some misapprehension as to just what accuracy can be obtained from repeating rifles. It is impossible to expect the semi-automatic rifle to deliver greater potential accuracy than such weapons as the Springfield and Mauser, and other equally well-designed arms, unless superior ammunition is developed, in which case such ammunition would be available for the repeating weapons as well as for the semi-automatic type.

Here again, however, we run into a state of confusion. Accuracy may mean various things. For example, there is accuracy from special barrels in special cradles, such as the Mann barrel which is assembled to a special V-block. Ammunition fired in this barrel produces extreme accuracy. Then there is accuracy obtained by placing a rifle in some form of machine rest, and firing groups of shots to determine the spread. Then, again, there is the accuracy which can be obtained by a skilled operator who utilizes various forms of special rests, special sights, or telescopes. There is also the accuracy which is obtained by a well-trained rifleman who uses the sling strap and possibly a sandbag rest with the very best of iron and sometimes telescope sights. And still again there is the accuracy which is obtained by average riflemen who fire average rifles from average positions such as standing, sitting, kneeling, and prone, with or without sling, and usually without a forearm rest.

But with the semi-automatic rifles there is another factor. Under actual conditions, the operator of any rifle usually fires more than one shot, and the shots are fired in fairly rapid succession. The rifleman armed with the semi-automatic weapon is relieved of the burden of operating a bolt handle for every shot, and there will be substantially less recoil on his shoulder. This results in increasing the efficiency of the rifleman so armed, as compared with the rifleman who uses the repeating type of weapon. From the standpoint of combat efficiency, it cannot be denied that the semi-automatic rifleman, given a weapon having the same inherent accuracy as the Springfield and the same accurate ammunition, will prove several times more efficient—or, if you prefer, "accurate"—than the corresponding individual armed with the repeating weapon.

With some weapons, such as the submachine gun, it is necessary to reduce the efficiency of the weapon and its ammunition in order to obtain the automatic feature. In some instances it becomes necessary to weigh the conflicting factors in order to determine whether such an automatic weapon represents a substantial improvement over the repeating arm in view of the necessary loss of inherent accuracy, range, and trajectory in terms of a corresponding increased volume of fire.

Many authorities feel that accuracy in connection with automatic weapons should be divided into the two categories of (a) inherent accuracy of single shots grouped together and fired by an average rifleman in an average position with or without a reasonably available type of rest, and (b) "efficiency" which is obtainable by virtue of the ease of operation of the semi-automatic rifle. In other words, it is felt that when we speak of increased accuracy in a semi-automatic rifle, we are misusing the term accuracy because we really mean increased efficiency. It would of course be possible to increase one's efficiency and at the same time decrease the accuracy of the weapon slightly. That can be determined only by firing upon battle targets.

Attention is called to several accuracy tables which are included herein merely for the purpose of indicating actual test comparisons between repeating rifles and a semi-automatic rifle. The data on the semi-automatic rifle are presented merely for the purpose of showing what a semi-automatic rifle can do. Similar data on other types of semi-automatic weapons are not available at this time. To repeat, it is necessary to compare the actual experienced accuracy with the accuracy obtained in an illustrated type of semi-automatic weapon.

The following general figures should not be considered from the standpoint of the very best performances which have ever been obtained under the very best conditions, but rather they represent the general average which is experienced in such a weapon as the M1903 Springfield rifle, made at Springfield Armory, and fired with an average lot of government or commercial type ammunition.

It is assumed that the rifleman is reasonably trained, that he is using either the sling strap or a forearm rest, that he is using iron sights, that visibility is fair, and that the wind is normal.

At 100 yards 10 shots will usually group within 3-6 inches; 5 shots will usually group within 2-3 inches.

At 200 yards 10 shots will usually group within 6-10 inches, and often groups will go as low as 5-7 inches. The normal spread, or 80 per cent, will usually be in the vicinity of 4-6 inches.

At 300 yards 10 shots will group 9-15 inches. The normal spread will usually be about 8-10 inches.

At 500 yards 10 shots will group in 16-24 inches.

At 600 yards 10 shots will usually group in 18-30 inches, with 80 per cent in about 14-20 inches.

At 800 yards 10 shots will usually group in 30-40 inches.

At 1000 yards 10 shots will usually group in 34-50 inches. The normal spread will usually be 36-45 inches.

The average Springfield rifle with standard lots of ammunition is definitely capable of keeping 10 shots inside a 5-inch black bullseye at 100 yards, or a 10-inch black bullseye at 200 yards, or a 20-inch black bullseye at 500 yards. Groups are generally in direct proportion at intervening ranges.

Based on very extensive firing at standard United States Army targets or their equivalent in proportionate size at the above ranges, it has been found that with the same type of ammunition specified in the foregoing, an average rifleman with a semi-automatic rifle is capable of producing practically the same groups as there outlined, even by rapid-fire. On more than one occasion 10 shots have been placed within 3 inches at 100 yards, within 5 or 6 inches at 200 yards, and within 20 inches at 500 yards, and on one occasion 14 consecutive shots were fired into the standard 20-inch bullseye at 600 yards. A 6-inch extreme vertical spread was obtained at 600 yards. On another occasion 10 shots were fired into 19 inches at 500 yards, but 80 per cent or 8 out of 10 were in 13 inches. At 1000 yards a rifleman fired over 10 consecutive shots into the standard 36-inch black bullseye. At 1000 yards 10 shots were grouped within 20-inch vertical spread.

ACCURACY AT 100 METERS

In a recent test conducted by the authors, a semi-automatic rifle was tested as follows. The rifle was selected at random for a 100-round accuracy trial. It was tested for nine groups rapid-fire, 10 shots in 11-18 seconds. The tenth 10-shot group only was slow-fire.

Some three minutes elapsed between each rapid-fire group for scoring. M2 loads were used. Total elapsed time was thirty minutes, approximately.

It is customary to fire the M1903 rifle in rapid-fire on the basis of 10 shots per minute at shorter ranges, and 10 shots per 70-80

Group	Diameter 10 shots (inches)	Diameter 8, 9 shots (inches)	E H x E V	Time (seconds)
1.	4¾	3 (9)	4⅞ x 2½	18
2.	7¾	4½ (8)	4½ x 7	11
3.	6	3 (8)	4 x 4½	16
4.	6	3½ (8)	4½ x 5	15
5.	4½	3½ (9)	4 x 2¾	17
6.	8	4¾ (8)	5 x 7½	16
7.	8	4¾ (8)	5 x 7½	11
8.	7	3¾ (8)	5 x 7	12
9.	6½	4¾ (8)	4 x 6¼	18
10.	3¾	2¾ (9)	1¾ x 3	Slow Fire
Average	6	3¾ (8)	4¼ x 5¼	

seconds at longer ranges up to 500 yards. In the British Service it is customary to fire the SMLE caliber .303 rifle in rapid-fire on the basis of up to 15 shots per minute. The target used by the United States Army for rapid-fire is a silhouette shaped to correspond to the head and shoulders of a man in the prone position, the extreme dimensions being 26 inches in width by 19 inches in height. This target is used at 200, 300, and 500 yards.

Based upon extensive firing tests, it appears that with a 10-shot capacity magazine, a rifleman armed with a caliber .30 semi-automatic rifle is capable of firing 10 shots in 10-15 seconds at 200 yards, obtaining in some cases groups of less than 8 inches and usually not over 12-15 inches.

At 300 yards from the prone position with sling it was found quite possible to fire 16 shots in 1 minute with all shots in the above-mentioned rapid-fire silhouette target, known as the "D" target.

At 500 yards it was found possible for a rifleman in the prone position with sling to fire 16 shots in 70 seconds with all shots in the "D" target bullseye.

On one occasion two strings of 10 shots each were fired at the rate of slightly less than 15 seconds per string at a range of 500 yards. The first group measured 28 inches in extreme breadth and the second, 26 inches. The combined spread of all 20 shots was approximately 32 inches, with 80 per cent in 23 inches.

At 600 yards 10 shots fired in 18 seconds grouped in a 22-inch extreme spread. Firing 20 shots in 60 seconds at 600 yards, a score of $9\frac{4}{100}$ was made on the "B" target, 20-inch bullseye. Firing 10 shots in 12 seconds gave a 26-inch spread. Firing 10 shots in 15 seconds at 600 yards on the "B" target gave a 26-inch extreme spread, with 9 out of 10 in 16 inches. There were 8 bullseyes, score 47.

Using one of the new model 1940 M1 Garand rifles we obtained the following score in July, 1940.

With 28 shots loaded and fired in one minute, prone with rest, range 600 yards, "B" target 20-inch bullseye, the score was 16 bullseyes, 10 "fours," 2 "threes." The score value was 90 per cent.

At 1000 yards it is possible for a rifleman armed with a semi-automatic to fire at the rate of 20-30 shots per minute deliverable fire, keeping practically all the shots within a 5-6-foot circle.

On one occasion 10 shots were fired in 28 seconds at 1000 yards, giving an extreme vertical spread of 20 inches, extreme horizontal of 38 inches.

It is possible in any event for a rifleman with a semi-automatic to fire at least into a 10-12-foot circle at 1000-1200 yards, delivering the fire at a rate of 20-30 shots per minute. With reference to limited bursts of 5-10 shots delivered at this range, the rate of fire would be about 2 seconds per shot. In bursts of 5 shots, for example, delivered at a range of 1000-1200 yards, the semi-automatic rifle would have very much the effect of a burst of buckshot, and would cover an area within which one or two enemy soldiers might be located. Attention is called to the fact that if a rifleman with a semi-automatic could obtain one hit per 5-10 shots at 1000-1200 yards, his battle efficiency would be far greater than any soldier has previously been capable of producing with the conventional repeating weapon.

In this connection, attention should be paid to the mobility of rifle-armed troops as compared with the mobility of machine-gun units. The subject of ammunition supply has been covered in another chapter, but it should be remembered that machine guns generally fire many, many rounds per combat casualty and are much more difficult to move about than semi-automatic rifles. Further information and data on accuracy will be found in other connections elsewhere in this book.

With reference, therefore, to semi-automatic rifles, it is believed that with weapons capable of firing ammunition of higher-powered category, such as the caliber .30 U.S. and others of that type, the semi-automatic rifle is capable of maintaining practically the same inherent accuracy as rifles of the M1903 type, and is capable of accurate fire at the same extreme ranges, but, in addition, is capable of projecting its fire much farther by virtue of its ability to deliver accurate bursts of 5-10 shots at ranges in excess of 600-1000 yards.

The history of weapons shows a very decided trend towards improvement which maintains practically all the features previously achieved, with new features added. It is not likely that any attempt to reduce the inherent accuracy, effective range, and efficiency of the weapon issued to the individual soldier will ultimately be successful.

We now turn from our consideration of accuracy in semi-automatic weapons to a brief study of machine-gun accuracy, or rather, accuracy in terms of full-automatic fire.

Contrary to the impression which prevails in some quarters, it is generally desirable in full-automatic weapons to obtain the smallest possible bursts or "burst groups." The conception of the machine gun as a bullet squirter which sprays projectiles all over the landscape in the fashion of a garden hose is a very unfortunate one. Battle efficiency depends upon the projection of effective fire. Effective fire means fire which takes effect upon profitable targets. Old Mother Earth is not generally a profitable target. Where, however, old Mother Earth is more or less infested with the enemy, then it is desired to project the fire upon those areas where the enemy is found. Thus, for example, with enemy units which are approaching or retreating through avenues or passes, or which are marching upon roads, or which are crossing road junctions, or which are advancing in small groups along trails or on open ground, it is highly profitable to place accurate long-range fire upon such areas, or at close range directly upon such groups.

It is customary to attempt to place flanking or enfilading fire upon the enemy, due to the nature of the bursts from an automatic weapon. As has been stated elsewhere in other connections in this book, burst fire from automatic weapons forms what is described as a cone, or band, upon the ground, this band being long or deep, and comparatively narrow, especially at shorter ranges.

Fundamentally, the problem is the same as that which faces the single rifleman. A machine gunner, however, is perhaps more like the shot gunner, because a burst from a machine gun is not unlike a burst of shots from a shotgun. The machine gunner treats the burst as one unit of projectiles, and it is his purpose to place that burst, or unit, on the target. Thus, accuracy in this connection is quite as important to the machine gunner as to any other gunner.

But there is also another factor which must be considered; namely, the danger of hitting your own troops. Because of the comparative lack of mobility of heavy machine guns, the gun crews must set up their guns and fire to the flank or over the heads of their own troops. It would not be safe to fire under such conditions unless the weapons fired were reasonably accurate. In this connection, however, accuracy means not only the accuracy of the ammunition, the inherent accuracy obtainable in the weapon by firing single shots from a machine rest, but it also means the accuracy of the weapon as a whole, including its mount, the stability of its mount, the accuracy with which it is fitted onto the mount, the way in which the recoil of the weapon in firing is translated into the gun and mount, the correct headspacing of the weapon (as for example the heavy Browning machine gun M1917), and the proper siting and fixing of the mount on the ground. In many machine guns the cyclic rate of fire actually affects the size of the bursts, as, for example, if the cyclic rate is too high, the gun and barrel may be out of position with respect to each shot in such a way as to create a certain amount of climb. The factor of vibration is of material importance in connection with the reduction in size of bursts fired from conventional machine guns.

Guns in which the moving parts are generally well distributed as to mass along the axis of the bore, usually tend to produce much better groups than weapons which have a comparatively irregular distribution. With all due respect to the very excellent

M1917 heavy Browning gun, the Vickers-Maxim, and others, attention is called to the fact that the distribution of weight on these weapons is not at all conducive to accurate groups. This necessitates considerable attention to the mount, to the bedding of the mount, to the tightening of all joints, and to the regulation of the cyclic rate.

A great deal has been written on the subject of machine-gun accuracy. The authors, having read a reasonable number of such essays, feel that in the interest of improving accuracy in such weapons as the heavy Browning machine gun M1917, nothing better has been presented on the subject than an article appearing in the *Infantry Mailing List*, Volume XV, page 195. With the kind permission of the *Infantry Mailing List*, it is our privilege to include that very excellent article in this book. Before doing so, however, the authors wish to digress for the moment to illustrate the importance to the machine gun of this *Mailing List* article. The following is therefore a personal experience narrative.

In August, 1939, a machine-gun company conducted marksmanship qualification firing with the heavy Browning gun. Before going to the range, all the officers read the above-cited *Infantry Mailing List* article very carefully, and discussed all the points with the non-commissioned officers of the company.

Prior to applying the points brought out in the *Mailing List* article, the guns of this company were far from giving satisfactory groups. Fired on the standard 1000-inch machine-gun targets, virtually none of the guns were capable of placing consistent bursts substantially within the target squares. Following the information given in the *Infantry Mailing List* article, the company spent a day overhauling the guns. Particular attention was given to head-space and other factors.

The following day, record firing commenced at 1000 inches. It should be understood that a score on the 1000-inch target used by this organization of 150 points is within the average required for expert rating. Imagine the company commander's joy when he discovered that the first 20 scores turned in contained no targets with a score of less than 160, and with quite a number of targets scoring above 170. As an illustration of the accuracy obtained by this company at long range, it was noted that one of the guns of this company, when fired at 1000 yards on a 6x6-foot target, placed a full 40-round burst within that target.

When the results of this qualification firing were tabulated, this machine-gun company found itself the holder of the machine-gun qualification record for machine-gun companies of the United States Marine Corps. One can always depend on a good story about the Marine Corps, but this time it is necessary to give full credit to the Infantry School at Fort Benning, Georgia, and to the author of the article, Major W. H. Schildroth.

We now take pleasure in presenting the article from the *Infantry Mailing List* of 1937-38.

TUNING MACHINE GUNS

The record course in machine-gun marksmanship is based upon 1000-inch firing. Scoring spaces are 3 by 2 inches.[1] In order for the men to qualify as experts only 13 per cent of the shots can be out of the scoring spaces. To obtain this accuracy the men of the organization must not only be well drilled in the fundamentals of machine-gun marksmanship, but the guns themselves must be capable of grouping with this 3 by 2 inch scoring space. If the guns are not able to do this, the organization will fail to make a high score. This will hold true even though the men have received the best of training. It can safely be said that to a large degree the percentage of high qualifications obtained in an organization rests squarely upon the mechanical efficiency of the guns. It amounts to this: good grouping guns make good scores.

All commanders of machine-gun units realize this. As a consequence, great stress is laid by them on the size of the shot group. We not infrequently find entire organizations firing their record course with one or two guns. Why? Because those guns will group smaller than the others. Besides, the men soon acquire confidence in the guns. With these particular guns they believe they can make good scores. It would be unwise to destroy this confidence by forcing them to use others.

Yet, to use one or two guns is obviously not good procedure. Naturally we would like to find a remedy. A search for one will soon resolve itself into an attempt to answer these questions: (1) Are we attempting to make the guns do the mechanically impossible? (2) Do we lack the

---

[1] New course now under consideration.

necessary mechanical skill for obtaining small-shot groups? (3) Can most guns be made to do our bidding?

We believe that shot groups sufficiently small for marksmanship purposes are not difficult to obtain with almost any gun. But, we also believe it is necessary to know those factors that affect the size of the shot group, and to what degree, before the shot groups can be made larger or smaller at will. How can we get that knowledge? If we would like to know definitely how to make the machine gun shoot the group we desire, if we want a convincing reason—one easy to accept because of its soundness—we must have some means other than mere speculation or conjecture.

An attempt has been made at The Infantry School to find out those factors that change the size of the shot groups. It was done by a series of experiments with one gun, followed by verifying experiments with a number of other guns. Every effort was made to fire the guns under the same conditions. The experiments were based upon the conviction that changes in the shot group were caused by certain factors. A tentative list of these factors, the product of long and close association with machine guns, is given below:

1. Muzzle gland adjustment.
2. Headspace adjustment.
3. Loose elevating screws, play in elevating screw housing.
4. Loose traversing screws, play in traversing screw housing.
5. Vibration due to looseness in the cradle.
6. The cyclic rate.
7. Mounting of the tripod.
8. Riding the gun.
9. Friction in the recoiling parts and the feeding mechanism; worn parts; heavy oil.

A method of solving the problem quickly presented itself. By changing one of the above factors, noting its effect on the shot group, while keeping all other factors constantly and properly adjusted, we should arrive at conclusions that would in some measure give us the answer. At least, we should have at our command information available for analysis. With that in mind we proceeded with the experiments.

It should be realized that the experiments are by no means exhaustive or conclusive, but even in the early stages certain significant facts emerge that are of value to the machine gunner. To really clinch these facts a longer period of experiment at The School and in the regiments is needed. But here at least we can show the trend.

MUZZLE GLAND ADJUSTMENT

With all the factors believed to affect the size of shot groups correctly adjusted, a series of bursts was fired at a blank target. (See

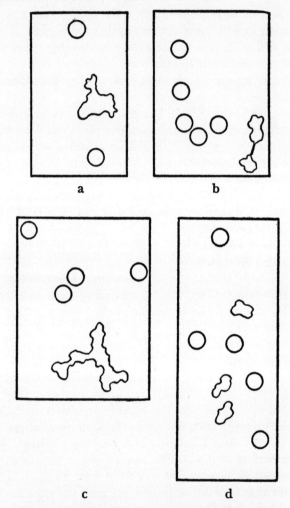

Figure 34. Result of muzzle gland looseness.

Figure 34.) Notice the progressive increase in size of the shot groups.
Investigation showed that the muzzle gland, tight to begin with, was
now loose. This was due to the packing becoming compressed by the

moving barrel and thus creating a looseness in the muzzle gland. The next group (see Figure 35) was fired with the muzzle gland tightened. Notice the decrease in the size of the shot group. Just as we had always

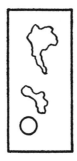

Figure 35. What happened to *d* group, Figure 34, when muzzle gland was tightened.

thought, loose muzzle gland—large group; tight muzzle gland—small group. Incidentally, we learned that the front packing does not seat itself until after the firing of about 150 warming-up rounds. During this warming-up period it was discovered that the muzzle gland adjustment had an appreciable effect upon the size of the shot group. To keep the groups small, initially, it was necessary to keep the muzzle

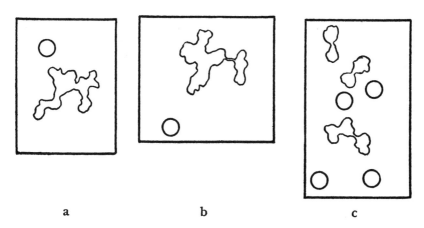

a   b   c

Figure 36.a shows group with muzzle gland unloosened. Note that it took three bursts before dispersion became great as in c.

gland tightened after each burst. However, when the packing had seated itself, it was found that the muzzle gland needed little adjusting and that the shot groups remained constant and small. Upon getting similar results with other guns we concluded that the muzzle gland adjustment does affect the size of the shot group, but not to the extent we had previously supposed. We also discovered that when the packing is well seated, a change in the shot group on account of change in muzzle gland adjustment did not manifest itself at once. It required two or three bursts before the size of the shot group was altered (see Figure 36).

HEADSPACE ADJUSTMENT

Look at Figures 37, 38, and 39. Figure 37 was obtained with headspace adjustment correct. Figure 38 was obtained with headspace loosened three notches. Figure 39 was obtained with headspace loosened six notches. Figure 40 was obtained with headspace again correct. Look at those changes in the shot group. Yes, loose headspace is

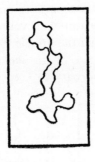 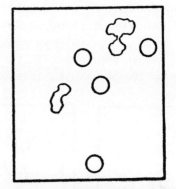

Figure 37. Shot group with   Figure 38. Shot group with
headspace correct.   headspace 3 notches loose.

quite an element in determining the size of the shot group. If it is not properly adjusted the gun will not group, although it will function smoothly. Therein lies the deception. With the gun firing perfectly, all other factors correct, but with headspace only three notches loose, it is impossible to get a small group. This is an important factor in tuning a machine gun. The evidence indicates that small changes in headspace adjustment will produce large changes in the size of the shot groups. Of the two factors investigated so far, it seems that the headspace adjustment has considerably more effect on the shot group than the muzzle gland adjustment.

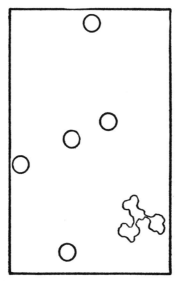

Figure 39. Shot group with headspace 6 notches loose.

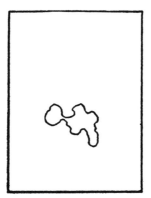

Figure 40. Shot group obtained when headspace employed in Figure 39 was corrected.

It is perhaps best at this time to explain what we mean by correct headspace adjustment. Headspace adjustment is correct when the taking up of one or two notches on the barrel will prevent the release of the firing pin.

Figure 41 was obtained with both headspace and muzzle gland adjustment very loose.

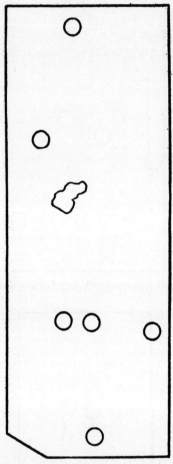

Figure 41. Shot group with headspace and muzzle gland loose.

LOOSE ELEVATING SCREWS, PLAY IN ELEVATING SCREW HOUSING

This experiment was fired with a one-sixteenth inch play in the elevating screw. (See Figure 42). Note particularly the vertical dispersion. The next shot group (see Figure 43) was obtained with no play in the elevating screw. The result obtained is self-explanatory.

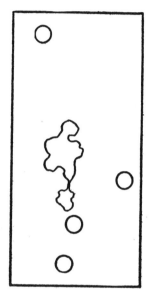

Figure 42. Shot group with play in the elevating mechanism.

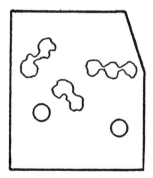

Figure 43. Shot group after play was taken out of elevating mechanism.

LOOSE TRAVERSING SCREWS, PLAY IN TRAVERSING SCREW HOUSING

Figure 44 was obtained by firing the gun with side play in the traversing screw. The next figure (Figure 45) was obtained with this play taken out of the traversing screw. It shows a reduction in the horizontal dispersion of the shots.

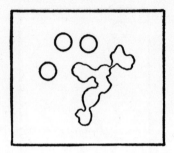

Figure 44. Shot group with play in traversing mechanism.

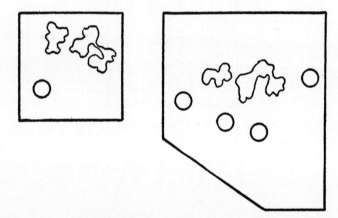

Figure 45. Shot group after play has been taken out of traversing mechanism.

Figure 46. Shot group due to looseness in the cradle.

VIBRATION DUE TO LOOSENESS IN THE CRADLE

The shot group obtained due to vibration in the gun because of looseness in the cradle is similar in nature and size to that obtained by a loose traversing screw. (See Figure 46.)

THE CYCLIC RATE

The effect that this factor has upon the shot group is perhaps less known than that of the other factors. When the gun is firing with the cyclic rate best suited to it, there is a smoothness of operation which becomes quickly apparent. This smoothness of operation gives uniform performance. Quite frequently a shot is consistently thrown outside of

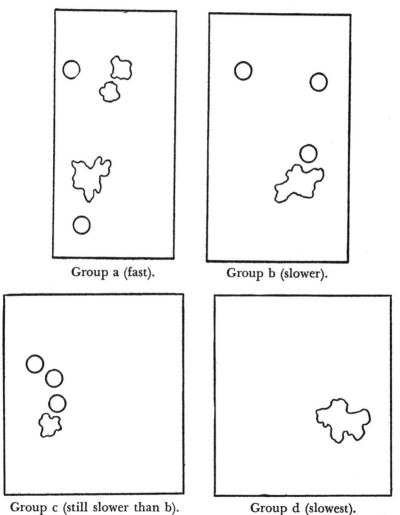

Group a (fast).   Group b (slower).

Group c (still slower than b).   Group d (slowest).

Figure 47. The effect of a change in cyclic rate on shot group.

a compact shot group. This often can be made an integral part of the shot group by changing the cyclic rate. The correct cyclic rate for any one gun can only be obtained empirically. However, there is no doubt that change in the cyclic rate affects the size of the shot group. A glance at the figure (Figure 47) will show what is meant. However, one should not jump to the conclusion that a slow cyclic rate means tight groups. The opposite is often true. Each sensitively balanced machine gun has its own individuality.

MOUNTING OF THE TRIPOD

The gun must be properly mounted on its tripod. Some support, such as a tent stake or the like, should be placed under the trail in order to increase its bearing surface. If this is not done, the shot group will have a large vertical dispersion. Figure 48 was obtained with support under the trail. Figure 49 was obtained with this support removed.

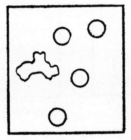

Figure 48. Shot group obtained with support under the trail.

RIDING THE GUN

Riding the gun is putting unnecessary pressure on the grip when firing the gun. This is one of the most prevalent methods of making a good grouping gun look bad. Shot groups of all descriptions can be obtained by riding the gun. They will vary in size and shape depending upon the amount and kind of riding done. All machine gunners know that a good shot group cannot be obtained if the gun is ridden. (See Figure 50.) Many low scores are attributed to reasons other than riding the gun. It is good practice to test the guns by experienced men whenever they seem to be grouping large. If an experienced gunner fires small groups, then we know the guns are not at fault.

These factors, together with others not mentioned, will also alter the size of the shot group, but no test was made at this time to dis-

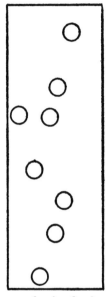

Figure 49. Shot group obtained when trail support was removed.

close their relative importance. In fact, we readily admit our test is not exhaustive, but we believe the factors which we have discussed are of such frequent occurrence that they constitute the greater part of machine-gun tuning. At the same time it is realized that with certain guns it will take considerable work in replacing bolts, barrel extensions, barrels, adjusting the buffer mechanism, and so forth, in order to obtain a delicate gun adjustment that will minimize vibration and permit the adjustments noted herein to be made effectively.

CONCLUSIONS

An examination of the evidence we have presented led us to these conclusions:

1. The factors in our list alter the size of the shot group.

2. The relative degree of alteration these factors have upon the size of the shot group is as follows:

First, riding the gun; second, headspace adjustment; third, loose elevating screws, play in elevating screw housing; fourth, improper mounting of the tripod; fifth, muzzle gland adjustment; sixth, loose travers-

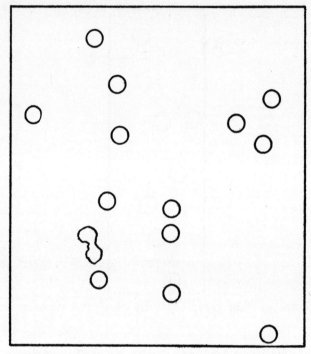

Figure 50. Result obtained by riding the gun.

ing screws, play in traversing screw housing; seventh, vibration due to looseness in cradle; eighth, the cyclic rate; ninth, other factors.

A machine gun is a high-pressure gas engine and, like all fast-vibrating mechanisms, it is extremely sensitive. It requires the care of a skilled operator to keep it tuned for best performance. A knowledge of the fundamentals of machine-gun tuning will aid us in training gunners so that we can get this best performance. Furthermore, it will enable us to change quickly from the close pattern ideal for marksmanship to the wide pattern more suitable for combat. If a knowledge of tuning a machine gun does this and nothing else, it is worth acquiring.

CHAPTER EIGHTEEN

Design Critique of Automatic Mechanisms

Methods of Actuation; Breech-Locking Systems; Shell Extraction; Gas vs. Recoil Action; Methods of Stocking

A DETAILED survey of the development of the semi-automatic rifle and the light-weight machine gun would demand a much larger volume than this. In this age of specialists, few men can devote much time to matters not directly connected with their more immediate work. Ordnance covers a wide range of scientific subjects, and many of the readers of this book are undoubtedly experts in specific fields. It is submitted, however, that those who are studying military science, and those who are interested in small arms, should especially appreciate the automatic or self-loading firearm. Moreover, those who are specialists may be interested in the tribulations of their fellow sufferers. This chapter is therefore dedicated to that legion of indomitable strugglers whose shattered hopes and lost causes are published in the United States Patent Office at ten cents per copy: the inventors of unsuccessful automatic weapons.

When we consider the multitude of mechanical military triumphs within the past four decades, we naturally are surprised at the tardy arrival of the service automatic. In numerous books and articles, such eminent authorities as Brigadier General Julian S. Hatcher and others have discussed the operation and design of all well-known automatic weapons. Their approach has been chiefly historical; ours will be analytical. We shall not be technical, so much as idealistic. We shall not necessarily narrate what others have done. Instead, let us suppose that we have been assigned a specific task; for example, the design of a simple, durable, rugged, reliable, understandable, military self-loading rifle which shall weigh little more than a Springfield, use .30 U.S. ammunition, contain few parts, require simple manufacturing operations, and function perfectly under all conditions in the hands of any rear-rank private.

Before beginning this analysis, the writers wish to state that no criticism of any inventor or invention, whether official or civilian, is intended, despite the fact that there shall be a free and honest expression of personal opinions in this discussion. Furthermore, remember one important fact: no invention is really a failure, because from the experimentation therein involved we all learn something more about the art which may be of immense value in our own work, even though it merely saves our time. There are many ways of skinning the cat, some good and some not. An inventor proves that a certain method is unsatisfactory, and his successors profit by the knowledge of "what not to do" thus imparted. Those who do achieve success are not legally or morally obligated to their unsuccessful predecessors on the above grounds; nevertheless, they should render tribute even to a negative contribution.

What must our automatic mechanism do? The process seems simple enough. When the bullet has departed from the barrel, and the residual gas pressure has dropped to a safe limit, the breechblock must automatically disengage from the breech and move to the rear of the frame or receiver, thereby extracting and causing to be ejected the empty shell case. A conventional mainspring having been compressed by this operation, the breechblock is then returned, loading a fresh cartridge from a conventional magazine, and locking the breech. Moreover, by these operations, or one of them, the hammer or striker is cocked. (See also Chapter Five.)

If we were considering a machine gun, the task would be simpler because we should not require a semi-automatic type of trigger mechanism. The forward movement of the breechblock could be utilized to fire the cartridge at the proper time; the sear would merely hold the breechblock in the open position. Stripped of belt-feed mechanisms, cooling apparatus, etc., the machine gun is a kid brother to the semi-automatic and easier to build, due to the much wider weight limitations.

Primarily, then, our task is complete when we have caused the empty case to be thrown from the gun, and compressed an adequate mainspring. We need not consider here the magazine, ejector, barrel, safety, stock, sights, mount, feed, cooling system, except in so far as provision must be made for these parts in conventional places on a finished arm.

However, we must not overlook secondary requirements. The production department, for example, will demand a weapon which can be cheaply manufactured within a reasonable time, with reasonable machine operations, without hairsplit adjustments. The ammunition department will demand a mechanism which can accept the standard service ammunition. Above all, the using arms demand a conventional-handling weapon, not a mechanical monstrosity. The tool was never made for the infantry that a recruit could not put out of order without taxing his destructive ingenuity a particle.

We have already been assigned our task or objective. We understand that our rifle or machine gun must be practical to build for experiments, economical to manufacture in production, and certain to function in combat. Our basic principle is Simplicity, which, paradoxically, is most difficult to apply, a fact recognized by the Supreme Court of the United States in patent opinions which affirm that "simplicity is the highest state of the art."

Therefore, we must adhere strictly to a simplified system in our automatic. Many ingenious contraptions have failed miserably for violation of Simplicity.

METHODS OF ACTUATION

Automatic weapons can be actuated, basically, by the employment of a gas cylinder, or by a retarded blowback method, or by the long- or the short-recoil system. We must accommodate high-powered ammunition such as the .30 U.S. We are not discussing such freaks as "blow-forwards," "blow-downs," "recoil-forwards," "primer-setbacks," and others, for reasons already set forth.

Two forces, or applications of the same force, are requisite:

1. The breechblock must be unlocked by some force set in motion by the explosion of the cartridge, which force must not

produce complete unlocking until the bullet has left the barrel, and the residual pressure has dropped to a safe limit.

2. The breechblock must be retracted by some force originated in the explosion, which force shall not act upon the breechblock until unlocking has been completed.

It is obvious that the explosion of the cartridge produces certain basic forces. Fundamentally, these are three:

1. The breechblock, which is employed to keep the shell from blowing back to the rear, receives an impact from the head or base of the shell. This blow is more accurately described as a violent push, because, upon ignition, the powder gas begins to build up from zero a pressure which rapidly reaches 50,000 plus or minus pounds per square inch, using the .30 U.S. load. But for the obvious fact that the breech cannot safely be opened at once, this force on the block would be a direct solution.

2. The above force causes the breechblock (or bolt if you are Springfield-minded) to go rearward. The block is locked to the whole gun. Therefore, the gun "kicks." If the barrel and breechblock are slidably mounted in the frame or receiver, then the kick or recoil may be utilized in some manner. Thus, we have, in effect, two aspects of the same force.

3. Expanding powder gas pushes the bullet through the tube, while forcing backward on the breechblock as described above. By putting a hole at some point along the barrel, gas may be taken into a cylinder underneath. A piston in the cylinder acted upon by the diverted gas, can be used in the gas-engine fashion.

The explosion, therefore, provides these forces in a normal weapon. By attaching various gadgets we might develop other movements, but to do so would violate Simplicity. Our objective is to harness the explosion by adding a minimum number of automatic parts to the conventional rifle. Bear that point in mind throughout this discussion. Moreover, it is submitted that one large or complicated part is less desirable than two or three very small and simple parts.

Gas-actuation method

What shall we try first? With plenty of gas available, the use of a gas cylinder and piston is logical. The gun can be made on engine principles. By this method the movement of the piston will unlock the breechblock and retract it. Or we might use the piston to unlock the breech and then use the residual pressure in the chamber to retract the block.

Where shall the gas port or ports be located? Powder gases are not beneficial to a rifle barrel; they are even less so to a cylinder. If the port is near the breech there is less carbon because the flame is hotter. But if located aft, then we must figure out a mechanical method of delaying the unlocking of the breech. Such an action would be very harsh. A recent experimental rifle developed by an arms company discloses a short-stroke (one-tenth inch) piston which gives an impetus to the operating rod. The gas port is near the breech. If we put the port at or near the muzzle we may have more carbon. The cylinder must be located at the port. A gas tube must be provided, as well as a piston and a connecting rod. Carbon may clog a gas port so located. The cylinder must be strong and durable, otherwise a dent may prevent operation. The size of the port must be determined or the gas force will be too great or too little. A weapon of this type may need to be cleaned faithfully. It may have inherent disadvantages in the field.

The United States semi-automatic rifle, M1 caliber .30 (Garand) is the world's outstanding gas-operated shoulder automatic rifle. References to this product of Springfield Armory and to the inventions of Mr. John C. Garand are found elsewhere in this book.

The Garand was improved in 1940 by changes in the gas port and cylinder design. Based upon numerous exhaustive tests, including certain lengthy trials followed in close detail by the authors, the Garand appears clearly to have overcome objections habitually raised against gas actuation in principle.

Another outstanding modern gas-operated automatic is the British Bren light machine gun. Developed by the Czech at Brno and improved materially by the British technical authorities at Enfield Lock (Royal Small Arms Arsenal) during 1924-1934, the Bren (B-R plus E-N) is very much the world's leading gas-operated full-automatic weapon, incorporating many universal and important features in a weapon of this type, including *inter alia* a removable barrel, carbon-scraping bipod device, self-opening breech cover, automatic bolt stop on last shot, positive breech action, and simplified, positive ignition.

Time, space, and other factors prohibit a further discussion of gas actuation. Later comparisons will be made in other connections.

Blowback-actuation method

The blowback method is worth our careful consideration. Here we have the most fundamental force. The breechblock wants to open up. However, we must delay the opening. Moreover, we must complete the unlocking movement in time to utilize the residual gas pressure in the chamber for retraction of the breechblock. The problem of timing, therefore, is more acute with this type than with the average gas-actuated system wherein the piston performs both tasks.

Bear in mind that the weapon must accommodate high-powered military cartridges, such as the .30 U.S. With the .22 long rifle load we could use a breechblock having sufficient weight to delay the unlocking by its inertia. For a .30 service load the block would have to weigh 27 odd pounds.

Several methods have been devised to retard the unlocking of the block or bolt mechanically. The most appealing point in such a system is the consolidation of the automatic parts in the breech. However, there is one serious difficulty. The conventional cartridge case does not lend itself to such a system unless adequate lubrication is provided, such as grease or wax or oil on the cases or in the chamber. Thus, the Schwarzlose machine gun has an automatic oil pump; the .30 Thompson rifle (not the .45 T.S.-M.G.) had oil pads in the magazine, and special wax was used on the cases for the Pedersen rifle.

If we use a rotating bolt, having its lugs and locking abutments beveled at the proper pitch, the bolt will automatically unlock upon firing, and can be made to do so on time for retraction. That is the so-called "Blish screw-breech" principle, and was used in the Thompson semi-automatic rifle. There is some diversity of opinion as to the proper description of the Blish principle. However, being empiricists, we respectfully submit that the head of the bolt begins to give way before the pressure has subsided sufficiently. The result is that the case, unless lubricated, splits, or the primer blows out. The average military cartridge case demands a fixed support until the pressure has dropped below 15,000 odd pounds per square inch. If during the interval of higher pressure the head of the bolt or block gives way while unlocking, more than a few thousandths of an inch, the case will rupture. Movement of the head away from the shell during lower pressure causes the primer to be unsupported at a crucial moment. Therefore, the primer will pop out, even though the case does not rupture.

Why should the average service case rupture under such circumstances? Why does it not move back all together in the chamber? The neck and shoulders of the brass case are turned out thinner than the rear portion of the body of the shell. As the powder is ignited, the pressure swells the case to the chamber walls, pushes the bullet through the tube, and pushes rearward against the bolt or breechblock. The thin brass neck serves to seal the chamber from gas leakage, in the manner of a gasket on an engine. Therefore, the forward portion of the shell refuses to move back. But the thicker portion or base of the case does not adhere so tightly to the chamber. Therefore, unless this base is supported, it gives way. The case cannot stand more than ten or fifteen thousandths of an inch stretch without rupturing. This rupture occurs, usually, about one-half inch from the extracting cannelure.

As the pressure drops, the entire shell adheres to the walls sufficiently to resist rearward movement without rupture. At such times, however, the removal of support from the base of the shell, allows the primer to be blown out by the remaining pressure. Primers may stand around 15,000 pounds per square inch, rarely more. If lubricant is applied to the case, this wall friction is reduced, allowing the case to move without any difficulty in the chamber.

Mechanisms, such as the Pedersen and Thompson, designed to make this blowback force work at a mechanical disadvantage during the interval of critical pressure, inevitably encounter the aforesaid rupture of cases unless lubrication is provided. With the conventional cartridge, only the "rearward" force is available for unlocking power. Hence some movement rearward must take place during the unlocking interval. If we were able to store up the force of the explosion against the breechblock or bolt, or to transmit it to a separate part outside the chamber, we might avoid the rupturing which occurs with a direct application of that force. However, such a method appears exceedingly dubious.

We find that indirect methods, whereby the force of the explosion is transmitted to an actuating member, do not furnish sufficient power, unless the head of the bolt or breechblock moves an appreciable distance. Lubrication is required for such a movement.

With conventional military rifle cartridges, no retarded blowback system can in all probability be devised without making provision for adequate lubrication. Moreover, we must remember that dirt and grit in the chamber might overcome the effect of our lubricant in the field. If we used unfixed ammunition, this movement would be quite unobjectionable. However, unfixed ammunition would at this date hardly be practical in conjunction with automatic small arms. We must use conventional cartridge cases.

The following point is submitted as a matter of academic interest. Where the movement of the shell case, under pressure, is used to impart a movement to an actuating member, it will be found that the "wartime" .30-1906 loads require about half as much movement to produce the required force as do .30 M1 or M2 loads. Mr. John C. Garand experienced this difficulty in his primer-actuated rifle. There the .30-06 primer was permitted to set back about thirty-thousandths of one inch, which movement drove his actuator rearward, thus producing a delayed unlocking of the breechblock. But so much more set-back of the primer was required in this weapon when fired with the then new M1 loads, that Mr. Garand decided to devote his skill to another type of actuation. The above phenomenon is attributed to the progressive burning of the improved rifle powders with which the .30 M1 ammunition is loaded. Manifestly, a successful military semi-automatic must operate with the powders in current use. In fact, it should operate without much adjustment for any type of normal load.

The reader may recall that earlier in our discussion the blow on the breechblock was described as a violent push. The tendency to push is more marked in the action of M1 powder.

In this connection we can now dispose of those systems in which the blow or push of the explosion is transmitted to an actuating member. Prima facie, such a scheme seems to have possibilities.

Suppose you place a croquet ball under your foot, place a second ball in contact with the first, and then strike with your mallet the ball which is under your foot. The impact, transmitted through the first ball, causes the second to move across the croquet ground.[1]

Why not use the bolthead or face for the first ball, an actuator or "inertia member" for the second, and the explosion or thrust of the shell for the mallet? Would the actuating member move with enough force to unlock the breechblock or bolt?

Or suppose you assume that the explosion is the muscle of your good right arm, the bolthead the mallet, a fixed or slightly movable block the first ball, and an actuating member, in contact with that, the second ball.

Roughly, the explosion produces a blow of about 6500 pounds. It would seem that so much force ought to make the actuating member go back violently, so as to perform all of the necessary work. Alas, such is not the result.

To produce the above effect the shell and bolthead must be allowed to move an appreciable distance under pressure. The conventional case will not do that without a rupture, which we have discussed above. If the case did not rupture, wall friction would retard the movement of the case and the effect of the push would be lost.

To conclude: (1) The explosion is merely a push, not a sharp blow. (2) The normal friction of the case, unless lubricated, contributes to the reduction of actuating power. (3) Even if the shell is lubricated, there is not enough force to retract the bolt without the aid of residual gas pressure. (4) If a rotating bolt is used, the lugs must be beveled slightly to facilitate rotation under high pressure.

Recoiling barrel system of actuation

A recoiling barrel system is perhaps the most obvious of all. The reader will recall the original Maxim machine gun which

---

[1] The experimental Winchester rifle as tested in November, 1940, utilized the "croquet" principle in a gas piston actuator near the breech, which, hit by high pressure, moved the contacted operating slide violently rearward.

was patented back of the gay nineties. The force which produces lame shoulders on recruits can be utilized to actuate automatics.

As stated at the beginning of our discussion, there are two classes: the long recoil and the short recoil. As this chapter is not historical, we need not describe every invention by name. Instead, we shall first analyze the long-recoil system.

Suppose we take a barrel and mount it slidably on a frame. We lock our breechblock to the barrel. When we fire the gun, the barrel and breechblock recoil to the rear of the frame. There the barrel and breechblock are caused to separate by some means, whereupon a barrel-spring causes the barrel to move forward while the breechblock is held at the rear of the frame. Thus the empty case is removed from the chamber. Then the breechblock is returned by its spring, loading and locking the piece.

Substantially the above system is used in the Browning autoloading shotgun, Remington autoloading rifle and shotgun (Browning patent) and the famous "chaut-chaut" or Chauchard "machine rifle" used by the French during the first World War. Paul Mauser, the inventor of the Mauser and 1903 Springfield rifle, took out several patents on the long-recoil system as early as 1904.

The worst criticisms of this system are the length of barrel recoil and the number of tricky parts. The barrel movement requires a brake system. Two return springs are necessary. The locking system is complicated and not particularly rugged. Provision for the barrel movement necessitates a tube around the rifle barrel, and this tube retains heat excessively. Of course the movement of the barrel takes care of the unlocking and retracting of the breechblock. Using .30 U.S. cartridges, the recoil distance must be increased an undesirable amount, usually over four inches.

Semi-automatic rifles of the long-recoil type have been consistently rejected for military use on the above and other grounds. If the barrel is movable to the extent of more than one-half inch, the weapon will require a complicated receiver or mount, and is quite likely to prove undesirable. Moreover, such faults would disqualify the invention as a satisfactory solution to our problem of designing the ideal semi-automatic military rifle or light machine gun.

Short-recoil type of actuation

Next on our list is the short-recoil type of actuation. Again we mount the barrel slidably in the frame. The breechblock is locked to the barrel. When the piece is fired, the bolt and barrel recoil together for a short distance, during which interval the bullet leaves the muzzle and the residual gas pressure drops to a safe point. The breechblock is thereupon unlocked, and the momentum thrusts the breechblock to the rear of the receiver, thus causing the shell to be extracted and ejected. The unlocking of the breechblock is effected in some manner by the force of the recoiling parts.

The above system is employed in the Colt automatic pistol (Browning patent), in the Browning machine gun, and in the Maxim gun. However, on the Browning machine gun there are a number of special parts, such as the accelerator, which allows the moving barrel to impart an extra momentum to the breechblock.

The barrels on the Browning and Maxim machine guns move about five-eighths of one inch. This movement allows time for the pressure to drop. Due to the weight of the breechblocks in these guns, recoil momentum is the chief factor in their retraction.

The Colt automatic pistol utilizes in part the momentum of the initial movement of the heavy slide. However, residual gas pressure also can be employed to retract a breechblock. Evidence of this fact is found in such weapons as the Thompson, the Pedersen, and other blowback rifles.

Numerous Browning recoil-rifle patents were taken out after the war, but it appears that this famous arms expert, who was so eminently successful with his pistols, machine guns, and shotguns, never succeeded in developing a satisfactory shoulder rifle, except, of course, the Browning Automatic Rifle, gas-actuated, which weighs over fifteen pounds, and the sporting Remington model 8.

This question is often asked: If we have a service pistol, such as the .45 Colt automatic, why do we not make a rifle on a similar design? Among other reasons, the pistol ammunition is much more adaptable for use in an automatic than the conventional .30 U.S. cartridge. The reader will recall our discussion of wall friction, ruptured cases, etc. Moreover, the locking system used in the Colt pistol is not adequate to withstand pressure developed in rifle ammunition. There the lugs on the top of the barrel are caused to drop down from engagement with their recesses in the slide. Incidentally, for the purpose of this discussion, the slide on the Colt pistol is, in effect, a breechblock. As such it is locked to the slidably-mounted barrel, with which it recoils about one-eighth of an inch. This raises another major question: breech-locking systems.

BREECH-LOCKING SYSTEMS

Rotating bolt method

Practical methods of locking the breech of a high-powered rifle or machine gun, are comparatively limited. Military authorities can have little patience with complicated contraptions of any kind, especially on guns. You will recall our discussion on a previous page of the need for simplicity. The interrupted screw is in common use on cannon, but that system on the Ross rifle, for example, was not very satisfactory. One fact remains inescapable. The Mauser-type bolt system has been used throughout the world for the past forty-odd years. Those nations which do not actually use the Mauser bolt, have copied it. Name any nations in the world, if you can, that do not use a rotating bolt with locking lugs in their standard service rifle. In a few, the lugs engaged abutments located abaft the magazine. In a majority, the lugs are situated at the head of the bolt. Bolt-action rifles alone can handle the highest pressures. The locking system used in the model 1895 Winchester proved inadequate for the .30-06. The Mauser bolt system is simple, rugged, and relatively reliable.

Many inventors are inclined to ignore their locking system. You will find many patents which carefully side step this phase of their weapon. The inventor thinks he has a wonderful gun. He has everything figured out except the locking. If you question that, he is insulted. Unless the alleged automatic rifle design sets forth a reliable locking system, the so-called inventor has not made much of a contribution to the art of gun making.

Since the first World War, sporting-arms makers have adopted the rotating bolt in order to provide for the .30-06 and other high-powered loads. We submit that the ideal automatic should use a simplified bolt of the Mauser type. Such a bolt is found on the Garand. If an inventor can produce a stronger bolt of a similar type, so much the better, provided always that it is practical. In many cases the designer must make concessions in his locking system so that his automatic parts can function as such. Inventors should place primary emphasis on their locking system, and concessions in design should be made in the actuating parts, not in the breechblock.

Short-recoil system

Modifications of the short-recoil type of actuation have been numerous in the patent office. However, there are very few of these inventions in common use. The reader has undoubtedly observed that most automatic pistols use a short-recoil system. The Colt pistol (Browning patent), which we discussed above, and the Luger, are outstanding examples. But, as we have repeatedly pointed out, there is a substantial difference between pistol and high-powered rifle cartridges. Thereby hangs the tale of woe.

A hasty examination of patents in the short-recoil class discloses much misdirected ingenuity. Invariably, as in other cases, the inventor was seized with an idea. One idea brought up another, and each idea adorned the weapon. Probably the most consistent defect, however, has been the failure to provide an adequate locking system, a point upon which we have already commented.

Some designs disclose methods of unlocking a breechblock after or during the interval of recoil, in time, nevertheless, to utilize the residual gas pressure for retraction. It would seem that such a system is impractical, in view of the unsuccessful experiments in that direction. One fault is this: the barrel has a tendency to hit the receiver or frame rather violently at the end of its recoil. Paul Mauser mentions this fact in connection with one of his early long-recoil patents. Moreover, it seems impracticable to use a Mauser-type, rotating bolt with such a system, because by the time the bolt has rotated, the pressure has vanished. While the pressure is high, a rotating bolt of the Mauser type cannot be unlocked very well, unless the lugs are slightly beveled. But beveled lugs cause the bolthead to move back from the base of the shell, and such a removal of support produces blown-out primers, or ruptured cases, as previously explained. Therefore, many other kinds of locking systems have been tried out, at least, on paper. A great majority of these breech devices are far too complicated, if not too weak, for military purposes.

Suppose we could design a bolt or breechlock which would rotate or unlock under pressure, without allowing the cartridge case to be unsupported. Then we might have so much unlocking before the pressure has dropped that the net result would be a breech system of insufficient strength.

Barrel-recoil system

In view of the above complications, we might use the force of barrel-recoil to impart power to an actuator. The reader may recall our discussion of the "croquet ball" principle in connection with retarded blowbacks. Instead of a movable bolthead we use a movable barrel, in contact with the actuator. When the barrel recoils it imparts a momentum to the actuator which, in turn, causes the bolt to unlock by the action of a cam or similar means. There should be quite a substantial blow from the recoiling barrel which we could harness up.

The bolt or breechblock recoils with the barrel. The bolt is locked to the barrel and moves back upon firing. We could put the actuator in contact with the bolt to get the same effect. Another method would be to allow the bolt or barrel to move a short distance and then hit the actuator. Any one of these methods ought to cause the bolt to be unlocked and retracted with enough force to compress a mainspring.

Such is not the case, however. Where the barrel or bolt is in contact with the actuator, a movement of one quarter to one half of an inch produces just enough power to compress a conventional mainspring about five pounds. That is barely enough power to unlock the bolt, so residual gas pressure must be used for retraction. The amount of barrel movement required to unlock the bolt takes too much time. Thus the bolt unlocks too late to utilize the residual gas pressure. Moreover, the lugs must be beveled slightly to permit immediate rotation.

If the barrel is allowed to move a short distance, hit the actuator, and follow through, the mainspring is compressed about fifteen pounds. If it were not necessary to compress the mainspring, this force would be enough to unlock the bolt and retract it. Therefore, one inventor tried to arrange a method of multiplying the barrel movement so as to compress the spring by that power. Then he tried to rig up a device to connect the compressed spring with the bolt.

To utilize residual gas pressure for retraction and spring-compression we might try to make the bolt unlock at once. To do that we would require an objectionable number of parts. Moreover, while the barrel is moving to hit the actuator, time is lost. Hence it is virtually impossible to utilize residual gas pressure by this method, and that force is essential.

If we ever should succeed in making any of the aforesaid recoil-actuator systems perform their task properly, the result would be another of those "mechanical monstrosities." We recall a remark attributed to the late John Browning, who, when shown a new "automatic" creation of some inventive genius, asked where the cheese was located. The gun looked more like a rat trap than a rifle.

SHELL EXTRACTION

Extraction of empty shells has not been considered in our previous discussion, but we cannot avoid the problem. A large percentage of jams occur in the extraction of cases. Of course if every cartridge were lubricated, this difficulty would be nicely overcome.

The time of extraction has much to do with our problem. The reader will recall our previous discussion of the basic methods of actuation in this connection. Extraction may take place: (1) when no pressure whatever remains in the barrel or chamber; (2) when some pressure remains; (3) when there remains sufficient residual pressure to retract the breechblock.

The .30 U.S. case or its equivalent tends to stick in the chamber. Those whose rapid-fire string with the Springfield has been interrupted by a recalcitrant empty case will appreciate this fact. A good rifleman or machine gunner is always fussy with the chamber of his piece. A smooth, clean chamber is of paramount importance. On many guns it is difficult to gain access to the chamber. On the ideal automatic rifle or machine gun this factor should be considered carefully.

The conventional extractor consists of a hook or claw which engages the extracting groove or cannelure on the cartridge case. When the breechblock, on which the extractor is carried, moves back suddenly, the result is a violent yank on the cannelure and on the extractor. Once loosened, however, the shell comes out easily. Some rifles, such as the 1903 Springfield, have an extracting cam which gives the operator a leverage.

Before taking up automatic extraction, we wish to make this assertion, based on the bulk of our previous discussion: no automatic action is worth its salt unless it affords enough power to compress its own mainspring in a direct and simple manner.

Therefore, our breechblock must necessarily be retracted with a considerable amount of initial force in order that the mainspring shall be fully compressed. Consequently, we may conclude that in any automatic the extractor and cannelure will receive a very sudden jerk as the breechblock begins to move rearward. Conceivably the extractor may break or the brass cannelure may be ripped. Pistol cases do not stick so tightly, and with pistols, as usual, this problem is not so acute.

The extractor must be extremely rugged and durable, yet it must be sufficiently "springy" to slip over the cannelure in the process of loading. Moreover, the claw must have a wide bearing on the cannelure to distribute the jerk. Otherwise the claw or hook will rip through the thin brass head.

In mechanisms which use residual gas pressure for retraction, this process is not quite so difficult because the pressure, provided of course it is of the right amount, tends to push the shell out of the chamber. With mechanisms wherein little or no pressure remains, the shell sticks anyway. However, with residual pressure, the breechblock wants to go back, and does actually yank at the shell to an appreciable extent before the internal pressure can co-operate in the extraction process.

Where the strength of the brass is sufficient to resist the pressure within it, the wall friction of the case under such pressure is not enough to overcome the tendency of the whole case to move rearward. For example, a .45 ACP case will move under maximum pressure against a movable breechblock without any lubrication. A .30 M1 or M2 case loaded not over 15,000 pounds per square inch will also move under that pressure in the same manner. Suppose, then, a full .30 U.S. load is fired, and the case is allowed to move just after the pressure has dropped below, say, five to six thousand odd pounds per square inch, by which time the bullet has left the muzzle. The case will then tend to extract itself by virtue of this effect of the residual pressure.

If our cartridge cases are ever altered in the distant future, less taper on the cases and a heavier base would be desirable. The brass is very thin at the extracting cannelure. Compare the .30 U.S. with the .45 ACP in this connection.

Another consideration with reference to extraction and ejection relates to the momentum of the breechblock.

Harking back to elementary physics we recall that a heavy body has more momentum than a light body, both moving at the same speed.

The breechblock of the automatic moves rearward under momentum. During its travel it is decelerated by the resistance of the mainspring, and by the feed action (belt operation or magazine friction).

Light automatics, such as rifles, require light breechblocks. Heavy guns can indulge in heavier breechblocks, hence they can develop much more momentum and reduced deceleration. Therefore they need not start rearward at such high speed. Also, therefore, the action of the shoulder automatic must be more harsh, for it must overcome by initial, violent, suddenly developed retracting speed what it lacks in breechblock momentum.

This explains also why most shoulder automatics require reasonable support by the operator in firing unless their action is extremely harsh. The breechblocks of conventional semi-automatic rifles, for example, if held loosely in the fingers, expand their retracting energy through the friction contact with the frame in pushing back the body of the weapon instead of moving rearward in relation to it. Actions which avoid this peculiarity do so at the unwarranted expense of an excessively harsh action.

Shoulder weapons are habitually fired from the shoulder, not from the finger tips.

GAS VS. RECOIL ACTION

Because there has been considerable discussion over a period of some years relative to the merits of gas versus recoil actions, the authors have been asked to include some reference to this specific topic.

By way of introduction to a recently somewhat controversial subject, we wish to make the following statement:

When, as, and if the people of this country and our allies are so fully equipped with automatic weapons of any and all types, kinds, actions, and calibers, that no one including even the bugler of the local up-country home guards lacks a *shootable,* modern weapon, whether it be gas or recoil, then, *and only then,* shall any of us be entitled to engage in any free-for-all arguments about what type of action we should choose for the future in an attempt to improve and perfect our then existing supply of arms for the national defense—if that day should ever come!

On the strength of this statement of a deep and most serious conviction, the authors would have preferred to let the matter rest. However, on a purely academic basis we have agreed to present herewith the advantages and disadvantages of both gas and recoil actuation as they have been evaluated generally in the two weapons with which we are most familiar.

It is assumed first that the reader is acquainted with the essential elements in gas and recoil actions.

By way of full explanation, the Johnson short-recoil action is augmented to some extent by a proportion of residual pressure, which is operative in retraction after recoil has unlocked the bolt. However, recoil is the sole unlocking force, and the Johnson may properly be regarded as a short-recoil weapon.

The Garand and, to a lesser extent, the Johnson, as well as practically all other automatic weapons, depend upon momentum to carry the breechblock rearward after the initial thrust of impinging gas or of recoil. The speed of the breechblock rearward is not at all uniform, for the force of momentum is rapidly decreasing, as has already been discussed in this chapter.

The amount of work to be accomplished is practically the same for any given ammunition. The breech must be unlocked, the empty case must be extracted and ejected, the mainspring must be compressed, and the hammer or striker cocked.

Consider the gas-operated rifle. The moving parts which include the bolt, piston, and operating rod, will ordinarily weigh not over two pounds in a 9½-10 pound weapon, and may weigh even less. Assume, then, that momentum is to be built up in a 2-pound unit.

Gas expanding behind the bullet develops in the projectile a velocity of over 2600 feet per second. Thus the gas hits the inert piston assembly at very high speed. With the gas port near the muzzle, the pressure of the gas hitting the piston is in the vicinity of 10,000-15,000 pounds per square inch. With the gas port near the breech, as in the experimental Winchester, the pressure is nearer 40,000 pounds per square inch.

When gas pushes a bullet, the pressure starts from zero and builds up until it overcomes the resistance of the bullet. By comparison, the action of built-up gas suddenly hitting the piston is extremely harsh. If the moving parts are heavy, the action of the gas, of course, is not so harsh. Moreover, heavy parts develop more momentum and do not slow down so rapidly as light parts. The Hotchkiss machine gun, weighing nearly 50 pounds, is an excellent example of a gas-operated weapon having a comparatively heavy breechblock, piston and operating rod assembly.

With lighter parts, as in the Garand or experimental Winchester, the only substitute for weight must be speed. The resistance encountered in unlocking, extracting, cocking the hammer, ejecting, and compressing the spring, must be overcome by velocity. Since the rate of deceleration, or loss of velocity, is much greater in the lighter gun, the initial speed of breechblock travel must be higher in order that the necessary operations may be successfully accomplished.

This results in subjecting the parts to some strain. Breakage and wear may be increased. Extraction of the cartridge case is naturally harsh. The action may be more sensitive to any resistance such as friction caused by rough surfaces, dirt, lack of lubricant, and so on. The cams, links, toggles, etc., used to cause breech unlocking are inevitably subjected to harsh treatment, especially in gas-operated weapons having the Lewis or Garand type breechlock and cam system.

The short-recoil action differs in many of the above respects from gas actions.

In the short-recoil action of the Johnson rifle, the bolt assembly weighs one pound. The barrel assembly weighs about three pounds. Thus, the initial moving parts of the Johnson weigh four pounds, or more than twice the weight of the corresponding Garand or Winchester parts, or over 40 per cent of the total weight of the 9.5-9.8-pound Johnson rifle.

When the Johnson is fired, the bolt and barrel actually begin recoiling while the bullet passes through the barrel. The approximate velocity of initial recoil before the bullet leaves the muzzle, which recoil is *gradually* built up from zero, amounts to considerably less than 2 feet per second.

The velocity of recoil developed from the time the bullet leaves the muzzle until the bolt is fully unlocked is approximately 15 feet per second.

The average velocity of the bolt throughout its travel is about 11.6 feet per second.

The velocity of the bolt and barrel prior to unlocking is measurably less than the average velocity during unlocking, for the reason that the quite considerable inertia of these parts has to be overcome initially. However, the resistance encountered in the rotation of the bolt slows up the barrel considerably by the time the bolt is fully unlocked. This retardation in turn prevents the barrel from striking the receiver with undue force.

Primary extraction—that is, the initial loosening of the empty case—is accomplished by the momentum of the bolt. Residual pressure (about 1000-1800 pounds per square inch) is operative in continuing the retraction of the bolt. For this reason the average velocity of the bolt is not much below the velocity of the bolt and barrel during barrel recoil.

Unfortunately, no figures are available to the authors on the bolt velocities of the Garand or Winchester gas-operated rifles.[2] On the experimental Winchester a small piston is hit by gas via a port six inches from the breech. The piston is permitted to move about one-tenth of an inch in contact with the operating rod assembly. Momentum then carries the breechblock rearward, and, as on the Garand, the momentum of approximately a two-pound mass must also unlock the breech. The pressure of the gas when it hits the piston is around 40,000-45,000 pounds per square inch.

The Johnson-type action is unlocked by the momentum of a four-pound mass, moving at a much lower velocity.

As it is absolutely impracticable to commence unlocking the breech until the bullet is out of the muzzle, it is necessary on the Garand, and especially so on the Winchester, to provide for a delay of the unlocking. On the short-recoil type, as on the Johnson, there is no appreciable recoil until the bullet leaves the muzzle. (Actually about $\frac{1}{64}$th inch.)

Since the barrel is an indispensable rifle component, the useful employment of its mass of three pounds may be said to constitute a weight economy. On the gas-operated type rifle of 9 or 10 pounds one cannot afford to indulge in a 3-pound operating rod.

The fixed barrel of the gas-operated rifle is better adapted to the attachment of the bayonet than is the recoil type, and better adapted to the conventional employment of the conventional bayonet.

The fixed-barrel, gas-operated weapon is more readily adapted to the incorporation of wooden handguards around the entire barrel. Moreover, it can be stocked in the conventional manner.

Excess weight or friction may affect the action of the recoiling barrel.

The gas-operated rifle may be subject to fouling in the gas port, cylinder, and on the piston. So long as the bore is fouled, the gas parts may also be fouled. If a barrel rusts when not cleaned, the gas port, cylinder, and piston may rust, also.

At this writing, rifle bores must be cleaned carefully. Clean-

[2] In October, 1941, the U. S. Army announced the adoption of the Winchester Short Rifle M-1 (cal. .30 S.R. M-1) which, it is understood, is patterned after the experimental Winchester caliber .30-06 semi-automatic rifle.

bore primers are not as yet extensively used. Stainless steel prevents rust but does not absorb residue. Exhaustive tests of the new-model Garand did not disclose any especial difficulty resulting from fouling.

The barrels of the gas-operated Garand and Winchester must be cleaned from the muzzle instead of from the breech. Some argument has centered around this point. According to the best authority, muzzle wear from such cleaning is not serious. The average soldier may fail to clean thoroughly right at the muzzle. He fails to reach the area around a gas port located near the muzzle. He should clean the chamber separately.

Unless a special rod is used, the soldier may burr the bolt face in pushing the rod through the bore. Burring the bolt face of the Garand may hinder proper unlocking, as the bolt must rotate against the base of the case. Burring the muzzle should be avoided.

On the gas-operated Bren L.M.G. the barrel may be removed.

The short-recoil action of the Johnson permits removal of the barrel for cleaning. There is an absence of fouling in the operating parts.

There are certain minor points which may be mentioned. For example, it has been argued by some that the gas rifle kicks less than the recoil rifle, especially referring to the Garand and Johnson. Actually, the mathematically measured kick of the Johnson is 25 per cent less than the M1903 using .30 M1 ammunition.

METHODS OF STOCKING

Turning to considerations of the stocking method, it must be noted that barrels bedded in wood are prone to be affected adversely by expansion and contraction of the wood due to weather conditions. The recoiling barrel, mounted in a metal sleeve, is free from such influences. The stock cannot impair or affect the accuracy.

As for accuracy and barrel warping, some discussion has raged on that score. Recoil-action rifles are probably no less or no more accurate than the gas type, and the recoil type does not "walk" or warp. We personally fired a new 1940 Garand eighty rounds in several 3-clip (24-shot) strings of rapid fire. It held its zero well with each of two types of ammunition. Some of the earlier type Garands developed this difficulty, but the new Garand does not walk.

The proposition that a weapon of the Johnson short-recoil type cannot function when fired downwards, as into a trench, is entirely untrue. With a weight attached to the barrel and the rifle *held loosely in the fingers,* a failure to eject may occur.

Reports covering so-called abuse or "adverse service condition" tests during 1940 have been made public during 1941. Space does not permit detailed references to these reports.

According to the *Infantry School Mailing List,* Vol. VIII, 1933-34, June, at page 213, it is stated:

> The recoil-operated type utilizes the kick or recoil from the explosion to perform the necessary operations. It is generally conceded that this mechanical principle furnishes the best possibilities for the type of gun desired.

The record in the United States may be of interest. The service used the Colt gas machine gun and the Benet gas gun. The Army refused to take the gas-operated Lewis gun, finally adopting the short-recoil operated Browning, and the gas-operated Browning automatic rifle.

The service adopted the recoil-operated Colt pistol, and later the recoil-operated Browning .50 caliber gun, and recently a recoil-operated 37 mm. automatic cannon. The only gas arm prior to the Garand which is still in use is the gas-operated B.A.R., M1918.

The gas-operated Standard rifle was used commercially in the United States in 1911.

The Germans discarded the Mondragon gas rifle in 1914 and adopted the short-recoil Maxim gun in several models before and during the first World War. The Nazis now use the short-recoil-operated M34 L.M.G. Although they have several gas rifles in model form, the Germans have clung to recoil or manually operated weapons.

The British and French adopted gas machine guns—the Lewis, Bren, Light Hotchkiss, and Hotchkiss.

The War Department of the United States has repeatedly, officially, and publicly stated that the gas-operated Garand rifle is the finest military rifle in the world, and that no other rifle meets the military requirements as does the Garand. This is based on twenty years of intensive study, test, and development, and five years of manufacturing experience. It represents the opinions of experts who have devoted their entire lives as officers and civilian engineers employed by the government to develop a semi-automatic rifle.

At this writing several hundred thousand Garand semi-automatic rifles have been delivered to troops from the famous Springfield Armory where tremendous strides have been made in Garand production during the past five years.

With all due respect to the opinions of many experts and other interested persons and groups, in the last analysis neither the gas nor the recoil types of semi-automatic rifles are entirely beyond some form of criticism.

But they can both shoot!

While the authors have freely expressed their opinions on types of weapons, it has been our policy to avoid too specific or detailed commendation, comparison, or criticism of any particular weapon and all of its incidental design features. On these the reader must form his own conclusions.

Appendix One

The following charts include a brief description of the chief characteristics of most of the best-known automatic weapons, including those discussed in the text in various connections.

Appendix One

Name	Colt	Maxim and Vickers	Hotchkiss	Hotchkiss	Benet Mercie
Type of Weapon	Heavy Machine Gun	Heavy Machine Gun Several Models	Heavy Machine Gun Several Models	Light Machine Gun Several Models	Light Machine Gun
Nation Where Used or Developed	U.S.A. and others	Britain, Germany, Russia and others	France, Japan and others	Britain and others	U.S.A.
Caliber	.30 U.S. .303, 7.62 mm.	.303, 7.9 mm., etc.	8 mm.	.303	.30 U.S.
Actuation	Gas, radial lever	Recoil (aided by gas in Vickers)	Gas	Gas	Gas
How Fired, Normally	Full auto.	Full auto.	Full auto.	Full auto.	Full auto.
Weight Without Mount	35 lbs.	30 to 40 lbs. (slight variations)	52 lbs. 60 lbs.	27 lbs.	27 lbs.
Weight With Mount Used	96 lbs. Tripod	82–90 lbs. Tripod (also sled)	122 lbs. Tripod	32 lbs. Tripod "rest"	About 34 lbs. Bipod
Feed	Belt	Belt	Strip, metallic	Strip, metallic	Strip, metallic
Cooling	Air	Water	Air	Air	Air
Type of Locking	Canting block	Toggle block	Link and locking recess	Interrupted screw	Rotating Sermuture Nut
Cyclic Rate of Fire	400 RPM	500 RPM	About 400 RPM	550 RPM	About 500 RPM
Deliverable Rate	About 200	About 250	About 200	About 150	About 150
Date of Origin	1890	1888	1892	Prior to World War	1909

Appendix One

AUTOMATIC WEAPONS

Schwarzlose	Revelli	Browning			Lewis
Heavy Machine Gun	Heavy Machine Gun	Heavy Machine Gun	Light Machine Gun	Machine Rifle	Light Machine Gun (obsolete)
Austria, Hungary, Holland, Sweden and Czecho-Slovakia	Italy	U.S.A.	U.S.A. and Britain (aircraft)	U.S.A. and others	Britain (U.S.A.)
7.9 mm., 6.5 mm., etc.	6.5 mm.	.30 U.S.	.30 U.S. .303	.30 U.S.	.303 (.30 U.S.)
Blow-back, oiled chamber	Recoil	Recoil	Recoil	Gas	Gas
Full auto.	Full auto.	Full auto.	Full auto.	Full or semi-auto.	Full auto.
44 lbs.	38 lbs.	32 lbs.	24 lbs.	16 to 19 lbs.	26 lbs.
88 lbs. Tripod	88 lbs. Tripod	87 lbs. Tripod	34 lbs.	22 lbs.	29 lbs. Bipod
Belt	Box, 50 rds. in cols. of 5	Belt	Belt	20 rd. Box, (bottom)	Flat circ. drum
Water	Water	Water	Air	Air	Induced air draught
Inertia of block, mech. adv.	Rotating wedge	Rising wedge	Rising wedge	Rising link	Rotary bolt
400 RPM	500 RPM	500 RPM	500–1200 RPM	500 RPM	550 RPM
About 250	About 250	About 250	About 200	100–200	150–200
Prior to World War	About 1910	1917	1917	1918	1914

Appendix One

Name	Bren—Z.B.	Light Hotchkiss	Chauchard	"M-34"	Parabellum
Type of Weapon	Light Machine Gun	Machine Gun	Also known as Chauchat, was used by France and U.S. during 1914–1918, a long recoil machine rifle in 8 mm. (French) caliber, weighing about 18 lbs. with circular magazine, full or semi-automatic. Now obsolete.	Light–Heavy Machine Gun	Light Machine Gun
Nation Where Used or Developed	Britain Czech Origin, Z.B.	France		Germany	Germany
Caliber	.303 7.9 mm.	7.5 mm.		7.9 mm.	7.9 mm.
Actuation	Gas	Gas		Recoil	Recoil
How Fired, Normally	Full or semi-auto.	Full or semi-auto.		Full or semi-auto.	Full auto.
Weight Without Mount	19 lbs.	19.7 lbs.		About 26 lbs.	22 lbs.
Weight With Mount Used	21 lbs. Bipod	About 22 lbs. Bipod		Bipod and tripod	Chiefly aircraft
Feed	30 rd. box (top)	25 rd. box (top)		Drum, belt or box	Belt
Cooling	Air	Air		Air	Air
Type of Locking	Wedge	Wedge type		Turning breech ring	Probably same as Maxim
Cyclic Rate of Fire	450 RPM	450–650 RPM		Probably 400–600 RPM	Probably 1000 RPM
Deliverable Rate	150–200	150–180		Probably 200	
Date of Origin	1925	Since World War		Since World War	World War

WEAPONS—*Continued*

S.I.A. Light Machine Gun	Nambu Light Machine Gun	Madsen Light Machine Gun	Bergmann Light Machine Gun	Gast Aircraft Gun	Eriksen Light Machine Gun
Italy	Japan	Denmark and others	Germany	Germany	Denmark
6.5 mm.	.256	8 mm.	7.9 mm.	7.9 mm.	7.9 mm.
Gas	Gas	Recoil	Recoil	Recoil, gas; two barrels	Gas
Full or semi-auto.	Full auto.	Full auto.	Full or semi-auto.	Full auto.	Full or semi-auto.
23.5 lbs.	21.5 lbs.	18 lbs.	26 lbs.	42 lbs.	24 lbs.
Special sling	23 lbs. Bipod	20 lbs. Bipod	Bipod and tripod		26.5 lbs. Bipod
25 rd. clips	30 rd. clip-fed hopper	25–40 rd. box (top)	Belt fed	Two 189 rd. drums	50 rd. strip box
Air	Air	Air	Air	Air	Air
Probably wedge	Probably wedge	Hinged block		Rotating ring	Block, rotary crank
700 RPM	600–800 RPM	450 RPM	About 400–500	1200 RPM	Probably 400–500 RPM
About 150–180	About 120–150	About 150–200	About 300	200–300	Probably 150–200
Since World War	About 1914–20	About 1916	About 1916	World War	Since World War

Name	Furrer	Praga	C.S.R. 6 "Fusil Mitrailleur"	Darne	Berthier
Type of Weapon	Light Machine Gun	Light Machine Gun	Light Machine Gun	Light Aircraft Gun	Light Machine Gun
Nation Where Used or Developed	Switzerland	Czecho-Slovakia	Belgium	France	Britain (not standard)
Caliber	7.45 mm.	7.9 mm.	7.65 mm.	.303	.303
Actuation	Recoil	Probably gas	Gas	Gas	Gas
How Fired, Normally	Full or semi-auto.	Probably full or semi-auto.	Full or semi-auto.	Full or semi-auto.	Probably full or semi-auto.
Weight Without Mount	18.5 lbs.	17.6 lbs.	18 lbs.	16 lbs.	About 19 lbs.
Weight With Mount Used	21 lbs. bipod —23 lbs. rest	Tripod	About 20 lbs. Bipod		About 21 lbs. Bipod
Feed	30 rd. box (side)	20–25 rd. charger	20 rd. charger	Belt	Probably 25 rd. box
Cooling	Air	Air	Air	Air	Air
Type of Locking	Toggle block	Probably wedge	Probably wedge	Probably wedge	Probably wedge
Cyclic Rate of Fire	480 RPM	Probably 450 RPM	Probably 500 RPM	Probably 500–1000 RPM	Probably 500 RPM
Deliverable Rate	200	Probably 120–180	Probably 100–150	Probably 200	Probably 150–200
Date of Origin	1925	Since World War	1915	Experimental	Limited— World War

WEAPONS—*Continued*

Johnson	*Garand*	*Garand*	*Pedersen*	*Krieghoff*	*Thompson*
Light Machine Gun	Semi-automatic Rifle	Semi-automatic Rifle	Semi-automatic Rifle	Semi-automatic Rifle	Semi-automatic Rifle
Developed in U.S.A. Adopted abroad	Developed in U.S.A. experimentally	Adopted by U.S.A. in 1936 as "M1" rifle	Developed in U.S.A. experimentally	Developed in Germany (sporting)	Developed in U.S.A. experimentally
.30 U.S.	.276	.30 U.S.	.276	7.9 mm.	.276
Recoil	Gas	Gas	Retarded blowback	Gas	Retarded blowback
Full or semi-auto.	Semi-auto.	Semi-auto.	Semi-auto.	Semi-auto.	Semi-auto.
12 lbs.	About 9 lbs.	About 9.75 lbs.	About 9 lbs.	About 8 lbs.	About 10 lbs.
About 14 lbs. Bipod					
Several types. 20 rd. charger box	10 rd. clip	8 rd. clip	10 rd. clip	3 rd. box	5–10 rd. box
Air	Barrel wood covered	Barrel wood covered	Semi-air-cooled	Semi-air-cooled	Semi-air-cooled
Rotary bolt, 8 lugs	Rotary bolt, 2 lugs	Rotary bolt, 2 lugs	Toggle block (greased ammunition)	Rising wedge	Screw block
300–900 RPM	About 800 RPM	About 800 RPM	About 800 RPM	About 600 RPM	About 800 RPM
200	20–60	20–60	20–60	Probably not over 30	20–50
1937–1940	1928	1929–1936	1925–1929	About 1935	1925–1929

Appendix One

Name	*White*	*Standard*	*Johnson*	*Johnson*	*Remington*
Type of Weapon	Semi-automatic Rifle	Semi-automatic Rifle	Semi-automatic Rifle	Semi-automatic Rifle (rotary feed)	Auto-loading Rifle (Browning)
Nation Where Used or Developed	Developed in U.S.A. experimentally	U.S.A. Marketed 1910–1912 (out of existence)	Developed in U.S.A.	Developed in U.S.A. Adopted abroad	Developed in U.S.A. by Remington on Browning patents
Caliber	.276	.35 Rem.	.30 U.S.	.30 U.S.	.25, .30, .35 Rem. .300 Sav.
Actuation	Gas	Gas	Recoil	Recoil	Recoil (long)
How Fired, Normally	Semi-auto.	Semi-auto.	Semi-auto.	Semi-auto.	Semi-auto.
Weight Without Mount	About 10 lbs.	About 10 lbs.	About 9 lbs.	About 9.5 to 9.8 lbs.	About 8.7 lbs.
Weight With Mount Used					
Feed	5–10 rd. box		5–10 rd. box	10 rd., clip-loaded, rotary	5 rd. box
Cooling	Semi-air-cooled		Air	Air	Barrel enclosed in tube
Type of Locking	Probably wedge	Probably wedge	Rotary bolt, 8 lugs	Rotary bolt, 8 lugs	Rotary bolt, 2 lugs
Cyclic Rate of Fire	About 500 RPM		600 RPM	600 RPM	500 RPM
Deliverable Rate	20–50		20–60	20–60	20–30
Date of Origin	1925–1929	1910	1906–1908	1909–1940	1909

Winchester Self-loading Rifle	Thompson Sub-machine Gun	Schmeisser Sub-machine Gun	Hyde Sub-machine Gun	Smith-Wesson Sub-machine Gun	Revelli (Villa Perosa) Sub-machine Gun
Developed in U.S.A. by Winchester	Developed in U.S.A. Used to limited extent by U.S.A.	Germany, Spain, etc.	Developed in U.S.A. Close copy of Thompson.	Developed experimentally by Smith & Wesson	Italy (chiefly aircraft)
.32, .351, .401 Win.	.45 ACP	9 mm. Luger	45 ACP	9 mm. (Luger)	Various pistol calibers
Blow-back	Blow-back	Blow-back	Blow-back	Blow-back	Blow-back
Semi-auto.	Full or semi-auto.	Full or semi-auto.	Full or semi-auto.	Semi-auto.	Full auto. two barrels
About 8.5 lbs.	About 10 lbs.	About 9 lbs.	About 9 lbs.	About 9 lbs.	13.5 lbs. (Note: two barrels)
					17 lbs. Bipod
5 rd. box	20 rd. box 30 rd. drum	20–30 rd. box	20 rd. box	20 rd. box	Two 20 rd. box magazines
Air	Air	Air	Air	Air	Air
Inertia block	Inertia block	Inertia block	Inertia block	Inertia block	Inertia block
600 RPM	400–800 RPM	400–800 RPM	400–800 RPM	400–800 RPM	Probably up to 1600 RPM
20–30	100–200	100–180	100–180	40–80	150–300
1910 approx.	1921	Since World War	Since World War	About 1938	Since World War

Appendix One

Name	Fedorou	Colt Browning			Luger-Parabellum
Type of Weapon	Sub-machine Gun	Automatic Pistol	Automatic Pistol	Automatic Pistol	Automatic Pistol
Nation Where Used or Developed	Russia	U.S.A. and others	U.S.A. and others	U.S.A. Also Fabrique Nationale, Belgium	Germany and others
Caliber	Pistol caliber	45 ACP (also .221 R.)	.38 ACP (9 mm. long)	.22, .25, .32, .380 (9 mm.)	7.65 9 mm.
Actuation	Recoil	Recoil	Recoil	Blow-back	Recoil
How Fired, Normally	Full or semi-auto.	Semi-auto.	Semi-auto.	Semi-auto.	Semi-auto.
Weight Without Mount	11 lbs.	39 oz.	39 oz.	13 to 34 oz.	About 31 oz.
Weight With Mount Used					
Feed	25 rd. belt	7 rd. box	9 rd. box	6–10 rd. box	7 rd. or more box
Cooling	Air				
Type of Locking		Vertical lugs (rings)	Vertical lugs (rings)	Inertia slide	Toggle block
Cyclic Rate of Fire					
Deliverable Rate					
Date of Origin	Since World War	1900–1911	1900–1911	1900	About 1895

WEAPONS—*Continued*

Mauser Automatic Pistol	*Webley* Automatic Pistol	*Mauser* Automatic Pistol	*Webley* Automatic Pistol	*Webley* Automatic Pistol	*Savage* Automatic Pistol
Germany and others	Britain	Germany	Britain	Britain	U.S.A.
7.63 mm.	.455	.32 auto. (also .25 auto.)	.32	.38 auto. 9 mm. long	.380
Recoil	Recoil	Blow-back	Blow-back	Recoil	Recoil
Semi-auto. (also full on some models)	Semi-auto.	Semi-auto.	Semi-auto.	Semi-auto.	Semi-auto.
About 40 oz.	36 oz.	20 oz.	18 oz.	31 oz.	19 oz.
10 rd. box (clip)	7 rd. box	8 rd. box	8 rd. box	8 rd. box	8 rd. box
Link block	Vertical lugs (rings)	Inertia slide	Inertia slide	Vertical lugs (rings)	Rotating barrel
About 1895	Prior to World War	About 1900	Prior to World War	Prior to World War	About 1910

Appendix One

Name	Steyr	Bayard	Walther HP	Walther	Hi-Standard	Reising
Type of Weapon	Automatic Pistol	Automatic Pistol	Automatic Pistol	Automatic Pistol	Automatic Pistol	Automatic Pistol
Nation Where Used or Developed	Germany	Belgium	Germany	Germany	U.S.A.	U.S.A.
Caliber	9 mm. Steyr	9 mm. Bayard	9 mm.	.22, .25, .32, .380	.22	.22
Actuation	Recoil	Recoil	Recoil	Blow-back	Blow-back	Blow-back
How Fired, Normally	Semi-auto.	Semi-auto.	Semi-auto.	Semi-auto.	Semi-auto.	Semi-auto.
Weight Without Mount		33 oz.	29 oz.	16–24 oz.	Various models 30–40 oz.	About 31 oz.
Weight With Mount Used						
Feed	8 rd. box	8 rd. box	8 rd. box	7–8 rd. box	10 rd. box	12 rd. box
Cooling						
Type of Locking			Breech lock	Inertia slide	Inertia slide	Inertia slide
Cyclic Rate of Fire						
Deliverable Rate						
Date of Origin	Prior to World War	World War	Since World War	Before World War	Since World War	Since World War

WEAPONS—*Continued*

Besa	*Mendoza*
Heavy Machine Gun (tank type)	Light Machine Gun
Britain	Mexico
7.9 mm.	7 mm.
Gas (slight barrel recoil)	Gas
Full auto.	Full or semi-auto.
About 40 lbs.	18.5 lbs.
Tank mount	20 lbs.
Belt	Box
Air	Air
Wedge	Turning bolt
About 500 RPM	About 500 RPM
About 300	About 150–200
About 1936–38	About 1934

Astra	Dreyse	Frommer	Kommer	Lignose	Liliput	Mann
Ortgies	Sauer	Schmeisser	Simson	Vesta	Pieper	

All of these above-named are low-powered automatic pistols.

All of these weapons are of European origin and manufacture.

Calibers include .212, .25 (6.35 mm.), .32 (7.65 mm.), and .380 (9 mm.).

These pistols are all of the blow-back type.

All are fired semi-automatically.

Weights vary from about 10 oz. to 30 oz., the average being about 18 oz.

Magazines are of the usual detachable box type, holding 6–8 rounds.

The action depends upon the inertia of the slide (or block).

Most of the pistols originated about 1900–1914.

Appendix Two

The following table is submitted to aid those who desire to refer to the most common automatic weapons discussed in this book with especial reference to the ammunition for which such weapons are chambered.

AMMUNITION TABLE WITH REFERENCE TO TYPES OF AUTOMATIC WEAPONS

Caliber	Type of weapon or weapons used in	Normal Chamber pressure lbs. per sq. in.	Locking: blow-back or positive breech lock (action)	Effective accurate range (approx.)	Extreme effective burst range (approx.)	Whether effective against airplanes, vehicles, light armor	Weight of bullet (approx.)	Shape of bullet boat-tail or flat base	Rim or Rimless case
	I. Ammunition Used in Automatic Weapons Used or Developed in the United States								
.22 Long Rifle	Auto-loading sporting rifles and pistols	15,000	Blow-back	100–200 yds.	300–350 yds.	No (Very weak)	40 grains	Flat base	Rim
(.25, .32),.380, .38 ACP.	Self-loading (automatic) pistols	10,000–15,000	Blow-back	50–100 yds.	200–300 yds.	No (Very weak)	50–150 grains	Flat base	Rimless
7.63 mm., 7.65, or 9 mm. (Mauser or Luger)	Self-loading (automatic) pistols, machine pistols	15,000–20,000	Semi-locked	100–200 yds.	300–400 yds.	No (Weak)	80–100 grains	Flat base	Rimless
.45 ACP	Self-loading pistol, sub-machine gun	15,000	Semi-locked, blow-back	100–150 yds.	200–300 yds.	No (Weak)	230 grains	Flat base	Rimless
.32, .351, .401 W.R.A.	Winchester Self-loading sporting rifle	20,000	Blow-back	100–200 yds.	200–400 yds.	No (Weak)	150–200 grains	Flat base	Rimless
.25, .30, .300, .35 Remington	Remington Auto-loading sporting rifle	25,000–35,000	Locked (Long-recoil)	200–250 yds.	300–600 yds.	No	117–200 grains	Flat base	Rimless
	II. Ammunition Used in Certain Well-Known Types of Light and Heavy Machine Guns								
.303 British	Bren, Lewis, Vickers Machine Guns—SMLE rifle.	42,000	Locked (gas and recoil)	600 yds.	1500–1800 yds.	Yes	174 grains	Flat base	Rim

7.5 mm. (French)	Light Hotchkiss LMG, Lebel rifle, etc.	42,000–48,000	Locked	600–1000 yds.	2000–3000 yds.	Yes	174 grains	Boat-tail	Rimless
8 mm. (French)	Old Lebel rifle, Hotchkiss M.G.	42,000–44,000	Locked	600–1000 yds.	2000–3000 yds.	Yes	198 grains	Boat-tail (Balle D)	Rim
8 mm. (German) (7.9 mm.)	Mauser rifle, Maxim, M34 M.G.	42,000–44,000	Locked (recoil)	600–1000 yds.	2000–2500 yds.	Yes	154–170 grains	Probably Boat-tail (also flat base)	Rimless
7.62 Russian (Finnish)	Mozin rifle, Maxim and other M.G.	45,000	Locked	600 yds.	1500–1800 yds.	Yes	150 grains	Flat base	Rimless
6.5, 7.65 mm.	Mauser rifle, various M.G.	40,000–45,000	Locked	600 yds.	1500–1800 yds.	Yes	130–180 grains	Flat base	Rimless
Anti-tank, A–C, A–A, .50 cal.	Browning and other M.G. Cannon	50,000	Locked (recoil)	600–1000 yds.	2500–4000 yds.	Yes (Very)	800 grains	Boat-tail	Rimless
.30 M1906	M1903 rifle	50,000	Locked	600 yds.	1500–1800 yds.	Yes	150 grains	Flat base	Rimless
.30 M2 and	M1903 rifle, "M1" (Garand) semi-automatic rifle, and all U.S. and other cal. .30	38,000–45,000	Locked (gas)	600 yds.	1500–1800 yds.	Yes	150 grains	Flat base	Rimless
.30 M1	arms including the M1917; B.A.R. M1918; B.M.G. M1917, Johnson, etc.	48,000–52,000	Locked	1000 yds.	2500–4000 yds.	Yes (Armorpiercing loads with 170 grain flat base bullets)	173 grains	Boat-tail	Rimless

NOTE: 20 mm., 25 mm., 37 mm. calibers are used in certain automatic and semi-automatic cannon. Projectiles upwards of 0.5 lbs, muzzle velocities reach 3300 ft. per second. A typical 37 mm. load will penetrate 1.5 in. of best armor-plate at 1000 yds. Recoil actions are chiefly used.

Appendix Three

The following data is extracted from *The Infantry Mailing List*, Volume XXII, July, 1941, pages 203 *et seq.*

TABLE A

Note

In this and in subsequent tables where the infantry weapons are mentioned, they will be listed by their commonly accepted names rather than by their complete technical names, as indicated below:

Common Name	Abbreviations	Technical Name
Automatic Pistol............		Automatic Pistol, Caliber .45, M1911 or M1911A1.
Rifle, M1..................	R M1	U.S. Rifle, Caliber .30, M1.
Rifle, M1903 (or M1917).....	R M1903	U.S. Rifle, Caliber .30, M1903 (or M1917).
Automatic Rifle, M1918......	Auto R	Browning Automatic Rifle, Caliber .30, M1918, without Bipod.
Automatic Rifle, M1918A2....	Auto R	Browning Automatic Rifle, Caliber .30, M1918A2, with Bipod.
Heavy Machine Gun.........	H MG	Browning Machine Gun, Caliber .30, M1917.
Light Machine Gun..........	LMG	Browning Machine Gun, Caliber .30, M1919A4, Ground.
Antitank Machine Gun.......	AT MG	Browning Machine Gun, Caliber .50, HB, M2, Ground.
60-mm Mortar..............	60-mm Mort	60-mm Mortar, M2.
81-mm Mortar..............	81-mm Mort	81-mm Mortar, M1.
Antitank Gun..............	AT Gun	37-mm Gun, Antitank, M3.
or	or	
37-mm Gun................	37-mm Gun	37-mm Gun, Antitank, M3.

Appendix Three

Number of rounds per weapon *and echelon in which carried*

	On Individual Armed with Weapon	On Prime Mover or Am Truck	On Unit Am Tn	On Train of Higher Unit	Total	Remarks
Heavy Machine Gun..		6750		1500	8250	10% AP; 70% ball; 20% tracer
Light Machine Gun...		3000	2000	1000	6000	(Same % as next above)
Antitank Machine Gun		1200		1600	2800	80% AP; 20% tracer
37-mm Gun..........		160	40	100	300	90% AP; 10% HE
81-mm Mortar.......		100	50	150	300	70% M43; 10% M56; 20% M57
60-mm Mortar.......		60	60	100	220	100% HE
Automatic Pistol......	21		7		28	100% ball
Automatic Rifle						
In Rifle Sqd (AT Co)	(A)200		(B)820	600	1620	5% AP; 10% tracer; 85% ball
In Auto R Sqds of R Cos equipped with M1 Rifle.........	(C)320		(D)852	576	1748	Same % as next above
In Auto R Sqds of R Cos equipped with M1903 or M1917 Rifle............	(C)320		(E)860	540	1720	Same % as next 2 above
Per gun organically assigned to pedestal mount (AA on vehicle).........		(K)200		200	400	10% AP; 20% tracer; 70% ball
Rifle, M1						
In the rifle platoon..	40		(F)192	96	328	Same % as next above
In other units......	40					Same % as next 2 above
Rifle, M1903 or M1917						
In the rifle platoon..	40		(G)120	60	220	Same % as next 3 above
In other units......	40					Same % as next 4 above

(A) 80 by the automatic rifleman and 120 by the assistant automatic rifleman, all in 20-round magazines.

(B) 300 to be issued prior to combat—100 to the automatic rifleman and 80 to the assistant automatic rifleman in 20-round magazines; 120 to the assistant automatic rifleman in 60-round bandoleers; 520 retained in ammunition train as a reserve.

(C) 80 by the automatic rifleman, 120 by the assistant automatic rifleman and each ammunition carrier, all in 20-round magazines; 40 by each ammunition carrier in 5- or 8-round clips (see ammunition for the rifle).

(D) 468 to be issued prior to combat—100 to each automatic rifleman and 80 to each assistant automatic rifleman in 20-round magazines; 96 to each assistant automatic rifleman in 48-round bandoleers; 192 to each ammunition carrier in 48-round bandoleers (see ammunition for the M1 rifle); 384 retained in ammunition train as a reserve.

(E) 500 to be issued prior to combat—100 to each automatic rifleman, 80 to each assistant automatic rifleman and each ammunition carrier in 20-round magazines; 120 to each assistant automatic rifleman and each ammunition carrier in 60-round bandoleers. 360 retained in ammunition train as a reserve.

(F) 96 to be issued prior to combat in 48-round bandoleers; 96 retained in ammunition train as a reserve. (See ammunition for the Browning Automatic Rifle.)

(G) 120 to be issued prior to combat in 60-round bandoleers.

(H) In mobilization, all ammunition for the Rifle, M1 is packed and issued in 8-round clips in 48-round bandoleers in boxes.

(K) All in magazines.

TABLE B

AMMUNITION CAPACITY OF INFANTRY TRUCKS

1. The two types of ammunition carrying vehicles available within the infantry regiment when carrying no other loads will haul, without overload, ammunition of the various types in the amounts indicated below:

	Truck, cargo 1 ½-ton	Weapon carrier ½-ton
Caliber .30, rifle and automatic rifle...	35,000	11,500
Caliber .30, machine-gun, in belts.....	37,500	12,500
Caliber .50, machine-gun, in belts.....	9,000	3,000
60-mm Mortar	810	270
81-mm Mortar	300	100
37-mm antitank.	600	200

Appendix Three

TABLE C

CHARACTERISTICS OF INFANTRY WEAPONS

Weapon	Maximum Rate of Fire (Rounds per minute) a	Sustained Rate of Fire (Rounds per minute) a b	Projectiles		
			Maximum Range (yards)	Maximum Effective Range (yards) a	Effective Radius of Burst (yards) (Fragmentation)
Automatic Pistol.............	21 rounds in 12 seconds	10	1,600	50	
Rifle, M1903 (or M1917).....	10–15	10	3,450 k 5,500 l	600 k 600 l	
Rifle, M1....................	16–24	16	3,450 k 5,500 l	600	
Automatic Rifle, M1918......	100 c	40	3,450 k 5,500 l	600 k 600 l	
Automatic Rifle, M1918A2 ...	100 n 150 d	40 40	3,450 k 5,500 l	600 k 600 l	
Heavy Machine Gun.........	525	125	3,450 k 5,500 l	1,800 i 3,000 j k 4,000 j l	
Light Machine Gun..........	450	40–60	3,450 k 5,500 l	1,800 i 3,000 j k q 4,000 j l q	
Antitank Machine Gun.......	500	40–60	7,200	1,800 i p 4,000 j p	
37-mm Gun.................	25	20	12,750	1,800 i p	10 m
60-mm Mortar..............	30–35	18	1,935	f	15
81-mm Mortar..............	30–35	18	3,290 g 2,655 h	f	15 g 30 h
Hand Grenade, fragmentation			50	50	10–15

Characteristics of Chemical Mortar

Weapon	Maximum Rate of Fire	Sustained Rate of Fire	Maximum Range	Maximum Effective Range	
4.2 inch Mortar, Chemical....	20	5	2,400	f	

Notes

a. For other than full automatic weapons, personal proficiency is a controlling factor.

b. A variable factor, the time of endurance of which is limited by construction, heating, and other conditions influencing sustained or prolonged performance.

c. Semi-automatic.

d. Automatic.

e. Machine gun, caliber .30 (1919) A4 tank has same ballistic qualities.

f. Within limits of maximum range. Observation is a controlling factor.

g. Light shell.

h. Heavy shell.

i. Observed fire, distance varies with visibility.

j. Indirect fire.

k. M1906 or M2 ammunition.

l. M1 ammunition.

m. High explosive only.

n. Reduced rate automatic.

p. This range has no reference to armor penetration.

q. Gun not well suited to indirect fire.